Honda Tune-Up
for the
Mechanically
Impaired

39569

Paul Young
Illustrated by
Derek Lofgreen

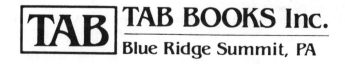

TAB **TAB BOOKS** Inc.
Blue Ridge Summit, PA

FIRST TAB EDITION
FIRST PRINTING

© 1992 by **TAB Books**.
TAB Books is a division of McGraw-Hill, Inc.
© 1981 First Edition published by Ten Speed Press as *Honda Tune-Up for Everybody*.

Library of Congress Cataloging-in-Publication Data

Young, Paul, 1949–
    Honda tune-up for the mechanically impaired / by Paul Young.
        p.   cm.
    Includes index.
    ISBN 0-8306-3427-4   ISBN 0-8306-3419-3 (pbk.)
    1. Honda automobile—Maintenance and repair—Amateurs' manuals.
I. title.
TL215.H58Y67   1992
629.28'722—dc20   92-7688
                                                                    CIP

TAB Books offers software for sale. For information and a catalog, please
contact TAB Software Department, Blue Ridge Summit, PA 17294-0850.

Acquisitions Editor: Stacy Pomeroy
Book Editor: Lori Flaherty
Director of Production: Katherine G. Brown
Book Design: Joanne M. Slike
Cover Design and Illustration: Denny Bond, East Petersburg, PA   HT3

Contents

Chapter 1
Spark Plugs

Chapter 2
The Ignition System

Chapter 3
Setting the Timing

Chapter 4
Valve Adjustment

Chapter 5

Carburetors & Fuel Injection

Chapter 6

Periodic Maintenance

Chapter 7

Tools

Acknowledgments

Honda Tune-Up for the Mechanically Impaired is the result of years of experience, research, and the suggestions and input of many people. I would like to thank three people in particular for their invaluable participation in the making of this handbook.

A special round of appreciation to my editor at Tab/McGraw-Hill, Stacy Pomeroy, for her efforts in seeing this handbook step-by-step from the drawing board into the homes of Honda owners.

To Derek Lofgreen, my illustrator, who is now probably wearing stronger lenses, many many thanks for your endless patience and commitment to fine work.

To my wife Fran, the greatest thanks for your support and encouragement, expert editorial assistance, and wonderful sense of adventure that, undoubtedly, helped you survive this project.

All about Tools

It doesn't take a box full of tools to tune-up and service a Honda. All you need is four basic tools: a ratchet wrench, a few sockets, a screwdriver, and an inexpensive spark plug adjusting tool. About $38 should cover the tools you'll need for everything in this manual.

I recommend Sears' Craftsman tools. Avoid Sears' Taiwan brand, however. Craftsman tools are good, quality tools used by many mechanics. There are other good brands out there, too. One place to find these brands is from the tool trucks you might have seen parked in front of automotive repair shops. These tool trucks cater to mechanics and sell only high-quality tools. The route driver will welcome your money, too.

Stay away from tools sold at supermarkets and discount automotive chain stores. These tools are not precision made. Often, just when you must depend on them—whammy—they slip and let go . . . ouch! Quality tools don't do this! A quality tool feels good in your hand and makes the job go smoothly. A quality tool doesn't wear out; it wears in and feels better with age. You can work with a quality tool; you can do things with it. The right tool makes the job happen. Chapter 7 fully illustrates and describes the tools you'll need to do everything in this handbook.

Introduction

Before you jump to conclusions and decide *Honda Tune-Up for the Mechanically Impaired* is only for the experienced do-it-yourselfer, I'd like to tell you some interesting things about this handbook. *Honda Tune-Up for the Mechanically Impaired* is written and illustrated specifically for Honda owners who might know little or absolutely nothing about their Hondas. So, if you don't know one end of a spark plug from the other, or a timing light from a headlight, this is just the book for introducing you to the fun and rewarding hobby of tuning and servicing your Honda.

While there are many excellent hobby books on stitchery, carpentry, ceramics, and most everything imaginable, there are no other how-to books on Honda care for the beginner. The days of feeling intimidated when it comes to getting involved under the hood of your Honda are over!

With *Honda Tune-Up for the Mechanically Impaired* to show you exactly what to do and how to do it, you'll find the rest surprisingly easy. There's nothing tricky, "grimey," or time-consuming about tuning and servicing your Honda. Every Honda owner can do these things with just a few basic tools, a couple of free hours and, of course, *Honda Tune-Up for the Mechanically Impaired* to demonstrate how to do things auto repair manuals never seem to include.

On a busy schedule? This handbook is designed so you can do a little under-the-hood car care and then drive your Honda until you get a chance to do more. Here's a welcome change from spending a car-less day while your Honda sits at a shop waiting for some mechanic "to get to it." The stopwatch at the beginning of chapters 1 through 5 illustrates the approximate time each part of the tune-up will take so you can decide when is a good time to put your Honda into tip-top shape.

Saving time and money and ensuring that your Honda has a long and happy road life are just a few of the benefits you receive from do-it-your-self Honda care. There's also a very nice sense of independence and accomplishment from keeping your own car in tip-top shape all by yourself. Knowing that your well-tuned Honda is producing a minimum of harmful pollutants is encouraging, too.

For me, when all is said and done, I endorse do-it-yourself car care because, nowadays, it's the only way I can be sure my car really gets everything it deserves.

To Tune
or Not to Tune

To get you and your Honda around town, up hills, down the freeway, or just around the corner, that little power pack under the hood of your Honda withstands a variety of tortures. Day in and day out, hundreds of times a day, your Honda's motor heats up, speeds up, slows down, and cools down. Not to mention that it has to start up each morning after a cold night outside.

All this is just the beginning! Depending on where and how you drive, your motor must endure bumps and ruts, water, dirt and dust, hot and cold, jackrabbit starts and even turns that feel like an amusement park ride.

To make matters worse, at times, your Honda's motor must endure all these abuses with a car full of your friends along for the ride. Quite a chore! Consequently, your Honda can't live without periodic tune-ups.

At freeway speeds and during quick acceleration, a Honda motor often spins more than 6,500 revolutions per minute (RPM). If you spin in a circle for one minute and count the number of turns, this would be your RPM. As you can imagine, 6,500 RPM is very fast, especially in the presence of hot, exploding gasoline and the other abuses I just mentioned.

Such strenuous activity causes some motor parts to slowly slip out of adjustment while others, including motor oil, actually wear out and require replacement. As these things happen, your Honda begins to feel tired and sluggish and gets less than great gas mileage. Some parts, like valves, if not periodically adjusted, can actually burn, creating the need for an expensive valve job.

In addition, when parts of the motor that need adjustment or replacement are not pulling their own weight, added strain is placed on other parts of the motor that are. Running out of balance, so to speak, can shortly result in motor, clutch, transmission, exhaust system, and drive axle problems.

So, a tune-up is simply putting the spunk back into your Honda by setting some parts back into adjustment and replacing others that have worn out. Plus, a tune-up is the best way to safeguard against expensive repair bills. Don't panic . . . as I said in the introduction, these are things every Honda owner can do with a few basic tools and this handbook as their guide.

Servicing your Honda is a little different than tuning it. Servicing includes such things as lubricating locks, doors, and trunk hinges; replenishing brake, clutch, power steering, and transmission fluids; changing filters; checking tire pressure and fan belt tension; and even the windshield washer fluid. Just like the motor, these other parts of your car are subjected to daily tortures that require periodic attention, which, if neglected, can cause your Honda to quickly grow old.

As a result of the tuning and servicing you'll be giving your Honda, it will maintain that characteristic new-Honda feel for a long, long time to come.

How often should you tune-up and service your Honda?

Some manuals, including your owner's manual, recommend a tune-up and service at ridiculously long intervals. My experience shows that after 3,500 miles of driving, motor oil is already dirty and thin. At 5,000 miles, a couple of valves are usually out of adjustment. At 6,000 miles, the spark plugs require adjustment, as do ignition points, engine timing, and possibly even the carburetor on older model Hondas. By 10,000 miles, the ignition points and condensor are ready for replacement on older model Hondas and the distributor rotor and spark plugs are ready for replacement on all models.

I always tune and service my automobiles at 3,500 mile intervals. Sometimes, I'm surprised to find how many things need adjustment or replacement. Other times, I'm happy to see how well everything remained just as I left it the last time I was under the hood. Driving conditions and temperatures have a big effect on your motor's ability to stay in adjustment, making it impossible to predict accurately what will stay in adjustment and for how long.

By faithfully following a 3,500 mile tune-up and service schedule, I usually get 145,000 miles out of a car and motor before it requires expensive repairs. So, why risk big repair bills when a tune-up and service at the the right time will keep your Honda "happy" and give you peace of mind?

Answers to Frequently Asked Questions

Q: *I don't know the first thing about my Honda. Can I actually tune and service it myself?*

A: Yes! *Honda Tune-up for the Mechanically Impaired* has been completely tested and perfected on beginners just like you. The first edition of this handbook was extensively tested and perfected on Honda owners who knew no more about their Hondas than where to put the ignition key.

Another thing everybody who tested this handbook had in common was a strong desire to be free of high-priced and sometimes, incompetent mechanics. Through the efforts and patience of these willing and forgiving Honda owners, it was possible for me to carefully develop this Honda handbook that is just right for beginners. Thanks again to everyone who made this handbook a reality.

Q: *How much money does do-it-yourself car care cost?*

A: The savings are big! The few things you need for a full tune-up cost between $20 and $40, depending on what gets replaced. Compare this to today's shop price of $225 to $350 for a full tune-up and you save enough for a nice little vacation the first time you take matters into your own hands.

Actually, you save in three ways when you do it yourself: First, you save on the big price of a tune-up. Second, the personal service you give your Honda should keep it running like new and out of the shop. Third, as a nice bonus, you save every day, because a well-tuned Honda gets better gas mileage. Besides being an enjoyable hobby, there are plenty of rewards that come with do-it-yourself car care.

Q: *How much time does it take to care for my Honda? I've never done it before.*

A: Not much time at all. Most mechanics can completely tune-up and service your Honda in about 1 hour. And that's without exerting themselves. So, if you plan to do everything in this handbook in one day, allow about 4 hours from start to finish.

Good news! If you're on a busy schedule, you can do just a little at a time, completing one chapter and then driving your Honda until you get a chance to go on. In each chapter, the approximate completion time is posted. Most chapters will take a complete beginner less than an hour to complete.

Q: *What about tools? Aren't they expensive?*

A: Tools to enable you to do everything in this manual cost about $38. For this much money you can get a quality brand tool that will actually help make the job go smoothly. Stay away from cheap discount tools—they only make a nightmare out of a simple task. For more about tools, see All About Tools on page xiii.

Q: *My car has a computer. Can I still tune it up myself?*

A: Yes. And with less work than if your car didn't have a computer!
Newer model Hondas, with their high-tech electronics, require far less adjusting and parts replacement than Hondas of the late 1970s, which relied on primitive moving parts. Honda Motor Co. actually switched to electronic components in an effort to reduce the need for parts replacement and to keep their cars in adjustment longer.

Q: *What if I only want to do some things myself and have my mechanic do the rest, will this be a problem?*

A: Do only as much as you want. Do any chapter you choose. Then, if your schedule gets crazy, it's okay! You can safely drive your car after completing each chapter. If weeks and weeks go by and you just can't find time to finish up, your mechanic can pick things up from where you left off. Be sure to show him your handbook so he can see for himself exactly what's been done.

If you do no other chapter, I recommend you do chapter 1 on spark plugs. This chapter takes 45 minutes to complete and in it, I show you how to examine the spark plugs for facts about your motor's condition. If you really want to check up on your mechanic, be sure to do the beginning of chapter 1.

Q: *Some shops charge only $40 for a tune-up. How do they do it?*

A: No shop will completely tune-up your Honda for just $40. Read the fine print and you'll realize you're paying $40 to have a set of spark plugs installed, and that's it. Yes, they do "scope check" your car. But, that fancy piece of equipment with the TV screen and the wavy lines is hardly necessary for a routine tune-up, particularly since few mechanics are able to accurately interpret the information a scope displays. To maintain your car's integrity, more needs to be done than just replacing spark plugs and ceremoniously connecting a scope.

Q: My mechanic doesn't always tune-up my Honda to run the way I like it. What makes you think I can?

A: You can because you care about your Honda. Let me explain. The faster your mechanic finishes with your car, the more money he makes. This is because your mechanic does not charge for the actual time it takes to tune-up your Honda. Instead, he charges you based on what is known in the business as "flat rate." Here's how flat rate works and why it's a threat to your Honda's happiness:

A book, known as *The Flat Rate Book* and often referred to as The Book, lists every conceivable repair your Honda might ever need and how much time each repair should take. Tune-ups and servicing and the time these procedures should take are listed in The Book.

Your mechanic, working fast, can often beat "book time" by 50 percent and more. Although a shop's posted hourly rate might seem reasonable, you pay for the hours listed in *The Flat Rate Book* and not the actual time spent tuning and servicing your Honda. For your mechanic, there is only a reward for a job done quickly. That might explain why your car isn't running like you know it should.

Q: What if I buy this handbook and later decide not to care for my Honda by myself, then what?

A: Whether or not you actually tune-up and service your Honda, you can benefit from this handbook. Have you ever had the feeling your mechanic was trying to sell you on work your Honda didn't need? Even if you don't actually put this handbook to use under the hood, just reading through it can arm you with the knowledge you need to be safe from unscrupulous or underqualified mechanics.

Q: My Honda is still under warranty. How will do-it-myself Honda care affect my warranty?

A: Caring for your Honda should not affect your warranty. Keep all receipts for parts and fluids purchased. Enter the work completed in the proper place in your warranty book. Be sure to include the date. Just to be safe, check with your dealer to ensure he requires no special method for keeping a record of what you have done yourself.

Q: What's going to happen to my hands?

A: Basic Honda care hardly dirties your hands. Grease-stained hands and broken fingernails come with heavy mechanical work. You'll be doing light tune-up and servicing, which is clean and easy on your hands, as well as your clothes.

Q: *What's my first step?*

A: That's easy—like the other steps in this handbook! Take *Honda Tune-up for the Mechanically Impaired* to the tool store and pick up the tools you need. At the beginning of each chapter the tools you'll be using are illustrated. See All about Tools on page xii.

Q: *Where will you be if I need you?*

A: I'll be available to help. Should you like to reach me with comments or questions, you can through the publisher's address at the beginning of the handbook. Be sure to include your return address so I can write back.

Happy Motoring!
Your Friend,
PAUL YOUNG

Spark plugs

Approximate Completion
Time: 45 minutes

*B*egin this chapter when the motor is cold to the touch. This is important because the spark plugs are screwed into the aluminum "head" of the motor, which expands and contracts faster than the threaded steel shaft of the spark plugs. When the motor is hot, the steel shafts of the spark plugs are ultra-tight in the aluminum "head." Attempting to remove a spark plug from a hot motor can severely damage the threaded spark-plug hole in the head, making it impossible to reinstall the spark plug. Be good to your "head."

Before you start

Spark plugs produce the spark that ignites the gas, which, in turn, creates the energy to run your motor and get you down the road. After thousands of miles of igniting gasoline more than 2,000 times per minute, the spark plugs need cleaning and adjusting or replacing. A sluggish feel to your Honda, decreased gas mileage, and hard starting are signs that spark plugs are ready for your attention. Figure 1-1 illustrates a typical spark plug.

By examining the texture and color of the combustion deposits on the electrodes of spark plugs, a mechanic can quickly and easily learn valuable information about a motor's internal condition. You, too, can do this! Along with basic instructions on how to remove and replace the spark plugs, I've included a simple spark plug check that will clue you in on your motor's internal condition.

If you have the feeling someone has been trying to sell you on motor work your Honda doesn't need, completing this chapter could arm you with the information you need to save yourself hundreds of dollars.

Fig. 1-1.
A typical spark plug.

What's ahead in this chapter

This chapter contains nine steps to cleaning, adjusting, or replacing spark plugs, as well as a troubleshooting section and a condensed "Second Time Around" section to speed you through your next check. The nine steps are:

STEP 1 How to locate and remove the spark plugs from the motor.

STEP 2 How to know if a used spark plug can still perform.

STEP 3 How to read a spark plug for information.

STEP 4 How to clean and file used spark plugs.

STEP 5 How to check the adjustment of a new and used spark plug.

STEP 6 How to adjust new and used spark plugs.

STEP 7 How to determine if a spark plug has a screw-on top.

STEP 8 How to put spark plugs back into the motor.

STEP 9 How to check the condition of the spark plug wires.

There is also a troubleshooting section at the end of the chapter as well as a section titled "The Second Time Around," a condensed version of this chapter to speed you through your next tune-up.

Tools

Figure 1-2 illustrates the tools you'll need to check or adjust the spark plugs in your Honda. For a more detailed description of these tools, see chapter 7. You will need:

☐ ratchet wrench with 3/8-inch drive. The 3/8-inch refers to the size of the drive peg.

☐ small file (optional). A small file can be used to shape the sparking surface of used spark plugs.

☐ stiff wire brush. A wire brush is used to clean used spark plugs.

☐ extension bar with 3/8-inch drive. A 2-inch or longer extension bar works fine for a motor with side-mounted spark plugs. For a motor with top-mounted spark plugs, a 6-inch or longer extension bar is necessary. To know which extension bar to purchase, see the section ''Which style motor does your Honda have?''

☐ spark plug socket with 3/8-inch drive. Hondas with top-mounted spark plugs use 5/8-inch spark plugs. See the subhead ''Which style motor does your Honda have?'' to know which size spark plugs are used in your Honda. Purchase a spark plug socket with a rubber insert that grips the spark plug. If you own a spark plug socket without this insert, you can still use it.

☐ wire gauge or feeler gauge. These tools are used for checking and setting the spark plug ''gap.''

☐ rubber hose. A short length (about 10 inches) of rubber tubing with a 3/16-inch inside diameter is an excellent tool for removing and replacing spark plugs. It is available at any auto parts store.

☐ ohmmeter (optional). An ohmmeter is an inexpensive tool used to check the internal condition of spark plug wires. If your spark plug wires are a few years old, you'll want to perform this test. I've seen this tool for as little as $6. Shown here, is one with alligator clip leads.

STEP I
How to locate and remove the spark plugs from the motor

Which style motor does your Honda have?

The spark plugs in your Honda are mounted either on the side of the motor as shown in FIG. 1-3 or on the top of the motor, hidden from view, as shown in FIG. 1-4. Open the hood and have a look. Does your motor have side-mounted or top-mounted spark plugs? In this chapter, if there's something special I want you to know about your particular style motor, I will tell you by referring to it as a side-mounted or top-mounted motor.

Locate spark plug No. I

Now that you know which style motor you have, look at the motor from the driver's side of your Honda. Using FIG. 1-3 or 1-4 as a guide (whichever shows your motor), locate spark plug No. 1. As these

Fig. 1-2
Tools used in this chapter.

Ratchet wrench with 3/8'' drive peg

Small file

Stiff wire brush

Extension bar with 3/8'' drive

Spark plug socket with 3/8'' drive

Wire gauge

Feeler gauge

Rubber hose

Ohmmeter

Fig. 1-3
A motor with side-mounted spark plugs and the location of spark plug No. 1.

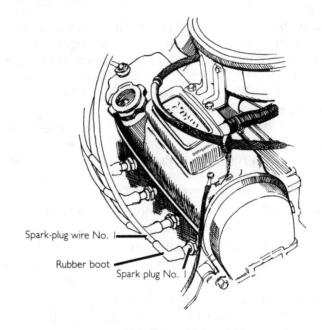

Spark-plug wire No. 1

Rubber boot

Spark plug No. 1

Fig. 1-4
A motor with top-mounted spark plugs and the location of spark plug No. 1.

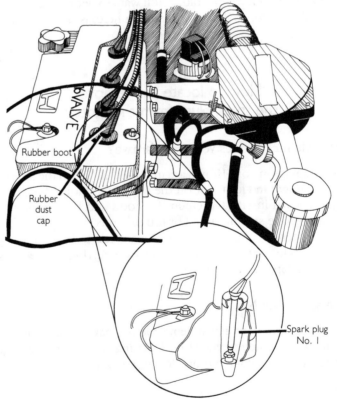

Rubber boot

Rubber dust cap

Spark plug No. 1

illustrations show, spark plug No. 1 is the spark plug closest to where you are standing. On motors with top-mounted spark plugs, you can't see spark plug No. 1 yet. It is, however, as shown in FIG. 1-4, under the dust cap of spark plug wire No. 1 and inside the valve cover.

Disconnect the spark plug wire from spark plug No. 1

Grab the rubber boot at the end of spark plug wire No. 1 and pull this rubber boot free from the spark plug. See FIG. 1-3 or 1-4 for a view of this rubber boot. To avoid damaging the spark plug wire, pull only on the boot—not the wire!

On some motors with side-mounted spark plugs, you must pull and also twist the rubber boot in order to release an inner lock that might be in use.

On motors with top-mounted spark plugs, peel back the rubber dust cap from the valve cover. This will make it easier to pull the connector free from the spark plug. See FIG. 1-4.

Stop! Do not disconnect more than one spark plug wire at this time! Each spark plug wire is attached to a specific spark plug. The spark plug wires are not connected at random. Therefore, you will service one spark plug at a time to avoid confusing which spark plug wire goes with which spark plug.

If you have some past automotive experience and are intent on removing all four spark plugs from the motor at once, before you do so, wrap a piece of masking tape around each spark plug wire and number each piece of tape. The wire you're removing now is No. 1. Thus, succeeding wires will be labeled 2, 3, and 4, in that order. In chapter 4, FIG. 4-7 illustrates this procedure.

Make sure the masking tape is on securely before you remove the spark plug wires from the spark plugs. As you remove the spark plugs from the motor, number them as well. This is important because, when you check the spark plugs for information about your motor's condition, you'll want to know from which cylinder you removed each spark plug.

Get your wrench "set" to use

Connect the ratchet wrench with the extension bar and spark plug socket as shown in FIG. 1-5. Spark plugs are removed from the motor by turning them counterclockwise. Take a minute to set your ratchet

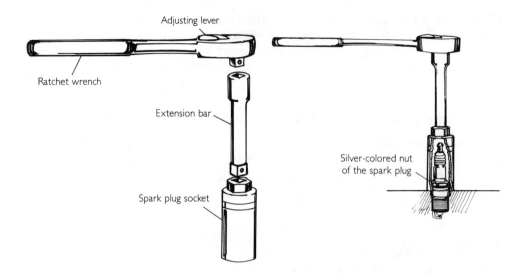

Adjusting lever

Ratchet wrench

Extension bar

Spark plug socket

Silver-colored nut
of the spark plug

wrench to loosen the spark plugs. Here's how to do it: Hold the spark plug socket in one hand. With the other hand, turn the ratchet wrench counterclockwise. If the spark plug socket turns in your hand, the ratchet wrench is set to remove the spark plugs. If the ratchet wrench makes a clicking sound and spins freely, see FIG. 1-5, and slide the adjusting lever on the head of the wrench. That's all there is to it; you're ready to go!

Slide your wrench down over the spark plug

Ensure the spark plug socket has slipped completely over the silver-colored nut of the spark plug as shown in FIG. 1-6. Figure 1-7 shows a good view of this silver-colored nut. If the extension bar gets in the way while working on a motor with side-mounted spark plugs, connect the spark plug socket directly to the ratchet wrench.

Many spark plug sockets have a black rubber insert that grips the porcelain shaft of the spark plug. This rubber insert prevents the spark plug from slipping out of the socket during removal. If your motor has top-mounted spark plugs, you might find removing the spark plugs a little difficult without this insert.

No matter from which style motor you're removing the spark plugs, if your spark plug socket has a rubber insert, you will have to push the spark plug socket down onto the silver-colored nut of the spark plug, thus forcing the porcelain shaft up into the rubber insert.

Loosen, but do not remove the spark plug

Turn the ratchet wrench counterclockwise to loosen the spark plug. Put a little muscle into it and the spark plug will "pop" loose and begin to unscrew from the motor. If the spark plug refuses to "pop" loose, skip ahead to the subhead "If the spark plug is stuck and won't pop loose."

Save your knuckles! A spark plug can "pop" loose under wrench pressure without warning. Before you begin to push or pull on your wrench, be sure nothing is directly in the path your hand will travel should the spark plug "pop" loose.

When applying muscle power to your wrench, don't let the spark plug socket tilt itself on the spark plug. You can accomplish this on side-mounted spark plugs by supporting the spark plug socket with one hand and turning the wrench with the other. On motors with top-mounted spark plugs, support the head of your ratchet wrench with one hand. If the spark plug socket tilts on the spark plug, it might crack the porcelain shaft of the spark plug, rendering it useless.

When the spark plug begins to unscrew, stop what you're doing. Don't remove the spark plug yet. On motors with side-mounted spark plugs, you're going to do a little cleaning up first. On motors with top-mounted spark plugs, there's a few things I want you to know before you completely unscrew the spark plugs.

If the spark plug is stuck and won't pop loose

Occasionally, a stubborn spark plug becomes just plain stuck in the motor. Rather than force it out and take the chance of ruining the threads in the motor, pour solvent around the base of the spark plug. Kerosene, turpentine, paint thinner, or any solvent will do.

An easy way to get the liquid to the base of the spark plug without making a mess is to roll a piece of notebook paper into a long, thin cone with a small point. Hold the small end of the cone at the base of the spark plug and slowly pour in the solvent.

Allow the solvent about 30 minutes to work its way in. Next, squirt some oil around the base of the spark plug. Allow another 30 minutes standing time. At this point, the spark plug should pop loose.

Side-mounted spark plugs

Once the spark plug begins to loosen, remove the socket wrench. With a clean rag, wipe all dirt and grease from the area where the spark plug will unscrew from the motor. This prevents grime from falling into the motor after the spark plug has been removed. When you're done cleaning up around the spark plug, remove the spark plug from the motor.

If your spark plug socket has a rubber insert, the socket will grip the spark plug while you lift it up from the motor and into your hand. If there is no rubber insert, get your hand down there and grab that spark plug before it falls to the ground.

Once a spark plug "pops" loose, it can no longer provide the resistance a ratchet wrench needs to ratchet, and you're left turning the spark plug back and forth. At this point, the best thing to do is remove the ratchet wrench from the extension bar and use your fingers. If you prefer to use the ratchet wrench, lightly grip the extension bar between your thumb and index finger to provide the needed resistance.

Top-mounted spark plugs

Before removing the spark plug, ensure that it's secure in the spark plug socket. The last thing you want is a spark plug to slip out of the spark plug socket and be left sitting at the bottom of the long tube that runs through the valve cover. To avoid this, be certain the porcelain shaft of the spark plug is tight in the rubber insert of the spark plug socket. Then, lift it up and out of the tube. A gentle push on your wrench just before the spark plug is completely unscrewed will ensure a tight fit.

When the spark plug becomes too loose to create the resistance your ratchet wrench needs to work, you have plenty of room to turn your wrench in complete circles. Support the extension bar with your fingers to protect the porcelain shaft of the spark plug.

Caution! After removing the spark plug, cover the top of the tube in the valve cover with a rag. This prevents any small objects from falling into the motor through the open spark plug hole.

If your spark plug socket does not have a rubber insert, before completely unscrewing the plug from the motor, push the 3/16-inch (inside diameter) rubber tube over the porcelain shaft. You can then use it to unscrew and lift the spark plug out.

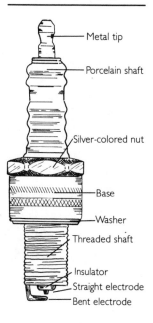

Fig. 1-7
The parts of a spark plug.

Metal tip
Porcelain shaft
Silver-colored nut
Base
Washer
Threaded shaft
Insulator
Straight electrode
Bent electrode

Identify the parts of the spark plug

With the spark plug now in your hand, take a look at FIG. 1-7, which illustrates the parts of a spark plug. Take a minute to study this illustration because knowing the parts of the spark plug will come in handy later in the chapter.

STEP 2
How to know if a used spark plug can still perform

Is this spark plug worn out? A spark plug with thousands of miles of use left in it has a straight electrode that is flat on top and a bent electrode that is not worn thin. Electrode condition is illustrated in FIG. 1-8.

    A little rounding around the edges of the straight electrode is okay, but when it's far from flat on top and close to being worn down to the insulator, don't reuse it in your motor. Likewise, a very thin, bent electrode qualifies a spark plug for the trash can. If one spark plug in your motor is worn out, the others will be worn out, too. Replace the spark plugs in your motor as a set.

    A worn spark plug does not produce the good, strong spark required to get the most power out of the gas entering your motor. Yes, you can reuse worn spark plugs, particularly if your motor has been running okay on them. The loss in gas mileage from these worn spark plugs will, however, soon cost you more than the $5 or $6 for a new set of spark plugs.

    If you do find the spark plug to be worn out, don't toss it in the trash until you complete the spark plug checks in STEP 3. These checks will supply you with valuable information about your motor's internal condition.

Special note for 1980 – 1991 Honda owners

All 1980–1991 Hondas are equipped with an electronic ignition. Often, this type of ignition system does not cause spark plugs to show visible signs of wear. No matter how flat the top of the straight

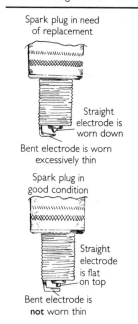

Fig. 1-8
Examine the condition of the bent and straight electrodes.

Spark plug in need of replacement

Straight electrode is worn down

Bent electrode is worn excessively thin

Spark plug in good condition

Straight electrode is flat on top

Bent electrode is **not** worn thin

electrode might appear or how thick the bent electrode, you should replace the spark plugs in your motor every 12 months.

The need for this annual replacement schedule is because the electricity passing through a spark plug tends to build resistance to the flow of electrons. This reduces spark plug efficiency. Although you might not see any visible signs of wear, the spark plug is becoming clogged inside.

STEP 3
How to read a spark plug for information

The quick and simple spark plug checks in this section will reveal some very useful information about your motor's internal condition. Mechanics use these same checks to diagnose most motor problems. In STEP 2, you might have found your spark plug to have plenty of life left in it. Due to conditions found in this step, however, I might tell you not to reuse it.

1. *Are the electrodes covered with wet, black, oily deposits?*
   If yes, replace this spark plug with a new one. An oily spark plug means badly worn motor parts. Be prepared for expensive trouble in the not-too-distant future. Bad oil rings, worn cylinders, a cracked piston, or bad valve guides are motor parts that might need repair. If a bluish-color smoke has been pouring out the tail pipe, the end is near! Your motor is burning oil.

   Sometimes, oil fouling occurs in new or just-rebuilt motors. The problem usually clears up once the motor is broken in.

> If you're not sure of the difference between oil and gas, smell the spark plug. Gas is watery and oil is sticky and usually black. Rubbing some of the substance from the spark plug between your fingers will also help you decide.

2. *Are there deposits bridging the space (the gap) between the bent and straight electrodes?*
   If yes, replace this spark plug with a new one. This is not a sign of motor trouble.

3. *Are the bent and straight electrodes melted or burnt? Is the insulator surrounding the straight electrode cracked? Are there metalliclike deposits on the insulator?*

A yes answer to any, or all, of these checks means this spark plug is to be replaced with a new one. Chances are, this spark plug is the wrong one for your motor. All auto parts stores have a *Spark Plug Application Chart*, which identifies the correct spark plug.

If this turns out to be the right spark plug for your motor, any or all of the spark plug conditions mentioned in check 3 can be caused by the following motor problems:

~ The air-to-fuel ratio entering the motor might be too lean, lacking sufficient gas. On both fuel injected and carbureted engines, a lean condition can be caused by a vacuum leak.

   A vacuum leak is air being drawn into the motor through some place normally sealed with a gasket. This excess air entering the motor "fans" the burning fuel mixture, creating a hotter burning explosion that can affect a spark plug in the ways mentioned in check 3. Your mechanic can find a vacuum leak using a special chemical.

~ The ignition timing might be too far advanced. The solution to this problem is covered in chapter 3.

~ The gas you are using might be too low grade. The next time you stop for gas, try another station or a higher-octane fuel.

~ Internal motor parts might be worn, requiring major work. Thoroughly check all other possibilities before considering this to be the problem with your motor.

4. *Is the insulator white with black spots?*
   If yes, this spark plug cannot be reused. A spark plug with a white insulator covered with black spots tells you the air/fuel mixture is too lean—not enough fuel—this is covered in chapter 5. This spark plug condition can also be caused by the motor timing being too far advanced. This is covered in chapter 3. This spark plug condition is often the result of someone not screwing the spark plug tightly into the engine. If the spark plug was very easy to pop loose, this is probably the reason it looks as it does.

5. *Are the straight and bent electrodes covered with gas?*
   If you discover gas on the electrodes, do not reuse this spark plug. This condition can mean the air/fuel mixture is too rich. A rich mixture is an air/fuel mixture containing an excess of gas. More about this in chapter 5.

   Gas-covered electrodes can also be caused by worn engine parts. Here's why: gas will explode completely only when it is ignited under pressure. Should certain internal motor parts become defective, a motor will develop leaks that prevent it from creating the pressure needed to completely explode gasoline. Some of this unexploded gasoline collects on the electrodes of the spark plugs. A cracked piston, worn compression rings, burned valves, or a "blown" head gasket are some parts that, when defective, can allow pressure to escape from the motor.

6. *Is the white porcelain shaft cracked?*

Should you discover even the slightest crack, replace the spark plug with a new one. A crack is not a sign of an engine problem, and chances are, you accidentally cracked the porcelain while removing the spark plug.

7. *Are the bent and straight electrodes covered with a black, fluffy, dry, carbon material?*

If yes, this might indicate any of the following conditions:

~ A damaged spark plug wire in need of replacement. See STEP 8, to test your spark plug wires.

~ Sticking or slightly burned valves.

~ A fuel mixture too rich due to a clogged air filter or a faulty carburetor or fuel-injection system. Chapter 6 covers air filter condition.

~ If the check engine light or the O2 (oxygen) sensor light is illuminated on the dashboard it probably has something to do with the condition of the spark plug. Usually, replacing the oxygen sensor will solve the problem. See chapter 6 for how to change the O2 sensor.

~ On carbureted Hondas, the choke valve might need to be adjusted or repaired. The choke valve cuts the flow of air to the engine during cold engine start-ups. This causes a fuel mixture heavy with gas, which is what a cold engine needs to run. Once the engine becomes warm, the choke valve should open and allow air to flow freely in with the gas. If the choke valve does not open, black carbon deposits result.

You can easily check the operation of the choke valve by yourself. To do this, first drive the car until the temperature gauge shows the motor to be warmed up to normal operating temperature. Then, see chapter 6 and remove the top of the air filter box to check the choke valve as instructed in STEP 2.

~ On a fuel injected car, a leaking fuel injector, a leaking cold start valve, or a malfunctioning fuel pressure regulator can cause black carbon deposits on a spark plug.

8. *Are the bent and straight electrodes coated with a black or yellow residue that is cinder or glazelike?*

If yes, this might not be the correct spark plug for your motor. Have an auto parts store verify the correct spark plug. If it turns out this is the correct spark plug for your motor, chances are, the deposits will go away as a result of this tune-up.

9. *Are the bent and straight electrodes coated with white deposits?* If yes, this might be the wrong spark plug for your engine. Have an auto parts store verify the correct spark plug. It is also possible the carburetor or fuel-injection system is adjusted too lean— not getting enough gas to the motor in proportion to air. Clogged fuel injectors or a faulty pressure regulator can cause this problem on a fuel-injected car. On a carbureted car, internal carburetor parts in need of replacement or cleaning can cause this spark plug condition.

On both fuel-injected or carbureted cars, this lean condition can be caused by a vacuum leak. Once again, a vacuum leak is air being drawn into the motor through an area normally sealed by a gasket. This excess air entering the motor "fans" the burning fuel mixture, creating a hotter-burning explosion.

10. *Do the bent and straight electrodes have some spotty deposits that don't look like anything I've told you about so far?* Don't worry about these spotty deposits. They are probably just the result of a little "blow-by" coming out of the combustion chamber when the fuel is ignited.

11. *Is there a light brown deposit on the bent and straight electrodes?* If yes, this is what you want! A light brown coating means everything is fine and your motor is in good shape. Completing the tune-up will help keep it that way.

Each of the four spark plugs in your motor is screwed into what is known as a cylinder. Hondas are four-cylinder motors. Thus, your motor has four spark plugs. Each cylinder in the motor has its own piston, with rings, valves, and bearings. For this reason, it's possible for a spark plug to show one section of your engine to be in perfect condition, while the spark plug from another cylinder might show an expensive repair is needed.

Yes, it is possible to find a mechanic who will repair the problem in just one cylinder. The entire motor, however, must be disassembled to get to that one cylinder, which makes it foolish to service just one cylinder when, no doubt, the others are also close to needing attention. "Tearing down" a motor and only fixing the problem cylinder is a well-known trick of dishonest used car dealers.

STEP 4
How to clean and file used spark plugs

With a stiff wire brush, clean any deposits from the bent and straight electrodes. Also, get the brush bristles down around the base of the insulator and up into the body of the spark plug. Now, close your eyes tight and blow hard on the electrodes and insulator and up into the body of the spark plug. Blow away all that loose dirt. Just one small speck of dirt can short-circuit a spark plug.

File the spark plug

If the end of the straight electrode is worn unevenly or appears a little pointed, you can level it with a small, fine-tooth file. Close your eyes and blow away the metal filings when you're finished. Some mechanics will tell you the scratch marks left from the file fill with carbon and decrease spark plug efficiency. Others will tell you filing the surface flat is necessary to get a good spark across the electrodes. It's six of one, half a dozen of the other. I like to file them myself.

STEP 5
How to check the adjustment
of a new and used spark plug

Checking the spark plug gap is nothing more than checking the distance between the bent and straight electrodes. This is a simple operation done with a feeler gauge or wire gauge. New spark plugs rarely come pre-adjusted for your motor, which means it's important to check their adjustment before installing them. Consult TABLE 1-1, The Spark Plug Gap Chart, and note the correct spark plug gap for your Honda.

Table 1-1 Spark Plug Gap Chart

Year	Model	Gap (inches)
1975–1979	All models	.030
1980	Accord & Prelude	
	All except California cars with automatic transmission	.030
	California cars with automatic transmission	.040
	Civic	
	Manual and automatic transmission	.040
1981–1991	All models	.042

The numbers on the spark plug gap chart are in thousandths of an inch. Mark the correct gap for your car so you can find it again easily. Don't let these numbers intimidate you; they're really no problem.

If you're using a feeler gauge, locate the blade stamped with the correct spark plug gap for your car. Some feeler gauge sets might not have blades as thick as .030 inch (thirty thousandths of an inch), which is the smallest spark plug gap on the chart. In this case, use the correct combination of smaller-numbered blades. For example, when held together, the .015-inch blade, the .010-inch blade, and the .005-inch blade equal a .030-inch blade. If you're using two or more feeler gauge blades in place of one thick one, squeeze them together when measuring the spark plug gap.

Most feeler gauge blades are marked in thousandths of an inch and in millimeters. Millimeters are designated on the blade as mm. For our purposes, use only the numbers marked in inches.

If you're using a wire gauge, locate the wire stamped with the correct spark plug gap for your car. Every wire on the wire gauge has its thickness stamped on the handle of the tool. Some wire gauge sets might not have the exact size wire asked for in the chart. In this case, use the wire closest to your motor's specifications.

Most wire gauge sets are marked in thousandths of an inch on one side of the tool and in millimeters, designated as mm, on the other side of the tool. For our purposes, use only the side marked in inches.

Gently slide the correct size wire or feeler gauge blade between the bent and straight electrode. If the wire or blade you are using will not fit, or the space between the two electrodes is wider than the thickness of the wire or blade, this spark plug is in need of adjustment. A spark plug is in adjustment when the blade or wire makes light contact with both electrodes as it is slipped in-between them. See FIGS. 1-9 and 1-10 for how to check the spark plug gap with a feeler gauge or wire gauge.

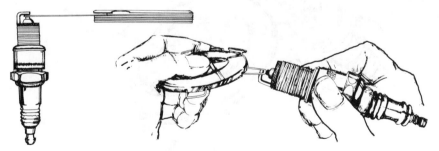

Fig. 1-9 (Left)
Insert a feeler gauge blade between the bent and straight electrode to check the distance.

Fig. 1-10 (Right)
Use a wire gauge to check the distance between the bent and straight electrodes.

Some mechanics claim a feeler gauge is not as accurate as a wire gauge. They reason it is possible to insert a feeler gauge blade at an angle and get an inaccurate measurement. If you're using a feeler gauge, be sure the blade goes in level and not at an angle.

STEP 6
How to adjust new and used spark plugs

Using a feeler gauge

To adjust your spark plug using a feeler gauge, bend the bent electrode closer to, or further away from, the straight electrode as necessary. To make the gap smaller, tap the bent electrode on a hard surface. The gap can be made larger by prying on the bent electrode with a small screwdriver or one of the thicker feeler gauge blades in the set.

As you already know, a spark plug is in adjustment when the correct size feeler gauge blade makes light contact with both electrodes as it is slipped between them.

Using a wire gauge

To put your spark plug into adjustment using a wire gauge, bend the bent electrode closer to—or further away from—the straight electrode, as necessary. Your wire gauge set has an attachment that will do the job as shown in FIG. 1-11. As you already know, a spark plug is in adjustment when the correct size wire makes light contact with both electrodes as it is slipped between them.

Fig. 1-11
Use a wire gauge to adjust the distance between the bent and straight electrodes.

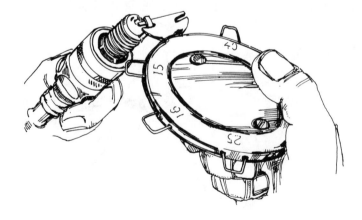

STEP 7
How to know if a spark plug has a screw-on top

A spark plug with a screw-on top is identified by a hole in the center of the top. If the top is solid and smooth, it is not a screw-on type and should be left alone. New spark plugs often come packaged with the screw-on top loose in the box. This is okay. Just screw the top on as shown in FIG. 1-12.

Ensure the screw on top is tight. Hold the nut of the spark plug, being careful not to disturb the electrodes. Use the fingers of your other hand to ensure the screw-on top is tight. It's okay to use pliers on the top, but be gentle. Turn the top clockwise to tighten it.

The top should screw down flush with the body of the spark plug. If not, it's on upside down. Take it off, turn it over, and put it back on.

STEP 8
How to put spark plugs back into the motor

Clean the porcelain shaft of a used spark plug

With a clean rag, wipe away any dirt and grease that can make a good conductor for electricity and cause a spark plug to short circuit.

Ensure the metal washer is against the base of the spark plug

If the metal washer is not against the base of the spark plug, move it as shown in FIG. 1-13.

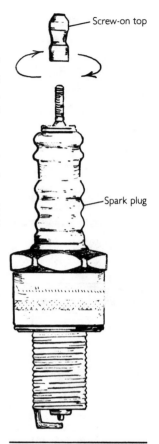

Fig. 1-12
Putting on the screw-on top.

Oil the threaded shaft of the spark plug

A few drops of oil on the threaded shaft of the spark plug is helpful. Not only does a little oil make it easier to put the spark plug back into the motor, but it helps prevent the spark plug from bonding with the motor during upcoming months of use. Once a spark plug has bonded with the motor, it is so difficult to remove that it usually causes damage to the motor.

When applying oil to the threads of the spark plug, don't squirt it all over. Put a few drops on your fingers and rub it in to lightly coat the threads. Be extra careful not to get any on the electrodes!

If you don't have any oil handy, pull the oil dipstick from the motor and use your fingers to remove the oil from the end of the dipstick. See chapter 6 for the oil dipstick location.

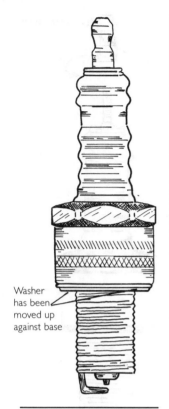

Washer
has been
moved up
against base

Fig. 1-13
Be sure the metal washer is up
against the base of the spark
plug all the way around.

Anti-Seize Compound is a product available at automotive stores that is designed specifically to prevent spark plugs from bonding with an engine. A few drops of oil works also, but I do know mechanics who use only Anti-Seize Compound.

Push the porcelain shaft of the spark plug into the rubber hose

Push the porcelain shaft of the spark plug into the rubber hose with the 3/16-inch inside diameter. Use this hose as your tool for getting the spark plug started back into its hole. A short piece of rubber hose is the perfect tool for getting a spark plug started back into the motor. Should the spark plug be going in at an angle and cross-threading, the hose will slip on the porcelain shaft of the spark plug and save the threads in the motor from damage. See FIG. 1-14.

Caution! Never use a wrench to start a spark plug back into the motor. Should you accidentally get a spark plug started in crooked, you might not feel it. Forcing a crooked spark plug into the motor will ruin the hole into which the spark plug screws. This is an expensive repair. If a spark plug is not going in while turning the rubber hose by hand, it is not going in correctly.

On motors with side-mounted spark plugs, the hole the spark plug screws into is on a slant. To get the spark plug started back into the hole, you must hold it at the same angle as the hole it is about to enter.

Continue turning by hand until the spark plug will turn no further. The spark plug should go most—if not all—the way in by hand.

Use the ratchet wrench when the spark plug becomes too tight to turn by hand. Now that you are sure the spark plug is going in correctly, pull the rubber tube from the spark plug. Slide the adjusting lever on your ratchet wrench so it will turn the spark plug in a clockwise direction. With your wrench, continue tightening the spark plug until it is set tightly into its hole.

Caution! Do not attempt to tighten the spark plug until it will turn no further. You will never reach this point; you'll end up damaging the hole into which the spark plug is screwed. What you should do is put the spark plug in so it is really snug—and then just a "drop" more (about $^1/_{16}$ of a turn) to firmly secure it.

Motors with side-mounted spark plugs

Reconnect the spark plug wire to the spark plug, ensuring a "snap-tight" fit. Look into the cap at the end of the spark plug wire. That metal tube in there fits over the top of the spark plug and grips it. Slide the rubber boot onto the spark plug, push it down firmly, and feel for the "snap" the metal tube makes as it engages the top of the spark plug. If the cap slides on and off without the metal tube snapping onto the top of the spark plug, you need to tighten up the fit.

To tighten up the fit, lightly squeeze the rubber boot with a pair of pliers as shown in FIG. 1-15. The metal tube inside the rubber boot will also get squeezed. If you squeeze too hard, the metal tube will become too small to fit over the top of the spark plug. Use a screwdriver blade to pry the tube apart and try again. Do not attempt to tighten the fit of connectors used on top-mounted spark plugs.

Motors with top-mounted spark plugs

Reconnect the spark plug wire to the spark plug by pushing the connector firmly into place. Reposition the dust boot. As you lower the spark plug connector down into the tube in the valve cover and over the top of the spark plug, make sure the connector goes over the top of the spark plug and does not get pushed to the side.

Fig. 1-14
A rubber hose makes a "safe" tool for starting a spark plug back into the motor.

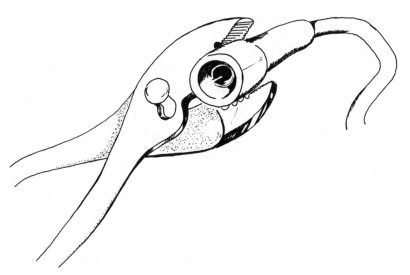

Fig. 1-15
If necessary, squeeze the metal tube inside the rubber cap on a motor with side-mounted spark plugs.

This is a safe stopping point

Now that you have completely serviced or replaced one spark plug in your motor, you can move on to take care of the other three, or call it a day and do the others as time permits. The choice is yours. Your Honda will suffer no damage if you drive it. I do suggest, however, that you get to the other plugs within a few weeks. In this way, if you're replacing worn spark plugs, they will all be equally worn the next time you work from this chapter. Plus, with four serviced or new spark plugs in your motor, you'll enjoy improved gas mileage and feel more power.

Service the three remaining spark plugs in exactly the same way as the one you just took care of. Be sure to service these three spark plugs one at a time to safeguard against confusing which spark plug wire goes with which spark plug. If you should decide to remove all three spark plugs at once, be sure to label the spark plug wires and the spark plugs as explained at the beginning of this chapter.

At the end of this chapter is a section titled ''The Second Time Around.'' You can use section to help speed you through the job of servicing the three spark plugs still in the motor. Refer back to the text should you need more details. After you have serviced all four spark plugs, start the motor to be sure you have correctly completed all procedures. If the motor seems to have developed a problem it didn't have previously, see the Troubleshooting section.

STEP 9
How to check the condition of the spark plug wires

Danger! Two of the following tests are performed with the motor running. During these tests, it is possible to accidentally receive an electrical shock from the spark plug wires. If you have a medical condition that makes it particularly dangerous for you to receive an electrical shock, do not do the two tests that are performed with the motor running.

The condition of the spark plug wires is just as important as the condition of the spark plugs. Cracked or broken spark plug wires will not deliver enough voltage to produce a strong spark across the electrodes of the spark plugs. This, in turn, results in incomplete fuel combustion and poor motor performance. An obvious clue to cracked spark plug wires is a motor that starts hard during damp or wet mornings, but starts right up later in the day after the motor is warmed up or the weather improves.

A simple test for cracked or broken spark plug wires is to watch the engine run in the dark. If you see blue or yellow sparking around the wires, this is a sure sign electricity is escaping. These wires are cracked and must be replaced. The leaping spark test is another good test for faulty spark plug wires.

If you saw no "sparking in the dark," here's another good test for cracks or breaks: Select a screwdriver with a well-insulated handle. Remove the insulation from each end of a 3-foot or longer piece of wire. Wrap one bare end of the wire around the metal shank of the screwdriver and twist it tightly. Wrap the other end tightly around the ground wire connector on the valve cover as shown in FIG. 1-16. Put your tool down someplace where the attached wire won't get tangled in the fan or moving belts when you start the motor. If your car has an automatic transmission, put the gear selector in park. Manual transmissions must be in neutral. Apply the parking brake and start the motor.

Pick up your screwdriver with the wire attached. Hold the screwdriver by the insulated handle and rub the screwdriver blade over the spark plug wires. Listen and watch for sparks leaping towards the blade. Sparks will jump as far as an inch to reach the blade. Should you discover any leaping sparks, replace that wire.

Caution! Should sparks leap during the above test, do not continue to make them leap. This might harm your car's computer.

Fig. 1-16 (Below left) Check the spark plug wires for cracks with a well-insulated screwdriver and a piece of wire.

Fig. 1-17 (Below right) Use an ohmmeter to check spark plug wire resistance.

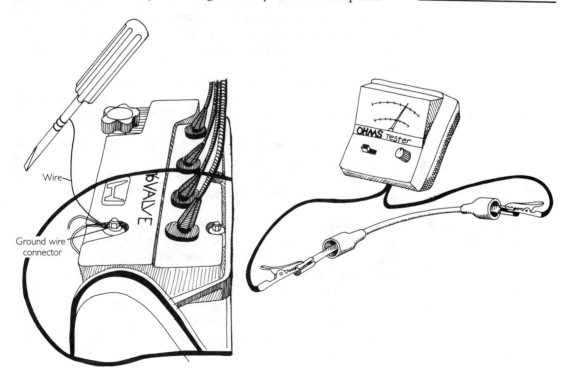

Wire

Ground wire connector

Check the coil wire

The plastic cap to which the other end of each spark plug wire is connected is known as the distributor cap. That short wire coming out of the center of the distributor cap is the coil wire. (Some models do not have a coil wire). Check this wire the same way you did the spark plug wires with the sparks in the dark or leaping sparks test and replace it if necessary.

Check the resistance of the spark plug wires

It is possible the spark plug wires will pass the "spark in the dark" test and the "leaping spark" test and still be in need of replacement. This is because, as electricity flows through the spark plug wires, the wires gradually build resistance to the flow of electrons. Eventually, this resistance becomes so great that it causes a substantial reduction in the flow of electrons, which results in a weaker spark at the spark plug and a noticeable reduction in motor performance.

A motor that starts up easily but severely lacks power or stops running when you step on the gas might well be a motor whose spark plug wires are too high in internal resistance. An inexpensive electrical tester known as an ohmmeter is used to measure the internal resistance of spark plug wires from end to end. Although I would normally advise you against buying tools and parts at discount chain stores, this is one tool you can safely buy there. For this purpose, you don't need a high-quality meter. I've seen ohmmeters for as little as $6.

To check the internal resistance of a spark plug wire, stop the motor and remove one spark plug wire from a spark plug and the distributor cap—the plastic unit at the other end of the spark plug wire. The spark plug wire is removed from the spark plug by pulling on the rubber boot at the end of the wire as shown in FIGS. 1-3 and 1-4. To remove the spark plug wire from the distributor cap, peel back the small rubber boot at this end of the spark plug wire, grasp the wire as close to the distributor cap as possible, and gently pull it free.

Caution! You don't want to confuse which spark plug wire goes to which spark plug. Remove, test, and replace one wire at a time. If your distributor has a center wire, known as a coil wire, don't forget to test it as well.

To test the spark plug wire, attach one lead from your ohmmeter to one end of the spark plug wire and the other ohmmeter lead to the other end of the spark plug wire (see FIG. 1-17). You must connect to the metal connector inside the ends of the spark plug wire. If the reading on your ohmmeter does not exceed 25,000 ohms, this spark plug wire is in good shape. Any reading in excess of 25,000 ohms means the wire should be replaced.

When you put the spark plug wire back into the distributor cap, make sure the metal connector at the end of the wire slips down into the distributor cap, contacting the metal surface inside.

Do yourself a big favor, and don't skimp on the quality of the spark plug wires you buy. Avoid the big discount chains and purchase your wires at an auto parts store that supplies shops and gas stations. If in doubt, ask a local shop to recommend a reputable parts store. Professional mechanics avoid discount chains because they can't afford to do a job twice due to the failure of a "discounted" part.

That's it, you're done! If you have replaced old, tired spark plugs and faulty spark plug wires, you're about to feel a real difference in motor power and see a substantial increase in gas mileage. Have fun!!

I recommend you do chapter 2 next and check the parts that are responsible for creating the "juice" that fires the spark plugs. If you like the way your Honda feels now, just wait until you've completed chapter 2.

Troubleshooting

If the motor doesn't run as well as it did before you began this chapter, you may have goofed. Ask yourself the following questions:

○ Did I screw the spark plugs securely into the engine? (page 17)

○ Did I crack the porcelain shaft on any of the spark plugs while loosening or tightening them? (page 7)

○ Did I gap the spark plugs correctly? (page 15)

○ Did I remember to tighten down the top of a spark plug with a screw on top? (page 17)

○ Does the metal tube inside the rubber cap snap securely over the top of the spark plug? (page 19)

○ Did I pull on any of the spark plug wires, causing them to become loose in the distributor cap (the unit the other end of each spark plug wire is plugged into)? (page 5)

○ If you tested the spark plug wires, did you plug them firmly back into the distributor cap, ensuring the metal end of the spark plug wire contacts the metal surface inside the distributor cap. (page 23)

The second time around

This section is a condensed version of this chapter to help speed you through your next tune-up.

Tools

- ☐ ratchet wrench
- ☐ extension bar
- ☐ spark plug socket
- ☐ feeler gauge or wire gauge
- ☐ 3/16-inch inside diameter rubber tubing and the optional wire brush and small file.

Procedure

The following is a condensed step-by-step version for checking and replacing spark plugs:

1. Turn the spark plug counterclockwise to remove it for inspection. Clean any dirt away from the spark plug hole before removing the spark plug.

2. Examine the bent and straight electrodes to determine if this spark plug still has a strong spark left in it.

3. Look the spark plug over for important information about your motor's internal condition. If there is a light brown residue on the spark plug, this is perfect.

4. If you're going to reuse the spark plug, clean and file it as necessary.

5. Check the adjustment of a new or used spark plug.

6. Adjust the spark plug gap if necessary.

7. Secure the screw-on top if one is used.

8. Be sure the washer is up against the base of the spark plug. Start the spark back into the motor by hand using a rubber tube as a guide. Tighten the spark plug securely when you're positive it is going into the motor correctly. Reconnect the spark plug wire to the spark plug. Check for a "snap-tight" fit.

9. Check the condition of the spark plug wires.

The ignition system

*T*he 1979 Prelude and Accord and all 1980 and newer model Hondas are equipped with an electronic ignition system. This system requires little servicing as compared to the mechanical ignition system found in earlier models. If you're the happy owner of a Honda with an electronic ignition, you can skip STEPS 1 through 8 of this chapter and begin with STEP 9.

Approximate Completion Time: 2 hours, 20 minutes

Before you start

Reading this section is completely optional. If you have the time, do take a few minutes and learn about the things you'll be doing in this chapter. There are two types of ignition systems used on Hondas— mechanical ignition systems and electronic ignition systems.

Mechanical ignition systems

Older model Hondas use a mechanical ignition system. In a mechanical ignition system, as shown in FIG. 2-1, the points and condenser, distributor cap, rotor, and coil produce the ultrahigh voltage that causes the spark plugs to spark. As you might remember from chapter 1, the spark plugs ignite the gasoline entering your motor. So, it follows that a "healthy" ignition system, one capable of producing a strong spark at the spark plugs, means more complete fuel combustion and, in return, better gas mileage and more power.

Electronic ignition systems

Electronic ignition systems are used on newer model Hondas. An electronic ignition system does not rely on the condenser and

Fig. 2-1
The ignition system.

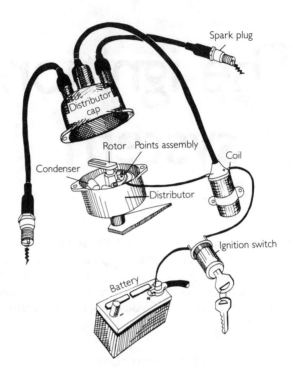

points found in a mechanical system. Instead, it uses a virtually maintenance-free electronic unit. An electronic ignition does, however, operate on the same basic principle as the mechanical system. If your Honda has an electronic ignition, I encourage you to continue reading this section and learn how an ignition system operates and also about the rotor and distributor cap, the two parts you will be servicing in STEP 9.

Worn ignition systems

A worn ignition system means a "tired" motor. Through use, the points eventually become worn, burned, and pitted, as does the distributor cap and rotor. When this happens, the spark plugs do not receive sufficient voltage to create a good strong spark, which results in reduced fuel combustion, poor gas mileage, and a loss in motor power. Worn ignition parts can also cause a motor to backfire, misfire, develop a rough idle, be difficult to start and, in some instances, not start at all. Although a condenser rarely shows visible signs of wear, it is replaced whenever new points are installed. The ignition coil does not require servicing.

How the ignition system works

The ignition system sparks the spark plugs. While the motor is running, the points are continually opening and closing, acting as a switch for what is known as the primary stage of the ignition coil. When the points are closed (touching each other), as shown in FIG. 2-11, the primary stage of the ignition coil is supplied with 12 volts from the car battery. When the points open (FIG. 2-5), these 12 volts are transferred to the secondary stage of the ignition coil, increased to 20,000 volts, and sent through the coil wire to the distributor.

Inside the distributor, the rotor receives this 20,000 volts. As it spins, the rotor transfers this voltage to each of the four spark plug wire terminals in the distributor cap. As you learned in chapter 1, the spark plug wires connect these terminals with the spark plugs. In this way, the distributor distributes voltage to each spark plug. At freeway speeds, this process is repeated more than 12,000 times per minute.

The condenser

The condenser plays a major role in the operation of your Honda's motor, because it absorbs excess electricity that would otherwise cause the points to arc and misfire, making the motor skip and backfire. In addition, by absorbing excess electricity, the condenser saves the points from quickly pitting and burning out.

A defective condenser can cause a motor to run intermittently—or not at all. More than one mechanic has done a major rebuild on a motor only to find that an intermittently faulty condenser was the problem. Whenever new points are installed, be sure to put in a new condenser.

Inspecting the ignition system

A periodic check of the ignition system ensures that your Honda operates at peak performance and gets optimum gas mileage. The points, condenser, rotor, and distributor cap play an important role in the operation of your Honda's motor. The condition of the points, distributor, and rotor should be checked periodically and new parts installed as needed to be sure your Honda has zippy performance and good gas mileage.

The points and condenser should be replaced after every 10,000 to 12,000 miles. They might, however, need to be replaced sooner. In STEP 4, you'll examine the condition of the points. If you find them to be burned, pitted, or worn, they should be replaced.

Tools for 1979 and Newer
Accords and Preludes
and 1980 and Newer Civics

No. 2 Phillips head screwdriver

Tools for 1978 and Older
Accords and Preludes
and 1979 and Older Civics

Feeler gauge

Points file (optional tool)

Offset screwdrivers

Medium-sized screwdriver

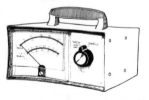

No. 2 Phillips head screwdriver

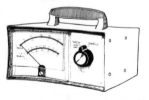

Tach and dwell meter (optional)

Fig. 2-2
The tools used in this chapter.

The points and condenser are replaced as a pair. The distributor cap and rotor will often last 30,000 miles or more and are replaced when an inspection shows it is time to do so.

What's ahead in this chapter

STEPS 1–8 are for 1978 and older Preludes and Accords and 1979 and older Civics. All other models, see STEP 9.

STEP 1 Locating the points and condenser.

STEP 2 How the points operate.

STEP 3 How to determine the condition of the points.

STEP 4 How to remove and install the points and condenser.

STEP 5 How to position the points for checking and adjusting.

STEP 6 How to check the points adjustment.

STEP 7 How to adjust (gap) the points.

STEP 8 How to check the condition of the rotor and distributor cap and lube the distributor cam.

STEP 9 How to check the condition of the rotor and distributor cap on Hondas equipped with an electronic ignition (1979 Preludes and Accords and all 1980 and newer models).

At the end of this chapter is a troubleshooting section and a section called "The second time around," a condensed version of this chapter to speed you through your next tune-up. There is also a section on how to adjust the points using a dwell meter.

Tools

Figure 2-2 illustrates the tools you'll need in this chapter. For a more detailed description of these tools, see chapter 7.

☐ No. 2 Phillips screwdriver

☐ feeler gauge

☐ points file (optional)

☐ offset screwdrivers

☐ medium-size screwdriver

☐ tach and dwellmeter

STEP 1
Locating the points and condenser

Locate the distributor cap

Remember to skip to STEP 9 if your Honda has an electronic ignition, as mentioned at the beginning of this chapter. Open the hood, stand on the passenger's side of your Honda and have a look at the motor. As shown in FIG. 2-3, the black, brown, or light green plastic object with the five thick, black wires coming out of it is the distributor cap. The points are located underneath the distributor cap, inside the distributor.

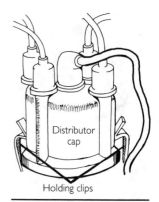

Fig. 2-3
The distributor cap and holding clips.

Remove the distributor cap

Look on either side of the distributor cap and find the holding clips that secure the distributor cap to the distributor. Use your thumbs to flip the clips from the cap. Figure 2-3 illustrates the position of these holding clips. If the clips are on tightly, you might need to use a pair of pliers to pull them off.

Lift the distributor cap from the distributor. Do this without removing the wires from the distributor cap. With the clips off, you can remove the distributor cap. Don't worry—nothing will fly out as the cap comes off. A tap on the side will help free the cap if it is stuck.

Caution! You don't want to remove the wires from the distributor cap. Each are plugged into a specific terminal. Simply move the distributor cap, with wires attached, to an unobstructed area so you can access the inside of the distributor.

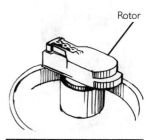

Fig. 2-4
View of the rotor with the distributor cap removed.

Remove the rotor

Once the distributor cap is removed, you can see the rotor, which is shown in FIG. 2-4. Pull upwards on the rotor and remove it. With the rotor out of the way, you have a clear view of the points assembly shown in FIG. 2-5.

Locate the condenser

On some models, the condenser is located inside the distributor, opposite the points assembly, as shown in FIG. 2-6. On other models, the condenser is screwed to the metal body of the distributor as shown in FIG. 2-7. If the condenser is not mounted inside the distributor, it is definitely mounted on the body of the distributor as shown in FIG. 2-7. Although an "outside" mounted condenser might

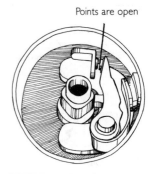

Fig. 2-5
The points assembly.

Fig. 2-6
A condenser mounted inside the distributor.

Condenser

Fig. 2-7
A condenser mounted to the outside body of the distributor.

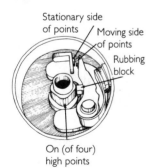

Stationary side
of points / Moving side
of points
Rubbing
block

On (of four)
high points

Fig. 2-8
How the distributor points work.

not be in the exact location illustrated, it will, however, be close by and on the body of the distributor.

STEP 2
How the points operate

Do not skip this step! You're about to find out that the points operate in a very simple way. But, unless you see how they work before you take them out of the distributor, you'll have one tough time getting them back in so they work like they should. Please, do not skip this step! Do the following four things to learn how the points operate:

1. Complete STEP 1 of this chapter.
2. If your car has a stick shift, put it into neutral with the parking brake applied. If your car has an automatic transmission, put it in park and apply the parking brake.
3. Have a friend sit in the car to operate the starter—with the key— on your command. The motor will not start because the distributor cap has been removed. **Caution!** Keep hands, hair, clothing, etc., away from the motor.
4. When you command your friend to turn over the motor with the key, watch the inside of the distributor. Do you see the two small metal parts that are opening and closing? These are, as shown in FIG. 2-8, the points. The points open ever so slightly (.020 of an inch), so look closely.

Did you see the small piece of fiber or nylon rubbing on the shaft that is spinning in the center of the distributor? This is also part of the points assembly and is called the rubbing block. See FIG. 2-8. The spinning shaft is the *distributor cam*. Notice that the distributor cam has four high points on it, as shown in FIG. 2-8. When the rubbing block rides up onto one of these high points, it causes the points to open. When the rubbing block is on the low space between the high points, the points are closed. Notice also that only one side of the points assembly moves—the side in which the rubbing block is attached.

Okay! Now that you have seen how the points work, you'll have no trouble completing this chapter.

STEP 3
How to determine the condition of the points

I've already told you this earlier, but because you're about to examine the condition of the points, I'll say it again. Normally, the points and condenser need to be replaced every 10,000 to 12,000 miles. It is possible, however, that they might need to be replaced sooner. If you find the points to be burned, pitted, or worn, they should be replaced at this time. Replace the points and condenser as a pair.

Separate the points

Pull the points apart with a screwdriver so you can see their condition. Figure 2-9 illustrates where to place the screwdriver.

Inspect the points for damage

Inspect the faces of the two points as shown in FIG. 2-9. New points are smooth and shiny. If your points are burned, pitted, or worn, you should replace the points assembly. A grayish coating also indicates that it is time to replace the points assembly. See STEP 4.

Look for a small metal bump sticking out from one of the points. The points might appear to be in good condition except for a small metal bump sticking out from one of them. If you see one of these bumps, use your points file to remove it. Do not use sandpaper or emery cloth on the points, because this will cause the points to arc. Use only a points file. If you don't file this bump, replace the points. If your points do not need to be replaced with new ones, skip to STEP 8.

You can drive your Honda to purchase new points and a condenser

You can use your Honda to go to the parts store to pick up a new set of points and a condenser. If you find the points need replacement or you would like to pick up a new set of points so you can see what yours should look like, you can use your Honda for a trip to the

Fig. 2-9
Use a screwdriver to separate the points.

Inspect these
two surfaces

Fig. 2-10
Removing and installing the points assembly and condenser on models with a condenser mounted inside the distributor.

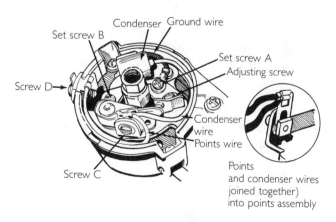

parts store. See STEP 8, which tells you how to put back the parts you removed. Pick up a small tube of distributor cam lube while you're at the parts store.

Did you get the right parts from the parts store? People do make mistakes and manufacturers have been known to mislabel parts packages. So double-check and be sure you have purchased the right parts before removing the points assembly and condenser from your Honda. Simply compare what you have just bought with the points assembly inside the distributor. If the details do not look the same, return the parts.

STEP 4
How to remove and install
the points assembly and condenser

This step is divided into two steps—STEP 4-1 and STEP 4-2. STEP 4-1 covers models with the condenser mounted inside the distributor, as shown in FIG. 2-6. STEP 4-2 covers models with the condenser mounted outside the distributor, as shown in FIG. 2-7. Proceed to the step that covers your model.

STEP 4-1. Models with the condenser
mounted inside the distributor (FIG. 2-6)

Loosen the set screws that secure the points assembly and slip the points assembly and condenser free. You'll disconnect the wires next. With a medium-sized screwdriver, loosen set screws A and B as shown in FIG. 2-10. Turn each screw counterclockwise four full turns. With the screws loosened, use your fingers to work the condenser out of the distributor. Next, work the points assembly up and out of the distributor. Don't pull on the wires still attached to the points assembly.

Disconnect the wires attached to the points assembly

Hold the points assembly in one hand. With the other hand, use a medium-sized screwdriver to loosen screw C, shown in FIG. 2-10. Turn this screw about $1\frac{1}{2}$ turns counterclockwise and slip the wires, known as the points and condenser wires, free from the points assembly. The points and condenser wires are joined together as one at the points assembly. If screw C is designed to accept only a Phillips screwdriver blade, use the Phillips offset screwdriver to loosen screw C.

At the distributor, remove the other end of the wire you just removed from the points assembly. As you can see, one end of the points wire is still attached to the distributor. With a medium-sized screwdriver, loosen screw D, shown in FIG. 2-10. Do not remove this screw, just loosen it enough to allow this end of the points wire to be slipped free. Be sure no other wires slip free when loosening screw D.

Assemble the new points assembly

On the new points assembly, loosen the screw that will secure the points and condenser wires. See FIG. 2-10 and loosen screw C on the new points assembly about 1 1/2 turns. Don't remove the screw, just loosen it.

Lay the new points assembly in the distributor and position it to face the way it will when actually installed. With screw C loose, lay the new points assembly in the distributor. Do not slip the points assembly under set screws A and B at this time. Use FIG. 2-10 as a guide to positioning the points assembly correctly.

Lay the new condenser in the distributor and position it to face the way it will when actually installed. Using FIG. 2-10 as a guide, lay the new condenser in the distributor and position it to face as it will when actually installed. As with the points assembly, do not slip the condenser under set screws A and B at this time.

Connect the wires to the points assembly

Slip the points and condenser wires into place on the new points assembly and tighten screw C, as shown in FIG. 2-10. Be sure to run the wire from the condenser to screw C as shown in FIG. 2-10. The encircled illustration accompanying FIG. 2-10 shows where to slip the points and condenser wires into the points assembly. Tighten screw C to secure the wires in place. Because the points assembly has not been screwed into place, you can easily lift it up to work with screw C.

Connect the other end of the points and condenser wire to screw D, as shown in FIG. 2-10. Be sure to run the points wire between screw C and screw D as shown in FIG. 2-10. Securely tighten screw D. When you originally loosened screw D, I warned you to watch for any other wire(s) that might slip free from this screw. If a wire slipped free, be sure to put it back in place under screw D. Using FIG. 2-10 as a guide, check to be sure the points and condenser wires are routed correctly in the distributor.

When the motor is running, the plate on which the points and condenser are mounted turns back and forth an inch or more, depending on the motor's requirements. Also, the points are continually opening and closing, which means the arm with the rubbing block on it is constantly swinging back and forth. With all this action taking place in the distributor, it is important to route the points and condenser wire so that they won't interfere with anything. If necessary, remove the points and condenser wires from screw C and D and start over. Figure 2-10 illustrates exactly how these wires should be routed through the distributor.

Locate the peg of the new points assembly

Look at the bottom of the new points assembly. Do you see the small, round, metal peg protruding from the bottom? When you install the points assembly, this peg must fit into the hole provided for it in the distributor. This peg will usually slip into the hole automatically, but just in case it doesn't, I want you to be aware of it.

Slip the points assembly under the set screws

While slipping the points assembly under set screws A and B, it is possible for the ground wire to slip free from set screw A, as shown in FIG. 2-10. If this happens, slip the ground wire back into place. It belongs above the points assembly but below any washers on set screw A.

Position the points assembly

Be absolutely positive that the bottom of the points assembly is completely flush with the distributor. If the bottom of the points assembly is not flush/flat with the distributor, this means the points assembly did not slip under all the parts on the set screws and/or the small, round, metal peg on the bottom of the points assembly did not slip into the hole provided for it in the distributor. Your motor will not run correctly, if at all. So, take the time right now to position the points assembly correctly in the distributor.

If the points assembly doesn't fit

Sometimes, the washers on the set screws cause the points assembly to not fit flush. Look closely at the set screws. Is one or more of the set screw washers underneath the points assembly causing the points assembly to not fit flush with the distributor? If this is the problem, remove the points assembly from the distributor. Then, with your fingers, work the washers back up set screws A and B. Now, carefully slip the points assembly back into the distributor, paying special attention to the washers on the set screws. This can be a little frustrating at times, so stick with it, you'll get it.

Also, if the peg on the bottom of the points assembly is not in its hole, it will cause the points assembly to not fit flush. If this peg is causing the problem, you can get it into the hole by moving the points assembly around in whatever direction it will move until you feel the peg slip into the hole. While trying to get the peg into the hole, do not allow the points assembly to slip from set screws A and B.

If you absolutely can't get the peg to drop into the hole provided for it in the distributor, the problem is being caused by the position of the points adjusting screw shown in FIG. 2-10. With a medium-sized screwdriver, turn the points adjusting screw 1/4 turn in either direction, then try again to get the peg into the hole. The peg should go into the hole this time. If it will not, turn the adjusting screw another 1/4 turn and try again. Sometimes, the adjusting screw will only turn back and forth. If you meet with resistance, don't use force; simply turn in the other direction.

Fit the condenser into place above the points assembly

Fit the new condenser into place above the points assembly, but under the washers on set screws A and B. You might have to loosen (turn counterclockwise) set screws A and B a little in order to get the condenser into place. Tighten set screws A and B, shown in FIG. 2-10, but just enough to securely hold the points assembly and condenser in place.

Check again to be sure the points and condenser wires are running as shown in FIG. 2-10. Also, look once again to be sure the bottom of the points assembly is mounted flush/flat with the distributor. If everything is okay, you're ready to move on. Leave set screws A and B lightly tightened because you're going to have to loosen these screws to adjust the points in an upcoming step. So for now, just make these screws tight enough to hold the points assembly and condenser in place. Go to STEP 5.

STEP 4-2. Models with the condenser mounted outside the distributor (FIG. 2-7)

Loosen the set screws that secure the points assembly and slip the points assembly free. You'll disconnect the wire next. With a medium-sized screwdriver, loosen set screws A and B as shown in FIG. 2-11. Turn each set screw counterclockwise four full turns.

With the set screws loosened, use your fingers to work the points assembly out of the distributor. See that wire still attached to the points assembly? Don't pull on it, you'll remove it next.

Disconnect the wire attached to the points assembly

Hold the points assembly in one hand. With the other hand, use the medium-sized screwdriver to loosen screw C shown in FIG. 2-11. Turn this screw about 1 1/2 turns counterclockwise and slip the wire, known as the points wire, free from the points assembly. If screw C

Fig. 2-11
Removing and installing the
points assembly on models with
a condenser mounted to the
body of the distributor.

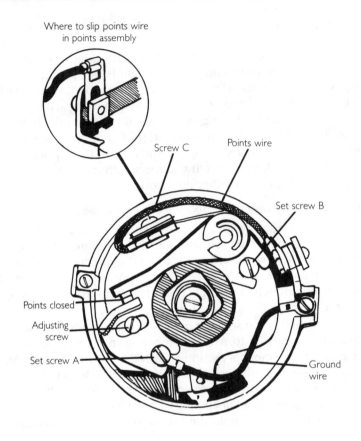

Where to slip points wire
in points assembly

Screw C

Points wire

Set screw B

Points closed

Adjusting
screw

Set screw A

Ground
wire

is designed to accept only a Phillips screwdriver blade, use the Phillips offset screwdriver to loosen screw C.

On the new points assembly, loosen the screw that will secure the points wire. See FIG. 2-11 and loosen screw C on the new points assembly about 1½ turns. Don't remove this screw, just loosen it.

Assemble the new points assembly

With screw C loose, lay the new points assembly in the distributor and position it to face the way it should when it is actually installed. Use FIG. 2-11 as a guide. Do not slip the points assembly under set screws A and B at this time. You'll want to pick up the points assembly in just a minute.

With the points assembly positioned in the distributor, slip the points wire into place on the new points assembly and tighten screw C as shown in FIG. 2-11.

Be sure to route the points wire through the distributor as shown in FIG. 2-11. The encircled illustration accompanying FIG. 2-11 shows where to slip the points wire into the points assembly. Tighten screw C to secure the points wire in place. Because the points assembly has not been screwed into place, you can easily lift it up to work with screw C.

Locate the peg protruding on the new points assembly

Look at the bottom of the new points assembly. Do you see the small, round, metal peg protruding from the bottom? When you install the points assembly, this peg must fit into the hole provided for it in the distributor. The peg will usually slip into the hole automatically, but just in case it doesn't, I want you to be aware of it.

Fit the points assembly under the set screws

While fitting the points assembly under set screws A and B, it is possible for the ground wire to slip free from set screw A. The ground wire is shown in FIG. 2-11. If this happens, slip the ground wire back into place. It belongs above the points assembly but below any washers on set screw A.

Position the points assembly

Be absolutely positive the bottom of the points assembly is completely flush with the distributor. If the bottom of the points assembly is not flush/flat with the distributor, this means that the points assembly did not slip under all the parts on the set screws and/or the small, round, metal peg on the bottom of the points assembly did not slip into the hole provided for it in the distributor. Your motor will not run correctly, if at all. So take the time right now to position the points assembly correctly in the distributor.

If the points assembly doesn't fit

Sometimes, the washers on the set screws cause the points assembly to not fit flush. Look closely at the set screws. Is one or more of the set screw washers underneath the points assembly, causing the points assembly to not fit flush with the distributor? If this is the problem, remove the points assembly from the distributor and with your fingers, work the washers back up set screws A and B. Now, carefully slip the points assembly back into the distributor, paying special attention to the washers on the set screws. This can be a little frustrating at times, so stick with it, you'll get it.

Also, if the peg on the bottom of the points assembly is not in its hole, it will cause the points assembly not to fit flush. If the peg is causing the problem, you can get it into the hole by moving the points assembly around in whatever direction it will move until you feel the peg slip into the hole. While trying to get the peg into the hole, do not allow the points assembly to slip from set screws A and B.

If you absolutely can't get the peg to drop into the hole provided for it in the distributor, the problem is being caused by the position of the points adjusting screw shown in FIG. 2-11. With a medium-sized screwdriver, turn the points adjusting screw $1/4$ turn in either direction, then try again to get the peg into the hole. The peg should go into the hole this time. If it doesn't, turn the adjusting screw another $1/4$ turn and try again. Sometimes, the adjusting screw will only turn back and forth. If you meet with resistance, don't use force; simply turn in the other direction. Once the points assembly is in correctly, tighten set screws A and B, shown in FIG. 2-11, but just enough to hold the points assembly securely in place.

Check again to be sure the points wire is running as shown in FIG. 2-11. Also, check once again to be sure the bottom of the points assembly is mounted flush/flat with the distributor. If everything is okay, you're ready to move on. Leave set screws A and B lightly tightened because you're going to have to loosen these screws to adjust the points in an upcoming step. So, for now, just make these screws tight enough to hold the points assembly in place.

Unscrew the condenser from the side of the distributor

In STEP 1, you located the condenser. Relocate it and notice it is held to the outside body of the distributor with one, very small screw. Unfortunately, this screw is very easy to drop and lose.

> Because the screw on the condenser is easy to drop and lose, spread a rag under the distributor in the area where the screw might fall if you drop it. If access to this screw is obstructed, use an offset screwdriver.

Remove the condenser wire from the distributor

With the condenser detached from the outside body of the distributor, follow the wire coming out of the condenser to its other end. This wire is known as the condenser wire and it is held to the distributor with a small screw. Fortunately, you do not have to remove this screw, only loosen it.

Using a suitable screwdriver, loosen (turn counterclockwise) the small screw securing this wire. Once again, only loosen the screw enough to slip the condenser wire free. Don't let other wires slip free.

Fit the wire from the new condenser
into place and tighten the screw

Put the wire from the new condenser under the screw that secured the wire from the old condenser. Tighten this screw securely. If any other wires slipped free while loosening this screw, don't forget to put them back into place at this time.

Screw the new condenser into place on the distributor

Yes, it can be tough to get this tiny screw back into the little hole on the side of the distributor, especially when you can hardly get your hand back there to do anything. Just stick with it, you'll get it in. I suggest you spread a rag under the distributor in such a way that it will catch this screw if you drop it.

When you're finished mounting the condenser, it must be screwed tight against the distributor. Otherwise, the motor will not run properly. A loosely mounted condenser does not effectively absorb excess electricity from the points.

Put something sticky, like paper cement or gum, on the head of the condenser screw so you can stick the screw to the blade of a screwdriver or your fingertips. This technique is often helpful when it comes to getting small screws started back into hard-to-reach places.

STEP 5
How to position the points for checking and adjusting

This step must be completed whether or not you have installed new points. The points adjustment can only be checked or readjusted when the points are in the completely open position. You will remember from STEP 2, How the Points Operate, that the points are completely open when their rubbing block rides up onto one of the high points on the distributor cam. This step tells you how to align the rubbing block with one of the high points on the distributor cam so that the points will remain completely open. This step must be completed before proceeding to STEP 6.

Put manual transmissions into neutral; automatic transmissions into park. Apply the parking brake on both

Don't take chances! You're going to be operating the motor with the key. Sure, the car won't start because the distributor cap is off, but it can jump forward unexpectedly if the car is left in gear.

Fig. 2-12
Aligning the rubbing block with
one of the high points on the
distributor cam.

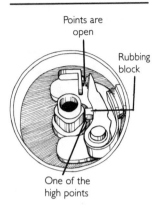

Points are
open

Rubbing
block

One of the
high points

To align the rubbing block with one of the high points on the distributor cam, causing the points to remain open (the position they must be in for checking and adjusting), have a friend sit in the car and "bump" the motor until this alignment occurs. Bumping the motor means to turn over the motor very briefly by momentarily turning the ignition key to the start position. Again, the motor will not start when it is bumped because the distributor cap is off.

After each bump of the motor, look to see if the distributor cam has stopped in such a position that the rubbing block of the points assembly is up on the highest spot of one of the high points on the distributor cam. When this occurs, the points should be open as shown in FIG. 2-12. The points absolutely must be in this position in order to complete STEPS 6 and 7.

Danger! If you have a medical condition that makes it particularly dangerous for you to receive an electrical shock, do not touch the car while the motor is being bumped. The chances of receiving a very small shock are slim, but possible. Play it safe!

It can take several tries for the motor to stop with the rubbing block up on one of the high points on the distributor cam. Sometimes, a little "bump" is all it takes. If the rubbing block is really close to being up on a high spot, you can grab the fan belt with your hand and pull or push on it to move the motor very slightly. To be safe, take the key out of the ignition.

Turn the ignition key to the OFF position when you're finished

Allowing the ignition key to remain in the ON position while the motor is not running will fry the ignition system in short order. In addition, you'll get an electrical shock in STEP 6 if you leave the key in the ON position. Double check that your friend in the car has turned the ignition key to the OFF position.

Important information for those of you who did not install a new points assembly

If the rubbing block on your points assembly is very worn, the points will open ever so slightly when the rubbing block is on the highest spot of a high point on the distributor cam. In extreme cases, the points might not open at all. This is because the rubbing block is so worn that it does not make contact with the distributor cam. If this is what is happening in your distributor, do not be con-

cerned with whether the points are open or closed; just get the rubbing block to align with the highest spot on one of the high points
on the distributor cam.

Extreme rubbing block wear is caused by lack of lubrication on
the distributor cam. If your car suffers from extreme rubbing block
wear, it has no doubt been running very poorly and maybe not at all.
After you adjust the points, I'll tell you how to lube the distributor
cam. Don't worry about the worn rubbing block. A little lubrication, along with adjusting the points, will make everything okay.

Important information for those who did install a new points assembly

The new points you just put into the distributor are far from being in
adjustment. This is obviously because they have never been
adjusted before. Chances are, this lack of prior adjustment means
the rubbing block is not yet making contact with the distributor cam
and thus, the points are not opening and closing when the motor is
bumped. If this is the case with your distributor, bump the motor
until the rubbing block is in line with the highest spot of one of the
high points on the distributor cam. During the actual adjustment of
the points, you will cause the rubbing block to contact the distributor cam and the points to open.

During the actual adjustment of the points, when the rubbing
block does contact the distributor cam, check to be certain the rubbing block is up on the highest spot of one of the high points on the
distributor cam. If this alignment does not occur, bump the motor
until it does. I'll remind you when you get to this point.

STEP 6
How to check the points adjustment

This step is for those who did not install a new points assembly. If
you did install a new points assembly, skip to STEP 7. Now that you
have the rubbing block up on one of the high points on the distributor cam (STEP 5 must first be completed before proceeding to check
the points adjustment), it is time to get out your feeler gauge set and
find the blade that reads .020 inch. All models use the .020-inch
blade.

Danger! If the ignition key is in the ON position, you might
receive a small electrical shock in this step. Be sure the ignition key
is in the OFF position.

Clean the end of the blade with alcohol, window cleaner, or
some other grease cutter. You do not want any grease getting on the

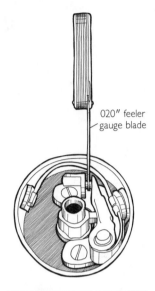

020" feeler
gauge blade

Fig. 2-13
Check the point gap with the
.020-inch feeler gauge blade.
Don't insert the blade at an
angle. This will cause a false
reading.

points. This can cause the motor not to run. Clean your feeler gauge blade even if it has never before been used. Manufacturers of feeler gauge sets often coat each blade with a thin coat of oil to prevent rusting during transport and shelf life.

Try to slide the .020-inch feeler gauge blade between the open points as shown in FIG. 2-13. If the points are in adjustment, the .020-inch feeler gauge blade will slip between them with a slight drag on it. This drag is caused by both points slightly touching the feeler gauge blade.

If the space is too small for the blade to slide into, the points gap is too small and the points will need to be adjusted. If the space is too large, the points will also need to be adjusted. If you are uncertain about whether the space is too large, try to slide in the .021-inch blade. If it fits, the points gap is too large.

STEP 7
How to adjust the points

If you did not install new points and found your old points to be in adjustment (STEP 6), skip this step and go to STEP 8. Complete this step if you installed new points or found your old points to be in good condition but in need of adjustment. STEP 5 must be completed before you start this step.

Danger! If the ignition key is in the ON position, you might receive a small electrical shock in this step. Be sure the ignition key is in the OFF position.

Loosen the set screws securing the points assembly

With a medium-sized screwdriver, slightly loosen set screws A and B that hold the points assembly in place. See FIG. 2-10 or 2-11. During the actual adjustment of the points, the points assembly will have to slide inside the distributor. These screws need only be slightly loose to allow for this movement. If you make the set screws too loose, the points assembly won't stay where you put it when retightening the set screws.

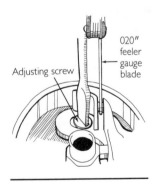

020"
feeler
gauge
blade

Adjusting screw

Fig. 2-14
Adjusting the points gap.

Adjust the points

Turn the points adjusting screw shown in FIG. 2-14 to adjust the points. Hold a medium-sized screwdriver in the adjusting screw. With your free hand, insert the .020-inch feeler gauge blade between the points as shown in FIG. 2-14. Turning the adjusting screw clockwise makes the points gap larger. Turning the adjusting screw counterclockwise makes the points gap smaller. If the points assembly does not move when you turn the adjusting screw, loosen the set screws a little more.

When the .020-inch blade slips between the points with a slight drag on it, the points are in adjustment. Once the points are in correct adjustment, securely tighten set screws A and B. Recheck the gap after tightening the set screws—it might have changed.

Recheck the position of the rubbing block. It must be on the highest spot of one of the high points on the distributor cam. After completing the adjusting procedure, check to be sure the rubbing block is on the highest spot of one of the high points on the distributor cam. If not, your adjustment is not accurate and the motor will not run correctly. Repeat STEP 5.

Did the points come out of adjustment when you removed the screwdriver from the adjusting screw to tighten the set screws? Try tightening the set screws just enough to allow you to adjust the points, yet have them stay in adjustment when you remove the screwdriver from the adjusting screw. Be sure to recheck the gap after securely tightening the set screws.

STEP 8
How to check the condition of the rotor and distributor cap and lube the distributor cam

Check the distributor cap for small cracks

Carefully examine the inside and outside of the distributor cap for hairline cracks as shown in FIG. 2-15. If you find even the slightest

Fig. 2-15
Check the condition of the distributor cap.

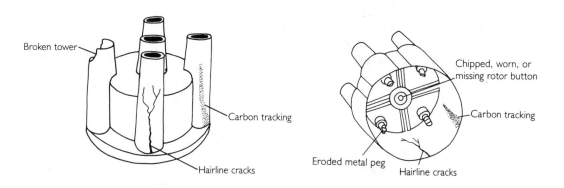

Broken tower

Carbon tracking

Hairline cracks

Chipped, worn, or missing rotor button

Carbon tracking

Eroded metal peg

Hairline cracks

hairline crack in the plastic, install a new distributor cap as soon as possible. Be sure to check the top of the cap around the spark plug wire terminals. If your motor has been running rough, this might well be the reason.

Check for carbon tracking

Carbon tracking, as shown in FIG. 2-15, appears as a small trail of black carbon deposits inside or outside the cap. You'll have to look closely on the inside and outside to identify carbon tracking because it is hard to see. As with small hairline cracks, a cap with carbon tracking must be replaced. Be sure to check the top of the cap around the spark plug wire terminals. If your motor has not been running smoothly, this might be the reason.

Check the distributor cap towers

Carefully peel back the rubber boot at the end of each spark plug wire and check for broken or cracked distributor cap towers as shown in FIG. 2-15. Sometimes, you can get away with a broken or cracked tower, but usually electricity takes full advantage of this break and escapes to a metal surface of the motor, causing the spark plug that would have normally received this voltage not to spark.

You can test the distributor cap towers with the Sparking in the Dark Test and/or the Leaping Spark Test in chapter 1, STEP 9. During the test, concentrate on the broken or cracked tower to know if electricity is escaping. Use epoxy cement to repair broken towers on otherwise good distributor caps.

Check the metal pegs

Are the four metal pegs inside the distributor cap charred or eroded in the location shown in FIG. 2-15? If so, plan to purchase and install a new distributor cap the next time you tune-up or sooner.

Check the rotor button

The small button in the center of the distributor cap, as shown in FIG. 2-15, is the rotor button. The voltage delivered by the coil wire passes through this button to the rotor. If this button is missing, chipped, or worn very small (possibly not touching the "springy" metal shaft of the rotor), replace this distributor cap with a new one.

Important information for switching distributor caps

Each spark plug wire is plugged into a specific terminal in the distributor cap. To avoid confusion about which wire belongs where in the new distributor cap, simply hold the new and old distributor caps side-by-side and transfer the wires one at a time. Don't yank on these wires. Peel back the rubber caps that seal the wires to the distributor cap and then work each wire free.

While transferring the spark plug wires, be positive that both distributor caps are facing the same direction. A distributor cap that is secured by holding clips has two flanges designed to accept the holding clips. Each flange is a slightly different shape. Use these flanges as guides for facing both distributor caps in the same direction. Be careful not to pull the spark plug wires free from the spark plugs.

Check the rotor

Check the rotor for hairline cracks and carbon tracking as shown in FIG. 2-16. Be sure to check the outside body of the rotor and also inside the tube portion that slips down onto the center shaft of the distributor. Inspect the metal edge of the rotor for burning, pitting, and corrosion (see FIG. 2-16). If your rotor displays any of these conditions, replace it.

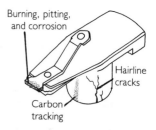

Fig. 2-16
Check the condition of the rotor.

One last thing to look for on the rotor are signs that it has made contact with the distributor cap. Check the plastic edge of the rotor. If you find it is chipped, it is either the wrong rotor for your distributor or it has been riding up on the distributor shaft, making contact with the distributor cap. In both cases, replace the rotor with a new one and have the parts person verify the correct rotor for your Honda.

Lube the distributor cam

Apply a very light film of distributor cam lube on at least two of the four high points on the distributor cam. Use only distributor cam lube. The cam lube prevents excessive friction, which in turn causes rapid and extreme rubbing-block wear. A worn rubbing block changes the points adjustment. You don't want this! You can use petroleum jelly as a temporary substitute for distributor cam lube.

Reinstall the rotor

The rotor will slide down onto the center shaft in the distributor only when it is on correctly. Place the rotor on the center shaft in the distributor and press down while turning it. When the key in the rotor lines up with the slot in the shaft, you will feel the rotor slip down onto the shaft.

You can tell the rotor is on correctly when it will not turn freely on the shaft. There is a certain amount of play in the distributor cam, so even when the rotor is on correctly, it will still turn a bit. This is actually the distributor cam turning. If the rotor will turn 1/4 turn or more, it is not on correctly. Be sure to push the rotor down as far as it will go.

Reinstall the distributor cap

When the distributor cap is on correctly, the cap will fit down evenly all the way around. Snap the holding clips in place. If the clips won't go back in place by hand, use a pair of pliers to pull the clips into position. That's it, you're done!

If you have replaced worn, burned, or pitted parts of your Honda's ignition system, you should now notice a real difference in motor performance and gas mileage. If you have already serviced the spark plugs and spark plug wires in chapter 1, all the components responsible for igniting the gasoline entering your motor are now in good shape. Your Honda should really "zip!"

I recommend you move on to chapter 3 on timing. In this chapter, you'll make sure the spark plugs are igniting the gasoline precisely when your motor stands to get the most power out it. Again, you'll experience another boost in motor power and fuel economy after completing chapter 3.

How to adjust the points with a dwell meter (optional)

Special note for everyone who just turned to this section from chapter 5: As you just learned in chapter 5, a tachometer is connected to the motor exactly like a dwell meter. To connect your tachometer, skip down to "How to attach a dwell meter to the motor," and connect your tachometer in the exact same way.

There are two ways to check the points adjustment (gap). As you already know, the feeler gauge method is one of them. When you adjust the points gap with a feeler gauge, you are actually setting the maximum distance the points will open.

The other method of adjusting points is accomplished with a dwell meter. When you adjust the points with a dwell meter, you are setting them for how many degrees of one distributor cam rotation they will stay closed or, in other words, for how long the points will remain closed before a high point on the distributor cam causes them to open. If you plan to adjust your points with a dwell meter, you should first complete this chapter, then attach your dwell meter.

How to attach a dwell meter to a motor

Connecting a noninductive dwell meter

The motor should not be running when attaching the dwell meter. If your meter does not have an inductive pick-up (the big connector that looks like a giant clothespin), it is a noninductive-type dwell meter. To connect it to the motor, first connect the black wire from the dwell meter to the negative (−) terminal of the battery. You'll see a (−) sign next to the negative terminal as shown in FIG. 2-17. To connect the remaining wire, closely examine the coil. You'll find a positive (+) sign next to one of the terminals and a − (for negative) next to the other terminal. Hook the remaining red wire from the dwell meter to the negative terminal of the coil as shown in FIG. 2-17. A connection to the positive terminal could result in motor damage.

Having trouble finding the coil? Follow the center wire running from the distributor cap to its other end and you've found the coil. You might have to peel back a rubber cover to access the negative terminal of the coil.

Connecting an inductive dwell meter

Begin by clipping the inductive pick-up around any spark plug wire. The center wire running from the distributor cap is not a spark plug wire; it's the coil wire, and you do not want to connect the pick-up to this wire.

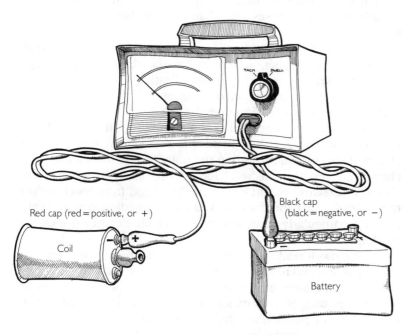

Fig. 2-17
Attaching a dwell meter to a motor.

Red cap (red = positive, or +)

Coil

Black cap
(black = negative, or −)

Battery

When the inductive pick-up is on correctly, the spark plug wire will slip freely inside the open area of the closed connector. On some inductive pick-ups, there is an arrow accompanied by the words, *spark plug*. Attach this inductive pick-up to the spark plug wire with the arrow pointing in the direction of the spark plug, not the distributor cap. Facing the arrow towards the distributor cap causes the meter not to work.

Connect the remaining wires to the battery. The black connects to the negative terminal (−) of the battery and the red wire to the positive terminal (+) of the battery. See FIG. 2-17.

How to read a dwell meter

Be sure the wires from the dwell meter are away from the fan and fan belts. Put the transmission in park or neutral, apply the parking brake, and start the motor. The dwell meter should read between 49 to 55. Any reading within this range is okay.

If your meter does not have a four-cylinder scale, multiply the eight-cylinder reading by 2 (e.g., a 26 on the eight-cylinder scale would be $26 \times 2 = 52$).

If the dwell reading is larger than 55, make the points gap bigger, which makes the dwell number smaller. To make this adjustment, stop the motor, remove the distributor cap, loosen the set screws, and turn the adjusting screw clockwise. Just a slight turn of the adjusting screw makes a big change in the dwell reading, so take it easy.

If the dwell reading is smaller than 49, you will have to make the points gap smaller, which makes the dwell number larger. Loosen the set screws and turn the adjusting screw counterclockwise. It might take a number of attempts to end up with a dwell reading within the 49 to 55 range. Stick with it!

Mechanics often use a quicker method to set the dwell. Here's how to do it: **Danger!** It is possible to accidentally receive a small electrical shock while adjusting the points using this method. The chances are very slim this will happen, particularly if you use a well-insulated screwdriver and keep your free hand from touching anything metal under the hood. If you have a medical condition that makes it particularly dangerous to receive an electrical shock, use caution.

If the dwell reading is not correct while the motor is running, stop the motor and remove the distributor cap and rotor. Then, have a friend sit in the car and "crank" the motor while you again verify the dwell reading on your meter. *Crank* the motor means to turn the key to the start position and hold it there. The motor will not start because the distributor cap has been removed.

To change the dwell reading, stop cranking the motor and loosen the set screws securing the points assembly. Put your screwdriver in the adjusting screw and while your friend cranks the motor again, you adjust the dwell while the motor is cranking. If the dwell reading is too high (more than 55), turn the adjusting screw clockwise until the meter displays the correct reading. If the dwell reading is too low (less than 49), turn the adjusting screw counterclockwise until the reading is correct. Personally, I'm partial to 52. When you have the dwell set correctly, tighten the set screws and recheck the reading. That's all there is to it!

Caution: Do not crank the motor for more than 30 seconds or you might burn out the starter motor. Wait a few minutes between each "cranking" session to allow the starter motor to cool off. Also, be sure to put your dwell meter on the fender of the car or in some other area where it will not be bounced to the ground by the cranking motor.

STEP 9
How to check the condition of the rotor and distributor cap on electronic ignition models

Locate the distributor cap

Open the hood, stand on the passenger's side of your Honda, and have a look at the motor. The black, brown, or light green plastic object with the four or five thick wires coming out of it, as shown in FIG. 2-18, is the distributor cap. You're going to check the condition of the distributor cap both inside and out. The rotor is located under the distributor cap.

Remove the distributor cap

See FIG. 2-19 and determine which drawing illustrates the distributor cap used in your motor. On distributor caps A, B, C, and D, and others that are similar, loosen the two mounting screws until the distributor cap can be separated from the distributor. If a clip with wires is attached to a mounting screw, completely remove this screw and slip the clip free. Do not pull on any wires.

To remove a distributor cap with the two holding clips E, use your fingers to flip the holding clips from the distributor cap. Use pliers if the clips are stuck. You might need pliers to pull the clips back into place when remounting the distributor cap.

To remove the last style distributor cap F, remove the three screws and then the distributor cap. You must pull the distributor

Fig. 2-18
Distributor cap location on
models with electronic ignitions.
The distributor cap on your
model might be in a different
location.

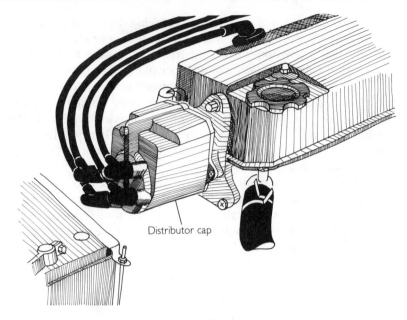

Distributor cap

Fig. 2-19 (Below)
Electronic ignition distributor
caps.

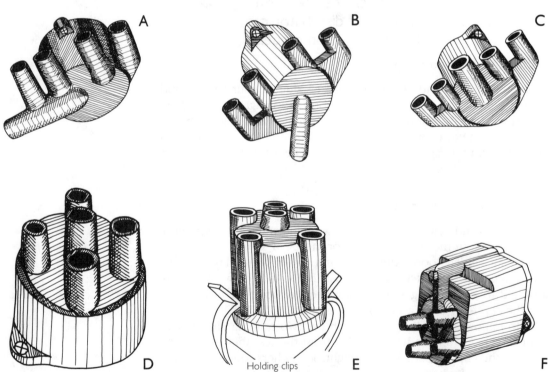

A

B

C

D

Holding clips   E

F

cap far enough from the distributor to permit the metal peg sticking out from the distributor cap to clear the distributor.

Check for small cracks

Carefully examine the inside and outside of the distributor cap for hairline cracks as shown in FIG. 2-20. If you find even the slightest hairline crack in the plastic, install a new distributor cap as soon as possible. Be sure to check the top of the cap around the spark plug wire terminals. If your motor has been running rough, this could be the reason.

Check for carbon tracking

Carbon tracking, as shown in FIG. 2-20, appears as a small trail of black carbon deposits on either the inside or outside of the distributor cap. Look very closely to identify carbon tracking; it can be hard to see. As with small hairline cracks, a distributor cap with carbon tracking must be replaced. Be sure to check the top of the cap around the spark plug wire terminals. If your motor has been running poorly, this might be the reason.

Check the cap towers

Carefully peel back the rubber boot at the end of each spark plug wire and check for broken or cracked distributor cap towers as shown in FIG. 2-20. You can sometimes get away with a broken or cracked tower, but usually electricity takes full advantage of the break and escapes to a metal surface of the motor. This means that the spark plug that would have normally received this voltage might not fire.

You can test the distributor cap towers with the Sparking in the Dark test and/or the Leaping Spark Test in chapter 1, STEP 9. During the test, concentrate on the broken or cracked tower to know if electricity is escaping. **Caution**! If sparks leap during the Leaping Spark Test, do not continue to make them leap. This can harm your car's computer. Use epoxy cement to repair broken towers on otherwise good distributor caps.

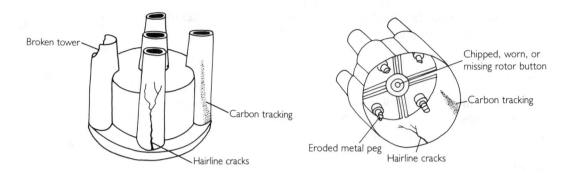

Broken tower

Chipped, worn, or missing rotor button

Carbon tracking

Carbon tracking

Eroded metal peg

Hairline cracks

Hairline cracks

Fig. 2-20
Checking the distributor cap on models with electronic ignitions.

Check the metal pegs

Are the four metal pegs inside the distributor charred or eroded in the location shown in FIG. 2-20? If so, plan to purchase and install a new distributor cap the next time you tune-up or sooner.

Check the rotor button

The small button in the center of the distributor cap, as shown in FIG. 2-20, is the rotor button. The voltage delivered by the coil wire passes through this button to the rotor. If this button is missing, chipped, or worn very small, possibly not touching the "springy" metal shaft of the rotor, replace this distributor cap with a new one.

Important information for switching distributor caps

Each spark plug wire is plugged into a specific terminal in the distributor cap. To avoid confusion about which wire belongs where in the new distributor cap, simply hold the new and old distributor caps side by side and transfer the wires one at a time. Don't yank on the wires. Peel back the rubber caps that seal these wires to the distributor cap and then work each wire free.

While transferring the spark plug wires, be positive that both distributor caps are facing the same direction. To verify that both are facing in the same direction, use the distributor cap flanges that accept the holding clips or the distributor cap mounting screw holes as a guide. (Some distributor caps are mounted with clips and others with screws.) Be careful not to pull the spark plug wires free from the spark plugs.

Remove the rotor

You're ready to remove the rotor from the distributor on all models except 1988–1991 Preludes and Civics. To remove the rotor from all distributors except 1988—1991 Preludes and Civics, simply pull the rotor straight out of the distributor. See the next section for 1988—1991 Preludes and Civics. Figure 2-21 illustrates a typical rotor. That's all there is to it. The thin plastic piece covering the distributor is the dust cap. Remove it and put it someplace for safe keeping. With the rotor in your hand, skip to the section titled "Check the rotor."

Removing the rotor from 1988 – 1991 Preludes and Civics

Before the rotor will slip off the shaft in the distributor of a 1988—1991 Prelude or Civic, there is a small screw that must first be located and removed. Start by removing the plastic dust cap from the distributor. Figure 2-22 illustrates removing this dust cap from a Civic. Your Prelude might not have a dust cap.

With the dust cap out of the way, you might be able to see the screw that has to come out before you can remove the rotor. Figure 2-23 shows the location of this screw. If you can see and access this screw at this time, skip to "Remove the rotor screw." Otherwise, continue on.

If you can't see the rotor screw

If you can't see the rotor screw, the reason is because the motor is stopped in a position with the screw out of view. To rotate the rotor and bring this screw into view, turn the motor with a wrench. This is very easy to do. You'll need a 17-millimeter socket, a short extension bar, and a ratchet wrench. Figure 1-5 illustrates a wrench assembly.

Sit behind the steering wheel and turn it as far as it will go to the left, as if you were making a sharp, left-hand turn. Once you have done this, hop back out of the car. Look into the front wheel well on the driver's side of the car and you should see a hole through which a 17-millimeter nut is visible. The exact location of this 17-millimeter nut is illustrated in FIG. 2-24.

Turn this nut to turn the motor until the screw in the rotor is visible. If you don't see the hole, it's because there is a rubber plug covering it. Find the plug, also shown in FIG. 2-24, and remove it. Don't lose the plug, you'll want to put it back when you're done.

Now that you have located this 17-millimeter nut and assembled your wrench, slip the 17-millimeter socket through the hole in the wheel well and onto the 17-millimeter nut. Turn the wrench counterclockwise to rotate the motor. If the wrench spins freely in this direction, slide the lever on top of the ratchet wrench and try again. The motor turns counterclockwise when it is running, so you want to turn it in this direction only.

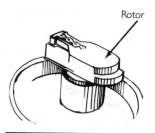

Fig. 2-21
The rotor.

Removing the dust cap

Dust cap

Replacing the distributor cap

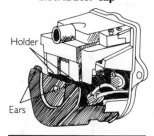

Holder

Ears

Fig. 2-22
Removing and installing the dust cap on 1988 – 1991 Civics. To remove the dust cap, pull down. To reinstall the distributor cap, slip the "ears" into the holder and the base into the slot in the distributor.

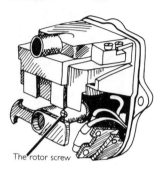

The rotor screw

Turn the motor $^1/_4$ turn and check if the screw is visible. When the screw is visible, remove your wrench from the 17-millimeter nut. You don't want to forget it and accidentally start the motor. Plus, you won't need to turn the motor again.

Remove the rotor screw

Remove the rotor screw by turning it counterclockwise, after which the rotor will slide easily off the shaft.

The rotor screw is easy to drop and lose. Spread a rag under the distributor in the area where the screw might fall if you drop it.

Fig. 2-24
Rotating the motor to access
the rotor-holding screw on
1988 – 1991 Civics and
Preludes.

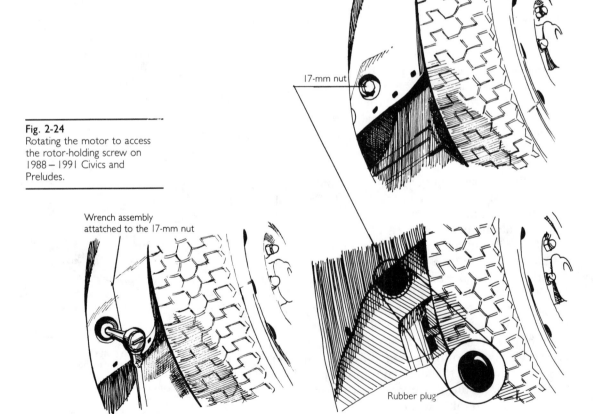

17-mm nut

Wrench assembly
attatched to the 17-mm nut

Rubber plug

Check the rotor

Check the rotor for hairline cracks and carbon tracking as shown in FIG. 2-25. Be sure to check the outside body of the rotor and also inside the tube portion that slips down onto the center shaft of the distributor. Inspect the metal edge of the rotor for burning, pitting, and corroding, also illustrated in FIG. 2-25. If your rotor displays any of these conditions, replace it.

One last thing to look for on the rotor are signs that it has made contact with the distributor cap. Examine the plastic edge of the rotor. If you find it is chipped, it is either the wrong rotor for your distributor or it has been riding up on the distributor shaft, in both cases making contact with the distributor cap. Replace this rotor with a new one and have the parts person verify the correct rotor for your Honda.

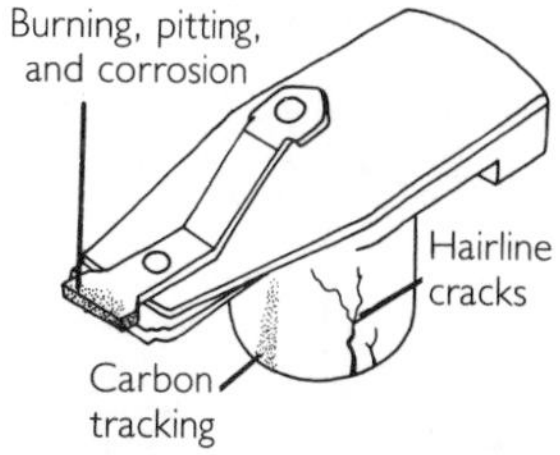

Fig. 2-25
Checking the condition of the rotor on models with electronic ignition of 1979 and newer Preludes and Accords and all 1980 and newer Civics.

Install the rotor on all models except 1988 – 1991 Preludes and Civics

Installing the rotor on your distributor is a simple task because the rotor will slide down onto the shaft only when it is on correctly. First, put the dust cover in place if one was removed. Then, place the rotor on the center shaft in the distributor and lightly press down while turning it. When the "key" in the rotor lines up with the slot or flat surface on the shaft (whichever your distributor has), you'll feel the rotor slip down onto the shaft.

You know the rotor is on correctly when it will not turn freely on the shaft. There is a certain amount of play in the distributor cam, so even when the rotor is on correctly, it will still turn a bit. This is actually the distributor cam turning. If the rotor will turn 1/4 turn or more, it is not on correctly. Be sure to push the rotor down as far as it will go.

Install the rotor on 1988 – 1991 Preludes and Civics

Slip the rotor back onto the center shaft in the distributor and replace and tighten the holding screw. This screw can be a bit tricky

> The best way to get the rotor screw back into its hole is to put a little chewing gum or paper paste inside the grooves of the screw head. You can then stick the head of the screw to the blade of the screwdriver during installation. Be sure to get the gum or paste out of the screw head once it's started back into its hole so it doesn't splatter inside your distributor when the rotor starts spinning.

to get started because there's absolutely no room to get your fingers in there to hold it. Once the rotor screw has been tightened securely, replace the plastic dust cap as illustrated in FIG. 2-22.

Install the distributor cap

Put the distributor cap back in place and tighten the screws that secure it. Slip any clips you removed back onto the distributor cap mounting screws. See FIG. 2-19.

That's it, you're done! You should feel more power from your motor and get better gas mileage with a new distributor. If you already serviced the spark plugs and spark plug wires in chapter 1, all the components responsible for igniting the gasoline entering your motor are now in good shape. Your Honda should really zip!

I recommend you move on to chapter 3 on timing. In this chapter, you'll make sure the spark plugs are igniting the gasoline precisely when your motor stands to get the most power out of it. Again, you'll feel another boost in motor power and fuel economy after completing chapter 3.

Troubleshooting

If the motor doesn't run as well as it did before you began this chapter, you might have goofed. Ask yourself the following questions:

○ Did I pull any spark plug wires loose from the distributor cap? Be sure all the spark plug wires are plugged firmly into the cap. (page 29)

○ Did I pull a spark plug wire from a spark plug when I removed the distributor cap? (page 29)

○ Did I gap the points with the rubbing block up on the highest spot of one of the high points on the distributor cam? (page 40).

○ Did I gap the points to .020 inch when the rubbing block was up on the highest spot of one of the high points on the distributor cam? (page 42)

○ Did I screw the condenser tightly against the body of the distributor? This does not apply to motors in which the condenser is mounted inside the distributor. (page 39)

○ Did I file the points with anything but a real points file? If so, you'd better buy new points if the car doesn't run.

○ If all else fails, here's what to do. "Bump" the motor so that the rubbing block is on the low part of the distributor cam. In this position, the points will be closed. With a screwdriver, pull the points apart. Do not touch the points with the screwdriver. Now, insert a dollar bill between the points and remove the screwdriver. Slide the dollar bill back and forth between the points to remove any grease or dirt.

The second time around

This is a condensed version of this chapter to speed you through your next tune-up. If your Honda has an electronic ignition, skip STEPS 1 through 8 and begin with STEP 9. See the beginning of this chapter for more details on electronic ignitions.

Tools

The tools needed for STEPS 1–8:

☐ medium-sized screwdriver

☐ feeler gauge set

☐ small tube of distributor cam lube

☐ offset screwdrivers—regular and Phillips

☐ dwell meter (optional)

☐ points file

The tools needed for STEP 9:

☐ No. 2 Phillips screwdriver

Mechanical ignitions

There are eight steps to servicing a mechanical ignition. The ninth step is for models with electronic ignitions only:

1. Remove the distributor cap and rotor.
2. See STEP 2, which tells you how the points operate.
3. Inspect the points for burning, pitting, or wear.
4. If the points are in need of replacement, remove and install new points and condenser.
5. Line up the rubbing block on the points assembly with one of the high points on the distributor cam.
6. Check the points gap; it should be .020 inch.
7. Set the points gap to .020 inch, if necessary.

8. Check the condition of the rotor and distributor cap. Lube the distributor cam. Put back the distributor cap and rotor.

9. For models with electronic ignition only (1979 Preludes and Accords and all 1980 and newer models). Check the condition of the rotor and distributor cap.

Setting the timing

A motor that is in "time" runs smoother and has more power. It's also more fuel efficient, making it less harmful to the atmosphere. For your Honda to pass its smog test, the motor must be in time.

Danger! If you have a medical condition that makes it particularly dangerous for you to receive an electrical shock, be careful not to touch any under-the-hood wires or objects while running the motor in this chapter. The chances of receiving a shock are very slim, but it pays to take no chances.

If you are the owner of a 1975–1979 Civic or a 1975–1978 Accord, complete chapter 2 before beginning this chapter. The reason is because the timing adjustment is affected by the procedures done (or not done) in chapter 2. The basic mechanical procedure is to complete chapter 2 and then set the timing. You can, however, set the timing without affecting any adjustments made in chapter 2.

The timing is checked and adjusted with the motor running at idle speed. Idle speed is the speed of the motor when you don't have your foot on the gas pedal. If your motor idles too fast or too slow, a timing check will not be accurate. I encourage you to see chapter 5, and check the idle speed of your motor before beginning this chapter. It only takes a few minutes to check and, if necessary, adjust the idle speed.

Approximate Completion Time: 45 minutes

Before you start

Before you begin to adjust the timing of your Honda, I'd like to fill you in on a little background information about motor timing. Reading this section is optional and you won't need to know the things I tell you here to complete this chapter. If you have the time, do take a few minutes and read this section to learn about the procedures you'll be doing.

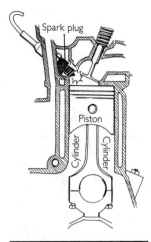

Fig. 3-1
A motor timed at TDC. The spark plug sparks and ignites the fuel the moment the piston reaches the top of the cylinder.

What is timing? *Timing* is nothing more than coordinating the ignition system of a motor to the movement of the power-producing parts inside the motor. When a motor is in "time," the spark plugs ignite gasoline in the motor at the exact moment the motor is able to turn the explosion into the greatest amount of power. If you'll just stick with me for a couple of minutes, you'll see how simple it is to time your Honda.

It takes a mechanic about five minutes to check and adjust your Honda's timing, including connecting the timing light. Although your first experience with timing your Honda might take you the good part of an hour, the next time, you'll be able to do it in no time. Here's what it's all about:

As a piston moves up its cylinder, it compresses fuel that has entered the cylinder. In FIG. 3-1, the spark plug is sparking and igniting the compressed fuel the moment the piston reaches the top of the cylinder. A motor timed to ignite its fuel when the piston reaches the exact top of the cylinder, as illustrated, is said to be timed at *Top Dead Center*, or *TDC*.

If the motor in FIG. 3-1 was timed to ignite the fuel before the piston reached the top of the cylinder (while it was still on its way up the cylinder), this motor would be timed at *Before Top Dead Center*, or *BTDC*. A motor that is timed so its spark plugs ignite the fuel as the piston is on the way back down the cylinder is timed at *After Top Dead Center*, or *ATDC*.

Your Honda's motor has four cylinders, each with its own piston. Almost all Hondas are timed so the spark plugs spark when the pistons are on the way up the cylinders (BTDC). The reason is simple. If your Honda is to get the full power from its gasoline, all gasoline that enters the motor must be completely ignited as the pistons pass by the top of the cylinders. This is important because the force of the exploding gasoline thrusts the pistons back down the cylinders. And because the pistons are connected to a rod that turns a crank, that turns the transmission, that turns the back wheels of your car, getting the most power possible out of each drop of gasoline makes a difference.

To compensate for the fraction of a second it takes for gasoline to become completely ignited, motor timing is set so the spark plugs spark a little before the pistons reach the top of the cylinders. When the timing is set correctly, the fuel will be completely ignited at the exact moment the pistons pass by the tops of the cylinders. Bang . . . big push!!

Honda motor timing is easy to check and adjust. The position of each piston in its related cylinder is measured in degrees before or after Top Dead Center. For example, some Honda motors are timed so that the spark plugs ignite the fuel when the pistons are 7 degrees Before Top Dead Center (7° BTDC). Although this might sound complicated, it's surprisingly easy to check and adjust the timing. This is because Hondas are equipped with a special measuring device that, when illuminated with a timing light, show exactly how many degrees before or after Top Dead Center the piston is when the spark plugs ignite the fuel. You then just turn the distributor to adjust the timing. It's that simple!

Chapter 2 covered how the points assembly is installed in your motor. It is this unit that determines when the spark plugs will spark—or the timing of your motor. Each time the points open, the spark plugs spark. Because the spark plugs spark only when the points open, you adjust the motor timing by altering when the points will open. This is easily done by loosening the distributor holding bolt and turning the distributor until the timing light shows the motor to be in correct time.

Models equipped with an electronic ignition work on a similar principle. The only difference is that it is an electronic unit instead of a points assembly that initiates the sparking of the spark plugs.

Your Honda is equipped with something known as a timing belt that, among other important things, plays a part in motor timing. Later, when you have a chance, read the information in chapter 6 about the timing belt.

What's ahead in this chapter

There are eight steps to timing your Honda:

STEP 1 How to connect an ac, dc, or neon timing light

STEP 2 How to check if your timing light is working

For all 1984–1991 Civics and all 1975–1979 non-CVCC Civics (other years and models, see STEPS 6–8):

STEP 3 How to illuminate the timing marks

STEP 4 How to check the timing adjustment

STEP 5 How to adjust the timing

For 1981–1983 Civics, all 1976–1991 Preludes and Accords, and all 1975–1980 CVCC Civics:

STEP 6 How to illuminate the timing mark(s)

STEP 7 How to check the timing adjustment

STEP 8 How to adjust the timing

Fig. 3-2
Tools used in this chapter.

Timing light

10 mm open- or
box-end wrench

Fig. 3-2
Tools used in this chapter.

Tools

Figure 3-2 illustrates the tools you'll use in this chapter. For a more detailed description of these tools, see chapter 7. You'll need:

☐ timing light. Owners of 1988 or 1989 Preludes with a carburetor (not fuel-injected models) will need a timing light that has an "advance" meter or scale. Your particular model cannot be timed without a timing light that has this feature.

☐ 10 millimeter open-end or box-end wrench

☐ pencil and paper

STEP 1
How to connect an ac, dc, or neon timing light

Warm up the motor

The timing is checked and adjusted when the motor is at normal operating temperature. Start the motor, and when the temperature gauge reaches normal operating temperature, turn the motor off. If you do not drive the car to warm it up before you turn it off, accelerate the motor a few times to release the mechanism that makes it idle fast in the morning. If your Honda doesn't have a temperature gauge, a five or six mile drive will warm it up. Stop the motor before beginning the next procedure.

Spark plug
wires

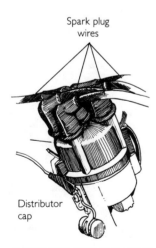

Distributor
cap

Fig. 3-3
The distributor cap and spark plug wires.

Locate the distributor cap and spark plug wires

This is the first step to connecting the timing light to the ignition system. If you have already completed chapters 1 and 2, finding the distributor cap and spark plug wires is "old hat." If you would like some help in locating these parts, see FIGS. 2-3 and 2-18 in chapter 2, as well as FIG. 3-3 in this chapter. The distributor on your Honda might be lying on its side or be different in shape than the one shown in FIG. 3-3.

Locate spark plug wire No. 1 and the distributor cap terminal it is plugged into

The timing light connects to this section of the ignition circuit. To avoid electrical shock, the motor must not be running. Locating spark plug wire No. 1 and the distributor cap terminal it is plugged into takes just a second. On some distributor caps, there are raised numbers stamped next to each of the spark plug wire terminals. If your distributor cap is this numbered type, find the terminal with the number 1 next to it. The spark plug wire connected to this terminal is spark plug wire No. 1. That's all there is to it. You have just found spark plug wire No. 1 and its terminal in the distributor cap. Some distributor caps display only the number 1 and no other numbers. This is fine because you're only looking for terminal No. 1.

If your distributor is not the numbered type, you'll need to locate the No. 1 spark plug. To do this, stand on the driver's side of your Honda and face the motor. You are now standing at the front of the motor. The No. 1 spark plug is closest to where you are standing. The spark plug wire attached to this spark plug is spark plug wire No. 1. The other end of this spark plug wire is plugged into the No. 1 terminal in the distributor cap. See chapter 1, FIGS. 1-3 and 1-4 for help.

Connecting a neon timing light

To avoid electrical shock, the motor must not be running. To connect a neon timing light to your Honda, remove spark plug wire No. 1 from the distributor cap and also spark plug No. 1. Pulling on the spark plug wire might damage it.

The correct way to remove the spark plug wire from the distributor cap is to peel back the rubber cap covering the terminal, grip the wire as close as possible to the now-exposed terminal, and work it free. At the spark plug end of the wire, pull on the rubber boot to free the wire.

As you can see, your neon timing light has two wires running from it. Plug one of these wires into the now-empty terminal in the distributor cap, pushing it in deep enough to contact the metal surface about half way down the terminal. Slip the remaining wire over the top of the wireless spark plug. It doesn't matter which wire goes to the spark plug and which goes into the distributor cap terminal.

You are now connected into the circuit that sparks the No. 1 spark plug. When the motor is running, every time the No. 1 spark plug sparks, your timing light will light up. Are you starting to get the idea? I'll meet you at STEP 2.

Connecting a dc timing light

dc refers to Direct Current, which is the type of current produced by a car battery. To avoid electrical shock, the motor must not be running. As you can see, there are three wires running from your dc timing light. Well, two of these wires might be stuck together like the cord on your living room lamp, but there are three wires.

Attached to the ends of the two identical-looking wires are connectors known as alligator clips. One of these alligator clips is "dressed" in black rubber insulation (must be from Los Angeles). Connect this clip to the negative (−) terminal of the battery. Connect the twin alligator clip, the one in the red rubber insulator, to the positive (+) terminal of the battery. All batteries have a + or a − next to the appropriate terminal. See FIG. 3-4.

The third wire is usually round and much thicker than the other two. At the end of this wire, you might find a large, red skirtlike insulator covering an alligator clip. If you own a more modern timing light, you'll find something that looks like a giant black clothespin. This is an inductive pick-up.

Connecting a "giant clothespin-type" connector

To attach a clothespin-type connector, just clip it around the No. 1 spark plug wire. As you already know, this is the spark plug wire running between the No. 1 spark plug and the No. 1 terminal in the distributor cap. When the inductive pick-up is on correctly, the spark plug wire will slip freely inside the open area of the closed connector. On some inductive pick-ups, there's an arrow accompanied by the words *spark plug*. Attach this connector to the spark plug wire with the arrow pointing in the direction of the spark plug, not the distributor cap. Reversing the arrow causes the timing light not to work.

Fig. 3-4
Connecting a non-inductive dc timing light to the motor.

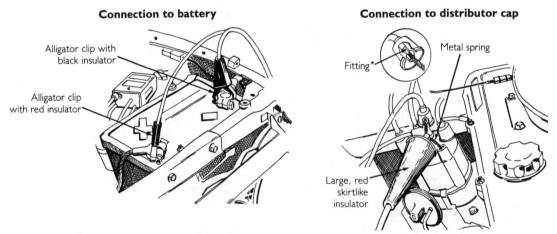

Connection to battery

Alligator clip with black insulator

Alligator clip with red insulator

Connection to distributor cap

Metal spring

Fitting*

Large, red skirtlike insulator

*If there is no fitting at the end of the spark plug wire, simply push the spring up against the end of the wire. This will usually permit the light to function; if not, instructions to correct the situation are provided at the necessary point.

You are now connected into the circuit that sparks the No. 1 spark plug. When the motor is running, your timing light will light up every time this spark plug sparks. Are you starting to get the idea? I'll meet you at STEP 2.

Connecting an alligator clip

This requires a little effort. At the distributor cap, remove spark plug wire No. 1 from the No. 1 terminal. Pulling on the spark plug wire might damage it. See Pro Tip 1.

Insert one end of the metal spring that came with your timing light into the now-empty terminal in the distributor cap, pushing the spring in deep enough to contact the metal surface, about half way down the terminal. Connect the free end of the spark plug wire to the other end of this spring. You can see in FIG. 3-4 that the spring slips inside the fitting located inside the rubber cap at the end of the spark plug wire. With the spring in place, clip the alligator clip onto this spring.

You are now hooked into the circuit that sparks the No. 1 spark plug. When the motor is running, every time this spark plug sparks, the timing light will light up. Are you starting to get the idea? I'll meet you at STEP 2.

Connecting an ac timing light

ac refers to Alternating Current, which is the type of current that comes from the wall sockets in your home. To avoid electrical shock, the motor must not be running. An ac timing light is connected exactly like a dc timing light. The only difference is that instead of hooking up the timing light to the car battery, you plug it into a standard electrical outlet. Plug the electrical plug into the wall socket and then connect the remaining wire to the distributor as explained in "Connecting a dc timing light."

STEP 2
How to check if your timing light is working

Put your timing light someplace where it won't be bounced to the ground as the motor leaps to a start. Also, be positive wires running between the timing light and the motor will not become tangled in the fan, fan belts, or other parts that spin by the rotating fan belts.

Start the motor

Caution! Do not start the motor until you have put an automatic transmission into park and firmly applied the parking brake. Put a manual transmission into neutral and firmly apply the parking brake.

Okay, here we go! Look at the end of the timing light with the glass or plastic lens, and you should see a light flashing on and off. Be sure to press the ON/OFF button or trigger if your timing light has one. If your timing light is working, skip to STEP 3 or 6, whichever pertains to your particular model. If your light fails to flash, see "If your timing light does not flash," which follows.

If your timing light does not flash

There is usually a simple reason why your timing light is not flashing. The following section takes you through several easy steps to correct this problem.

Jiggle the connectors

If your timing light fails to flash, jiggle the alligator clips attached to the battery. Sometimes, an oxidized battery cable connector will cause a poor connection and moving the alligator clips will cut through this oxidation.

Is your dc or ac timing light connected to the distributor cap with a spring connector?

If so, non-stock spark plug wires (replacement wires that did not come with the car when it was new) could be causing your timing light not to flash. At the end of the stock spark plug wires that came with your Honda is a metal fitting that plugs into the distributor cap terminals. This metal fitting also ensures an electrical connection is being made with the timing light spring. See FIG. 3-4 for an illustration of this fitting.

Turn off the motor and check for a fitting at the end of the spark plug wire. If there is no fitting, remove the timing light spring from the distributor cap. Plug the spark plug wire back into the distributor cap, and remove this same spark plug wire from the spark plug. Be sure to pull on the cap, not the wire.

With the spark plug wire free from the spark plug, use the spring to bridge the spark plug to the spark plug wire. To do this, insert the spring inside the rubber boot that slips over the end of the spark plug, making sure the spring contacts the metal fitting that normally fits over the top of the spark plug. Push the other end of the spring over the metal top of the spark plug. It is important that the spring not touch any other part of the motor. Should this happen, an electrical short will result.

*Is your ac or dc timing light connected with
a large clothespin-type connector?*

If so, is there an arrow along with the words *spark plug* on the
clothespin connector. If there is, be sure this connector is attached
to the spark plug wire with the arrow pointing in the direction of
the spark plug, not the distributor cap.

Is your timing light still not working? If your timing light just
doesn't seem to work and you're positive you have connected the
wires correctly to the battery, try reversing their positions. If your
timing light still does not work, it's time for a new one.

STEP 3
Illuminating the timing marks
with a timing light on all 1984 – 1991
Civics and all 1975 – 1979 non-CVCC Civics

Other years and models, see STEP 6.

Stop the motor and locate the timing pointer

Stand on the driver's side of the motor. Look down towards the bottom of the motor and locate the timing pointer illustrated in FIG. 3-5.

Start the motor

To see the timing marks, start the motor and point the flashing timing light at the timing pointer and the spinning wheel just below.

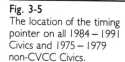

Fig. 3-5
The location of the timing
pointer on all 1984 – 1991
Civics and 1975 – 1979
non-CVCC Civics.

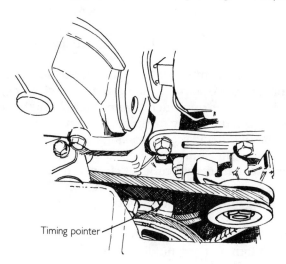

Timing pointer

With the motor running and the timing light flashing, point the timing light at the timing pointer. Do you see the wheel, known as a pulley, spinning just below the timing pointer?

Focus your eyes on the edge of the pulley that's just below the timing pointer and direct the timing light there to illuminate both the timing pointer and this edge of the pulley. Look closely, and you should see two, three, or four small grooves or lines cut into this edge of the spinning pulley. These cuts are known as timing marks. Some models have two timing marks, other models have three or four timing marks. For now, don't be concerned with counting the timing marks, just find them with the timing light. Figure 3-6 illustrates how to illuminate timing marks with a timing light.

Depending on the brightness of the sun as compared to the power of your timing light, it might not be possible to see the timing marks. Try lowering the hood a little to create some shade. This will enable the flashing light to illuminate the timing marks.

Did you see the timing marks?

If you saw any timing marks at all, skip to STEP 4. If you didn't see any timing marks, try slowly moving your light to illuminate the edge of the pulley up 5 or 6 inches to the left or right of the timing pointer. Also, try getting your light closer to the pulley, but be careful not to get your hands or timing light wires entangled in moving parts. If these things don't permit you to see the timing marks, it's possible you are connected to the wrong terminal in the distributor cap. Return to STEP 1.

If your timing light is hooked up correctly and you still can't see the timing marks, stop the motor and use a clean rag with solvent or some other grease cutter to completely clean the edge of the pulley into which the timing marks are cut. Chances are, the timing marks are full of dirt and grease, making them impossible to see. To clean a pulley, clean all the way around the edge of the pulley into which the timing marks are cut, first clean as much area as you can reach while the pulley is in its present position. Then, "bump" the motor in order to turn the pulley and expose the as-yet-uncleaned portion.

"Bumping" the motor means to briefly turn over the motor by momentarily turning the ignition key to the start position. Before

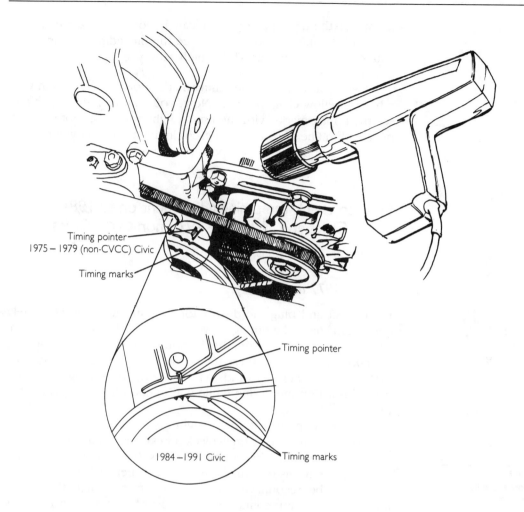

Timing pointer
1975 – 1979 (non-CVCC) Civic

Timing marks

Timing pointer

1984 – 1991 Civic   Timing marks

bumping the motor, put an automatic transmission into park or a manual transmission into neutral, and apply the parking brake. If you make a short, quick bump, the motor won't start.

Once the edge of the pulley is clean, restart the motor and have a peek at the timing marks. If you still can't see the timing marks, see ''Chalking difficult-to-see timing marks.''

Chalking difficult-to-see timing marks

If you haven't been able to see the timing marks, you will after you chalk them. With the motor not running, look at the edge of the pul-

Fig. 3-6
Illuminating the timing marks on all 1984 – 1991 Civics and 1975 – 1979 non-CVCC Civics.

ley where the timing marks are located. Do you see them? If not, "bump" the motor until you do. See the preceding section, "Did you see the timing marks?," which tells you how to bump the motor.

Once you've found the timing marks, color each of them with white or yellow chalk or paint. Now, you will definitely be able to see the timing marks with the timing light when the motor is running. A thin line of paint down each timing mark is all you need. A thick line will hide the exact position of a timing mark.

STEP 4

How to check the timing adjustment on all 1984 – 1991 Civics and all 1975 – 1979 non-CVCC Civics

Other years and models, see STEP 7.

1975 to 1977 models only

Disconnect and plug the distributor vacuum tubes. To accurately check and adjust the timing on your particular Honda, first disconnect the vacuum tubes from the distributor. When the motor applies a suction (a vacuum) to these tubes, the position of the timing plate in the distributor changes and, in turn, so does the timing. You don't want this action interfering while you're checking or adjusting the timing.

As shown in FIG. 3-7, there might be a unit attached to the distributor with one or two small black tubes connected to it. A couple of models don't have this unit or the tubes. If your model does have this unit and it has two tubes, be sure to label each tube because they must be reconnected to the spot from which they were removed. If the unit connected to the distributor on your model is

Fig. 3-7
Disconnecting the vacuum tube(s) from the distributor.

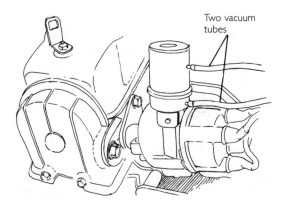

Two vacuum tubes

different in shape, no matter. The tube(s) must still be disconnected from 1975–1977 models.

After disconnecting the tube(s), cover or plug their ends to prevent the motor from sucking in air through the open ends. Air entering the motor this way makes it run faster and causes the timing reading not to be accurate. One last thing—don't "jam" anything into these tubes that you can't get back out again. The tapered end of a pencil usually fits perfect. Before using a pencil, break off the lead to safeguard against it breaking off inside a tube and getting sucked into the motor. Now, skip ahead to the section "Start the motor and flash the timing light on the timing marks."

1988 – 1991 Civics

To accurately check and adjust the timing on your rather sophisticated Honda, it is necessary to first "jumper" (insert a small wire) between the terminals of the timing terminal connector. Inserting a wire between these terminals takes control of your motor's timing away from the computer, allowing you to check base timing and, if necessary, readjust it.

Base timing is what the computer bases its calculations on. Without this jumper wire in place, the computer might not let you see base timing. In addition, without a jumper wire in place, the computer would change any timing adjustment you make to suit its own perception of what's best for the motor. The computer makes these changes based on engine speed, air pressure, ambient air temperature, coolant temperature, exhaust gas percentages, and a host of other things your home computer never thinks about.

To jumper the timing terminal connector on 1988–1991 models, turn off the motor. Using FIG. 3-8 as a guide, locate the timing terminal connector. On 1988 and 1989 models, the timing terminal connector is easily identified by its bright yellow rubber cap. On 1988 and 1989 models, you'll find this connector towards the back of the motor compartment on the driver's side. On 1990 and 1991 models, you'll find this connector under the passenger's side of the dashboard.

After finding the timing terminal connector, remove the yellow rubber cap, and insert a short wire between the two exposed terminals as illustrated in FIG. 3-8. Be sure to remove the insulation from each end of the wire or electrical contact will not be made. An unfolded metal paper clip will work in place of a wire. Just be sure this clip does not touch any metal surfaces near the connector or a short will result that could destroy the computer.

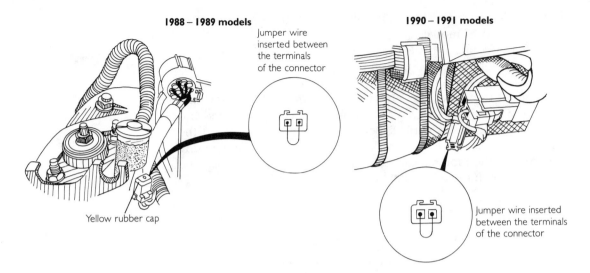

1988 – 1989 models

Jumper wire
inserted between
the terminals
of the connector

1990 – 1991 models

Jumper wire inserted
between the terminals
of the connector

Yellow rubber cap

Fig. 3-8
Jumpering the timing terminal
connector on all 1988 – 1991
Civics.

*Start the motor and flash the
timing light on the timing marks*

How many timing marks does your motor have? Now that you've
located the timing pointer and timing marks in STEP 3, with the
motor running and the timing light flashing, look again at the timing
marks and count them all. There might be more timing marks than
just the ones visible adjacent to the timing pointer. So, slowly move
your light to illuminate the edge of the pulley up 5 or 6 inches to the
left or right of the timing pointer and count all the timing marks you
see. Put ''Hondamatics'' into second gear and be sure to put on the
parking brake!

1975 – 1979 models

Are there just two timing marks? If so, just remember that there are
two timing marks and skip to the section ''Which timing mark is in
line with the timing pointer?''

Are there four timing marks? The 1975 – 1979 models with four
timing marks actually have two sets of timing marks with two timing
marks in each set. In other words, there are two pairs of timing
marks.

On motors with two sets of timing marks, forget about the set
on your left. The set on your right is the set used for checking motor
timing. From this point on, I want you to think of your motor as having only two timing marks, the set of two on your right. Now that
you know this important fact about your motor, skip down to the
section ''Which timing mark is in line with the timing pointer?''

1984 – 1991 models

All 1984–1991 models have four timing marks. You will see one group of three timing marks together. And, positioned just a few inches away to the right, another timing mark can be seen all by itself. For purposes of this chapter, forget about the timing mark all by itself. Only the group of three timing marks together is used for motor timing. From this point on, think of your motor as having only three timing marks.

Which timing mark is in line with the timing pointer?

With the motor running and the timing light flashing on the timing marks, determine which of the timing marks, if any, is in line with the timing pointer. If none of the two or three timing marks (depending on how many timing marks your motor has) is in line with the timing pointer, decide if all the timing marks are on the left side of the timing pointer or on the right side of the timing pointer. Or, are two marks straddling the timing pointer?

1975 – 1979 models

Your motor is in time if the left-most timing mark of the pair is in line with the timing pointer. The left-most timing mark of the pair of timing marks is known as the Before Top Dead Center (BTDC) timing mark. It is this timing mark that will be in line with the timing pointer if your motor is timed correctly.

Figure 3-9A illustrates the position of the timing marks when your motor is in time. Notice that the left-most timing mark (of the pair of marks) is in line with the timing pointer. This left-most timing mark, depending on the model and year of your car, is known as either the 2 degree before top dead center timing mark (abbreviated 2° BTDC), the 5° BTDC, or the 7° BTDC timing mark. It is not necessary to know how many degrees this mark is equal to on your model, just be aware that this left-most timing mark is the BTDC timing mark and your motor is timed correctly when it is in line with the timing pointer.

Figures 3-9B, 3-9C, and 3-9D illustrate different positions of the timing marks when the motor is not in time. These illustrations of motors out of time might be helpful, especially if you find it necessary to adjust the timing. In FIG. 3-9B, the "right" timing mark of the pair of timing marks is in line with the timing pointer. This timing mark is, on all models, the top dead center (TDC) timing mark. Because the TDC timing mark is in line with the timing pointer, this

Fig. 3-9
The meaning of the position of
the timing marks in relation to
the timing pointer on
1975 – 1979 models.

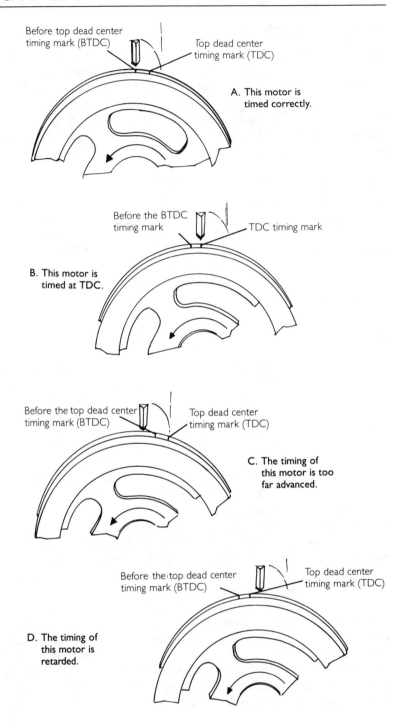

Before top dead center
timing mark (BTDC)
Top dead center
timing mark (TDC)

A. This motor is
timed correctly.

Before the BTDC
timing mark
TDC timing mark

B. This motor is
timed at TDC.

Before the top dead center
timing mark (BTDC)
Top dead center
timing mark (TDC)

C. The timing of
this motor is too
far advanced.

Before the top dead center
timing mark (BTDC)
Top dead center
timing mark (TDC)

D. The timing of
this motor is
retarded.

motor is said to be timed at TDC. In other words, the spark plugs are sparking when the pistons reach the top of the cylinders.

In FIG. 3-9C, the timing marks are all to the right of the timing pointer. This motor is timed at many degrees BTDC. Remember that the pulley into which the timing marks are cut is spinning counter-clockwise. In FIG. 3-9D, the timing marks are all to the left of the timing pointer. This motor is timed at many degrees after top dead center (ATDC). In other words, when the pistons have passed the top dead center position and are on their way back down the cyclinders.

If your 1975—1979 model is not in time, stay tuned. Before you proceed to STEP 5, I want to fill you in on a little secret. If you found both timing marks to be on the right side of the timing pointer as shown in FIG. 3-9C, someone might have timed the motor like this (at many degrees BTDC) to compensate for a problem. This is particularly true of motors with more than 100,000 miles that have never been rebuilt. After you set the timing back to the BTDC timing mark in STEP 5, you might find your Honda does not run well. See the "Troubleshooting" section on page 108 for more information.

If your model is in time, there's nothing more to do. So, stop the motor, disconnect the timing light, and reconnect the spark plug wire if it was necessary to disconnect it. If you disconnected one or more black tubes from the distributor, be sure to reconnect them. From here, chapter 4 on valve adjustment would be your next logical move. "For your information," which appears at the end of this step, explains why the motor is in time when the correct timing mark is in alignment with the timing pointer.

1984—1991 models

Your motor is in time if the middle timing mark (of the group of three timing marks) is in line with the timing pointer as seen in FIG. 3-10A. It's that simple! This timing mark is usually painted red and is know as the before top dead center (BTDC) timing mark.

Figures 3-10B, 3-10C, and 3-10D illustrate the position of the timing marks when the motor is not in time. These illustrations of a motor out of time might be helpful, especially if you find it necessary to adjust the timing.

If your 1984—1991 model is not in time, someone might have timed the motor like this (many degrees BTDC) to compensate for a problem. This is particularly true of motors with more than 100,000 miles that have never been rebuilt. After you set the timing mark in STEP 5 back to BTDC, you might find your Honda does not run well.

Fig. 3-10
1984 – 1991 models: The
meaning of the position of the
timing marks in relation to the
timing pointer.

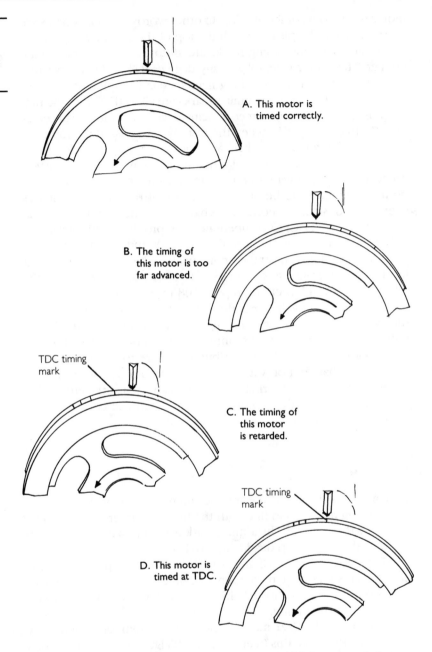

A. This motor is
   timed correctly.

B. The timing of
   this motor is too
   far advanced.

TDC timing
mark

C. The timing of
   this motor
   is retarded.

TDC timing
mark

D. This motor is
   timed at TDC.

See the "Troubleshooting" section on page 108 for more information.

If your model is in time, there's nothing more to do. Disconnect the timing light and, if necessary, reconnect the spark plug

wire. If your Honda is a 1988–1991 model, remove the jumper wire from the timing terminal and replace the protective cap. ''For your information,'' which follows, explains why the motor is in time when the correct timing mark is in alignment with the timing pointer.

For your information

Why is the motor in time when the Before Top Dead Center timing mark is in alignment with the timing pointer? As you know from the introduction of this chapter, checking the timing of your Honda's motor actually means checking that the spark plugs are sparking when the pistons are the correct distance from the top of the cylinders. To make this check, you connected a timing light into the circuit that sparks the No. 1 spark plug. Then, with the motor running, you pointed the flashing timing light at the timing marks.

Because the timing light is connected to the circuit that sparks the No. 1 spark plug, it flashes and illuminates the timing marks only when this spark plug sparks. And, because the timing marks are positioned in direct relationship to where the No. 1 piston is in its cylinder, you can tell where this piston is in the cylinder when the spark plug sparks by comparing the position of the illuminated timing marks to the timing pointer.

Honda engineers have positioned the timing pointer so that when the No. 1 piston is at the exact top of its cylinder, the Top Dead Center timing mark is aligned with the timing pointer. (If your motor has three timing marks, the fourth timing mark, which is off by itself, is the TDC timing mark.) Thus, if the timing light shows the TDC timing mark to be aligned with the timing pointer, you know that the spark plug is sparking when the piston is at the exact top of the cylinder. Remember: The timing light only lights up and illuminates the timing marks when the spark plug sparks.

The wheel into which the timing marks are cut is spinning counterclockwise. If the Before Top Dead Center (BTDC) timing mark is seen in line with the timing pointer, the spark plug is sparking at the correct time before the piston reaches the top of the cylinder.

STEP 5
How to adjust the timing on all
1984 – 1991 Civics and all 1975 – 1979 non-CVCC Civics

Other years and models, see STEP 8. Before doing this step, take a minute and read the preceding section ''For your information.''

This short section explains why the motor is in time when the Before Top Dead Center (BTDC) timing mark is in alignment with the timing pointer. You don't have to read this section to time your motor, but I thought you might find it interesting and helpful to know the "why" of what you'll be doing.

If you found your motor to be out of time, you'll find it easy to adjust. All you have to do is loosen the distributor holding bolt and slowly turn the distributor until the BTDC timing mark is in line with the timing pointer. The motor should not be running when you loosen the distributor holding bolt. Should the wrench slip, you could severely injure your hand on a moving motor part.

Loosen the distributor holding bolt

Stop the motor. Get out your 10 millimeter open- or box-end wrench. Using FIG. 3-11 as a guide, locate and loosen the distributor holding bolt, and turn it counterclockwise. Just loosen this bolt a turn or so to allow the distributor to rotate—but don't turn the distributor until you get to the part of the chapter where you do it with the timing light illuminating the timing marks.

Don't be alarmed if the distributor on your Honda is in a different location than the one shown in FIG. 3-11. It might be standing

Fig. 3-11
The location of the distributor holding bolt.

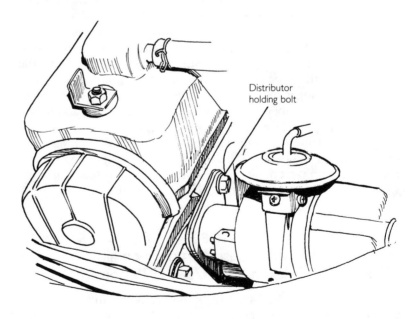

Distributor
holding bolt

upright. The distributor holding bolt will, however, be in the same place in relation to the distributor as illustrated. Some models have a black rubber cap covering this bolt. Remove the cap to access the bolt.

Which way to turn the distributor

Once again, don't turn the distributor until you get to the part in this chapter where you do it with the timing light illuminating the timing marks. When the time comes to turn the distributor, I'll tell you to start the motor and what to do.

Models with two timing marks

On models with two timing marks, turning the distributor clockwise moves the timing marks to the right (towards your right hand when facing the spinning pulley). This is known as advancing the timing. The spark plugs spark sooner when the timing is advanced. By sooner, I mean when the pistons are further from reaching the top of the cylinders. Turning the distributor counterclockwise moves the timing marks to the left. This is known as retarding the timing. The spark plugs spark later when the timing is retarded. By later, I mean when the pistons are closer to reaching the top of the cylinders.

Models with three timing marks

On models with three timing marks, turning the distributor counterclockwise moves the timing marks to the right (towards your right hand when facing the spinning pulley). This is known as advancing the timing. The spark plugs spark sooner when the timing is advanced. By sooner, I mean when the pistons are further from reaching the top of the cylinders. Turning the distributor clockwise moves the timing marks to the left. This is known as retarding the timing, and the spark plugs spark later when the timing is retarded. By later, I mean when the pistons are closer to reaching the top of the cylinder.

Are you wondering why a side-mounted distributor is turned in the opposite direction of an end-mounted distributor to make the same adjustment? The reason is because the distributor shaft turns counterclockwise in a side-mounted distributor and clockwise in an end-mounted distributor.

Examples to help you time your motor

The following examples can help you decide which way to turn the distributor to time your motor:

○ *If your motor has two timing marks and you found your motor to be timed with the TDC timing mark in line with the timing pointer* (FIG. 3-9B), turn the distributor very slowly clockwise to move the timing marks to the right (advancing the timing) until the BTDC timing mark is in line with the timing pointer.

○ *If your motor has two timing marks and you found your motor to be timed at many degrees before TDC* (FIG. 3-9C), turn the distributor very slowly counterclockwise to move the timing marks to the left (retarding the timing) until the BTDC timing mark is in line with the timing pointer.

○ *If your motor has two timing marks and you found your motor to be timed at many degrees ATDC* (FIG. 3-9D), turn the distributor very slowly clockwise to move the timing marks to the right (advancing the timing) until the BTDC timing mark is in line with the timing pointer.

○ *If your motor has three timing marks and all three timing marks were to the right of the timing pointer* as shown in FIG. 3-10B (advanced timing), turn the distributor very slowly clockwise to move the timing marks to the left (retarding the timing) until the BTDC timing mark (the one in the center of the group of three timing marks and usually painted red) is in line with the timing pointer.

○ *If your motor has three timing marks and all three timing marks were to the left of the timing pointer* as shown in FIG. 3-10C (retarded timing), turn the distributor very slowly counterclockwise to move the timing marks to the right (advancing the timing) until the BTDC timing mark (the one in the center of the group of three timing marks and usually painted red) lines up with the timing pointer.

○ *If your motor has three timing marks and the TDC timing mark is in line with the timing pointer* as shown in FIG. 3-10D, turn the distributor very slowly counterclockwise to move the timing marks to the right (advancing the timing) until the BTDC timing mark (the one in the center of the group of three timing marks and usually painted red) lines up with the timing pointer.

Set the timing

Start the motor. Hondamatics must be in second gear. Put the parking brake on securely! To turn the distributor and align the BTDC timing mark with the timing pointer, you can grasp the plastic distributor cap, but don't touch the wires because you might get an electrical shock.

Depending on which direction you are turning the distributor, the motor will either run faster or slower. If your motor should stop running while turning the distributor, turn the distributor a little in the opposite direction and then restart the motor.

When the motor is in proper time—the correct timing mark in line with the timing pointer—carefully retighten (turn clockwise) the distributor holding bolt, keeping hands clear of moving parts. Then recheck the timing. If it has not changed, turn off the motor. Now, that wasn't too bad!

Danger! If you have a medical condition that makes it particularly dangerous for you to receive an electrical shock, now is the time to be extra careful. The spark plug wires running from the distributor cap, if cracked, can deliver a strong electrical shock. Wear gloves or use a thick rag to grab and turn the distributor. Avoid touching the spark plug wires. If you don't touch the car with your body or free hand while turning the distributor, you won't make a good conductor for electricity and this will reduce any chance of electrical shock.

Disconnect the timing light

Stop the motor. Disconnect the timing light and, if necessary, reconnect the spark plug wire. If you disconnected one or more black tubes from the distributor, be sure to reconnect them. If your Honda is a 1988–1991 model and you "jumpered" the timing terminal, remove the jumper wire from the timing terminal and replace the protective rubber cap. That's it, you're done!

If you just put your motor into "time," be prepared for a smoother, more powerful, more fuel-efficient Honda. If you also completed chapters 1 and 2, the difference in your Honda will be so dramatic, you'll think you just got yourself a new car! From here, chapter 4, the valve adjusting chapter, would be your next logical procedure.

The "Second time around" and "Troubleshooting" sections are at the end of the chapter. For an explanation of how turning the distributor times the motor, see the section "For your information" under STEP 7.

How to illuminate the timing mark(s) on all 1981 – 1983 Civics, all 1976 – 1991 Preludes and Accords, and 1975 – 1980 CVCC Civics

Other years and models see STEP 3.

Locate the timing pointer

The timing pointer is inside the motor, covered by a rectangular-shaped black rubber plug with a pull tab. To find this plug and remove it, stand on the passenger's side of the motor and look for this plug in the side location shown in FIG. 3-12. See FIG. 3-15 for another view of this area.

If the plug is not in this side location, stand directly in front of your Honda and look in the front location, also shown in FIG. 3-12. See FIG. 3-15 for another view of this area. On models with a rear-opening hood, it's not possible to stand in front of the car and see the motor, so lean over from the passenger's side to spot this plug in the front location.

When you find this rubber plug, pull it from the motor. It can be stubborn. If this rubber plug is missing from your motor, you will see the square cut-out section where the plug should be located. It's a good idea to purchase a new plug because it keeps out dust and moisture.

Take a look into the square cut-out section of the motor that was covered by the plug. As shown in FIG. 3-12, the timing pointer is a pointed object visible through the cut-out.

1988 – 1991 fuel-injected Preludes and all 1990 – 1991 Accords

To accurately check and adjust the timing on your rather sophisticated Honda, it is necessary to first "jumper" (insert a small wire) between the terminals of the timing terminal connector. Before you go any further, now is a good time to take care of this procedure because you might not be able to see the timing marks in this step without this jumper wire in place. Inserting a jumper wire between these terminals takes control of your motor's timing away from the computer, allowing you to check "base" timing and, if necessary, readjust it.

Base timing is what the computer bases its calculations on. Without this jumper wire in place, the computer might not let you see base timing. In addition, without this wire in place, the computer would change any timing adjustment you make to suit its own

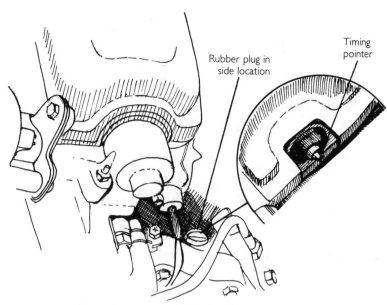

Rubber plug in
side location

Timing
pointer

Fig. 3-12
Locating and removing the
rubber plug covering the timing
pointer on 1975 – 1980 CVCC
Civics, all 1981 – 1983 Civics,
and all 1976 – 1991 Preludes
and Accords.

As seen from passenger's side of vehicle

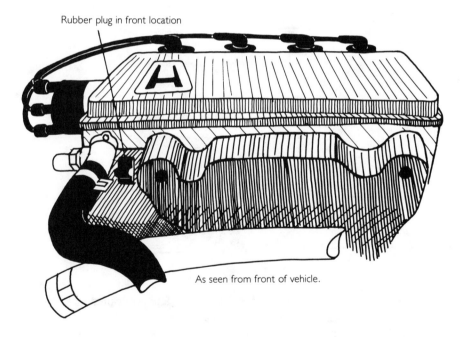

Rubber plug in front location

As seen from front of vehicle.

Fig. 3-13
Jumpering the timing terminal
connector on 1990–1991
Accords and 1988–1991
fuel-injected Preludes.

1990–1991 Accord

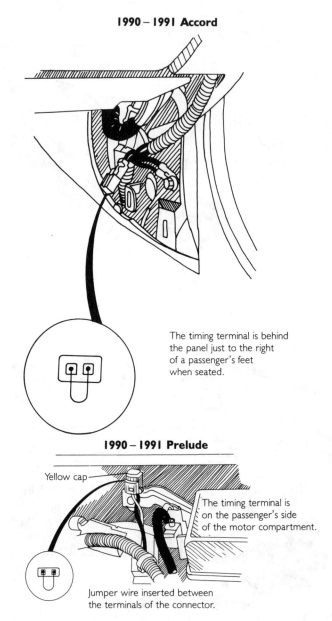

The timing terminal is behind
the panel just to the right
of a passenger's feet
when seated.

1990–1991 Prelude

Yellow cap

The timing terminal is
on the passenger's side
of the motor compartment.

Jumper wire inserted between
the terminals of the connector.

perception of what's best for the motor. The computer makes these
changes based on engine speed, air pressure, ambient temperature,
coolant temperature, exhaust gas percentages, and a host of other
things your home computer never thinks about.

To "jumper" the timing terminal, turn off the motor. Then,

using FIG. 3-13 as a guide, locate the timing terminal connector. This connector is easily identified by its bright yellow rubber cap. On 1988–1991 fuel-injected Preludes, you'll find this connector towards the back of the motor compartment on the passenger's side (FIG. 3-13). On all 1990 and 1991 Accords, you'll find this connector under the passenger's side of the dashboard (FIG. 3-13).

When you find the timing terminal connector, remove the yellow rubber cap and insert a short wire between the two exposed terminals as illustrated. Be sure to remove the insulation from each end of the wire or electrical contact will not be made. An unfolded metal paper clip will work in place of a wire. Be sure this clip does not touch any metal surfaces near the connector or a short will result that might destroy the computer.

1988 – 1989 carbureted Preludes (not fuel-injected)

Turn the advance knob on your special timing light to the 4° setting. As mentioned at the beginning of this chapter, your particular model requires a timing light with an advance scale. The reason for this special light is because your motor is missing the actual timing mark that designates correct timing. This special light compensates for the missing timing mark. Set the knob at the 4° mark, and you're in business.

On 1988 and 1989 Preludes with a carburetor (not fuel-injected), you must also disconnect and plug the distributor vacuum tubes. To accurately check and adjust the timing on your particular Honda, it is necessary to first disconnect the vacuum tubes from the distributor. When the motor applies a suction (a vacuum) to these tubes, the position of the timing plate in the distributor changes and, in turn, so does the timing. You don't want this action interfering while you're checking or adjusting the timing.

As shown in FIG. 3-7, there is a unit attached to the distributor with one or two small black tubes connected to it. If your model has two tubes, be sure to label each tube because they must be reconnected to the spot from which they were removed.

After disconnecting the tube(s), cover or plug their ends to prevent the motor from sucking in air through the open ends. Air entering the motor this way makes it run faster and causes the timing reading to be inaccurate. One last thing—don't "jam" anything into these tubes that you can't get back out again. The tapered end of a pencil usually fits perfect. Before using a pencil, however, break off the lead to safeguard against it breaking off inside a tube and getting sucked into the motor.

Fig. 3-14
The timing marks on 1975 – 1980 CVCC Civics, all 1981-1983 Civics, and all 1976-1991 Preludes and Accords.

CIVICS

1975 Civic

Manual transmission.   Automatic transmission.

1976 Civic

Sedan and station wagon with manual transmission.   Sedan with automatic transmission.   Wagon with automatic transmission.

1977 Civic

1978 and 1979 Civic

Fig. 3-14
Continued.

1980 Civic

1300

Non-California 1500
hatchback with
manual transmission.

Non-California 1500
wagon with manual
transmission.

California 1500 with
manual transmission.

1500 with automatic
transmission.

1981 Civic

All 1300 models with
manual transmission.

All 1300 models with
automatic
transmission.

Non-California 1500
hatchback with
manual transmission.

Non-California 1500
wagon and sedan with
manual transmission.

California 1500 with
manual transmission.

All 1500 models with
automatic
transmission.

Fig. 3-14
Continued.

1982 and 1983 Civic

All 1300 models with
manual transmission.

All 1500 models with
automatic
transmission.

All 1500 models with
manual transmission.

ACCORDS AND PRELUDES

1976 and 1977 Accord

Manual transmission.

Automatic transmission.

Manual transmission.

1978 Accord

Automatic transmission.

1979 Accord and Prelude

Manual transmission.

Automatic transmission.

1980 Accord and Prelude

Manual transmission.

Automatic transmission.

1981 Accord and Prelude

Fig. 3-14
Continued.

Manual transmission.   Automatic transmission.

1982 Accord and Prelude and 1983 Accord

California with manual
transmission.

Non-California and
high altitude with
manual transmission.

All with automatic
transmission.

1983 Prelude

 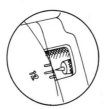 

Non-California with
manual transmission.

California with manual
transmission.

All with automatic
transmission.

1984 Accord

Non-California with
manual transmission.

California and high
altitude with manual
transmission.

All with automatic
transmission.

Fig. 3-14
Continued.

1984 Prelude

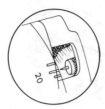

All with manual
transmission.

All with automatic
transmission.

1985 Accord

All with manual
transmission.

All with automatic
transmission.

1985 Prelude

All with manual
transmission.

All with automatic
transmission.

1986–1989 Accord, carbureted and fuel-injected
1986–1987 Prelude, carbureted and fuel-injected

Accord: 1986–1989
California, carbureted
with manual transmission.

Accord: 1986–1989
Non-California,
carbureted with
manual transmission.
(actual reading is 24°).

Prelude: 1986–1987
carbureted with
manual transmission.

Prelude: 1986–1987
carbureted with
automatic
transmission.

Fig. 3-14
Continued.

Accord: 1986–1989
fuel injected with
manual transmission.

Prelude: 1986–1987
fuel injected with
automatic
transmission.

Accord: 1986–1989
fuel injected or
carbureted with
automatic
transmission.

Prelude: 1986–1987
fuel injected with
automatic
transmission.

1988–1990 Prelude, carbureted only

Manual and automatic
transmission.

1990–1991 Accord, all

Manual and automatic
transmission.

1988–1991 Prelude

All with manual
transmission.

All with automatic
transmission.

To see the timing marks (all models)

Point the flashing timing light at the timing pointer. The timing marks are grooves cut into the wheel spinning just below the timing pointer. See the illustrations that make up FIG. 3-14 and locate the one for your motor. With the motor running and the timing light flashing, hold the flashing timing light just above the timing pointer as shown in FIG. 3-15. Look to see the timing mark or marks FIG. 3-14 shows your motor to have. Some motors have only one timing mark and others have two, three, or more.

The timing marks are thin lines cut into the edge of a wheel that spins just below the timing pointer. A portion of this spinning wheel is visible through the cut-out from which the rubber plug was removed. It is on this visible portion of the wheel that you will see the timing mark(s). Normally, the timing mark(s) are painted different colors. If the colors have worn from the timing mark(s), don't worry, I'll tell you what to do when the time comes. If the illustration of your motor shows numbers or the letter T alongside the timing mark(s), you need not be concerned with seeing them on your motor because they don't apply to the work in this chapter.

On models illustrated with two or more timing marks, you might not see all of the timing marks that the illustration in FIG. 3-14 shows your motor to have. This is because:

○ The space surrounding the timing pointer might be too small for all the timing marks to fit into it at once. In other words, when the timing light illuminates the timing marks, some of them are still back inside the motor and not within the area being illuminated. This isn't a problem, I just want you to know what's going on.

○ Another reason for not seeing all the timing marks on motors with two or more timing marks might be because the timing is out of adjustment. This, too, would cause some timing marks to be back inside the motor when the timing light is illuminating the area around the timing pointer. This is not a problem and I'll tell you what to do as we go along.

Did you see any timing marks?

If you did see one or more timing marks, skip to STEP 7. If you didn't see any timing marks, try getting your timing light closer to the spinning wheel. Be careful not to get your hands or any wires entangled in moving parts.

If you are using a neon timing light or are in bright sunlight, you might need to lower the hood to create some shade. This will help the flashing light illuminate the timing mark(s).

Side location of timing pointer

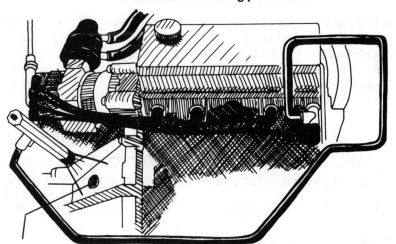

Timing pointer inside

Fig. 3-15
Illuminating the timing marks on 1975 – 1980 CVCC Civics, all 1981 – 1983 Civics, and all 1976 – 1991 Preludes and Accords.

Front location of timing pointer

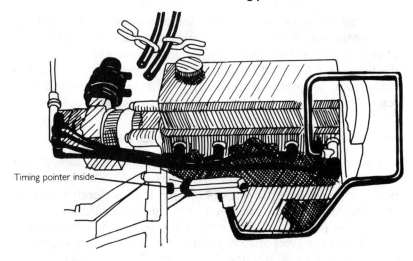

Timing pointer inside

If you still can't see the mark(s), it is possible you are connected to the wrong terminal in the distributor cap. Return to STEP 1. Owners of 1988 – 1991 fuel-injected Accords and Preludes: did you "jumper" the timing terminal earlier in this step? If not, here's your problem.

If you still can't see any timing marks

If you still can't see any timing marks, don't worry. If none of the preceding information solves the problem, your motor is probably out of time to the point that the timing mark(s) are not visible within the space that surrounds the timing pointer. Don't worry, everything is okay. Go to STEP 7.

STEP 7
How to check the timing adjustment on all 1981 – 1983 Civics, 1975 – 1980 CVCC Civics, and 1976 – 1991 Preludes and Accords with one timing mark

See STEP 7-1 if your model has more than one timing mark.

Is the timing mark in line with the timing pointer?

With the motor running and the timing light flashing, stand on the passenger's side of your Honda and illuminate the timing mark. Is the timing mark directly in line with the timing pointer, on the left (your left) side of the timing pointer or on the right (your right) side of the timing pointer?

If the timing pointer on your Honda is located in the alternate front position as shown in FIG. 3-12 and you are able to stand in front of your Honda and see the timing pointer without interference from the hood, feel free to do so. Please, however, for purposes of this explanation, imagine you are seeing the timing mark from the passenger's side of your Honda, leaning over the fender.

How to know if the motor is timed correctly

If the timing mark is directly in line with the timing pointer, your motor is in time. It's that simple. Disconnect the timing light and, if necessary, reconnect the spark plug wire. If your Honda is a 1988-1991 model and you "jumpered" the timing terminal connector, remove the jumper wire and replace the protective rubber cap. If your Honda is a 1988 or 1989 Prelude with a carburetor, reconnect the distributor vacuum tubes. The Second Time Around and Troubleshooting sections are at the end of this chapter. From here, chapter 4 on valve adjustment would be your next logical step.

Take a minute to read the "For your information" section, which appears at the end of this step. This section explains why the motor is in time when the correct timing mark is in alignment with the timing pointer.

If the timing mark is on the left or right side of the timing pointer, or not visible at all

Proceed to STEP 8. Before you proceed to STEP 8, however, I want to fill you in on a little secret. If you found the timing marks to be to the left side of the timing pointer (advanced timing), someone might have timed the motor like this for a reason. This might be particularly true if your motor has more than 100,000 miles on it and has never been rebuilt. After you reset the timing in STEP 8, you might find that your Honda does not run well. See the last entry in the Troubleshooting section at the end of the chapter for more information.

Also, before timing your motor, if your schedule permits, take a minute to read the "For your information" section, which follows. This section explains why the motor is in time when the timing mark is in alignment with the timing pointer. You don't have to read this section to time your motor, but I think you might find it interesting and helpful to know the "why's" of what you'll be doing.

For your information

Why is the motor in time when the timing mark is in alignment with the timing pointer? As you know from the introduction of this chapter, checking the timing of your Honda's motor actually means checking that the spark plugs are sparking when the pistons are the correct distance from the top of the cylinders. To make this check, you connected a timing light into the circuit that sparks the No. 1 spark plug. Then, with the motor running, you pointed the flashing timing light at the timing marks.

Because the timing light is connected to the circuit that sparks the No. 1 spark plug, it flashes and illuminates the timing mark only when this spark plug sparks. And, because the timing marks are positioned in direct relationship to where the No. 1 piston is in the cylinder, you can tell where this piston is in the cylinder when the spark plug sparks by comparing the position of the illuminated timing mark to the timing pointer.

Honda engineers have positioned the timing pointer so that when the piston is at the exact top of the cylinder, the timing mark will be aligned with the timing pointer. Thus, when the timing light shows the timing mark to be aligned with the timing pointer, you know that the spark plug is sparking when the piston is at the exact top of the cylinder. Remember: the timing light only lights up and illuminates the timing mark when the spark plug sparks.

The wheel in which the timing mark is cut is spinning clockwise when viewed from the passenger's side of the vehicle. If the

timing mark is seen to the left of the timing pointer, you know that
the spark plug is sparking sometime before the piston reaches the
top of the cylinder. If the timing mark is seen to the right of the timing pointer, you know that the spark plug is sparking after the piston
has reached the top of the cylinder and is on its way back down. In
either case, it is necessary to adjust the timing.

STEP 7-1: How to check the timing adjustment on all 1981 – 1983 Civics, all 1975 – 1980 CVCC Civics, and all 1976 – 1991 Preludes and Accords with two or more timing marks

Where are the timing marks
in relation to the timing pointer?

With the motor running and the timing light flashing on the timing
marks, stand on the passenger's side of your Honda and observe and
remember the position of the timing marks in relationship to the
timing pointer.

To remember what you see, you might find it helpful to draw a
picture. Do be sure your drawing is accurate, however. Each timing
mark in the motor might be painted a different color. When drawing
your picture, note the color of each timing mark. If you do not see
all the timing marks that the illustration in FIG. 3-14 shows your
motor to have, be sure to label the colors of those timing marks you
can see.

If the timing pointer on your Honda is located in the alternate
front position as shown in FIG. 3-12, and you are able to stand in
front of your Honda and see the timing pointer, feel free to do so.
Please, however, for purposes of this explanation, imagine you are
seeing the timing marks from the passenger's side of your Honda,
leaning over the fender.

How to know if your motor is in time

To know if your motor is in time, compare your drawing to the timing chart in TABLE 3-1. If the color has worn off of the timing marks
on your motor, see the timing chart in TABLE 3-2. In TABLE 3-2, your
motor is in time when the timing mark specified is in line with the
timing pointer. The information for each model is presented in the
order the timing marks appear when viewed from the passenger's
side of the car.

Viewed from the passenger's side, the timing mark furthest to
your right is called the first timing mark; the timing mark to its
immediate left is called the second timing mark; and for motors with
more than two timing marks, each successive timing mark is designated as third, fourth, etc. See FIG. 3-14 to know how many timing

Table 3-1 Colored Timing Mark Chart

Year	Model	Timing Mark Color
	Civic	
1975–76	All models	Red
1977	Non-California	Red
	California sedan	Red
	California wagon, manual transmission	Red
	California wagon, automatic transmission	White
	High-altitude, manual transmission	Red
	High-altitude, automatic transmission	White
1978–79	Non-California, manual transmission	Yellow
	Non-California, automatic transmission	Red
	California	Red
	High-altitude	Red
1980	Non-California, manual transmission	Red
	Non-California, automatic transmission	White
	California	White
	High-altitude	Red
1981–1983	Not covered in this section	See STEPS 3–5
1984–1991	Not covered in this section	See STEPS 3–5
	Accord	
1976–77	All models	Red
1978	Non-California	Yellow
	California	Red
	High-altitude	Red
1979	Non-California, manual transmission	Yellow
	Non-California, automatic transmission	Blue
	California, manual transmission	White
	California, automatic transmission	Black
	High-altitude, manual transmission	White
	High-altitude, automatic transmission	Black
1980	All models except for California sedans	White
	California sedan, manual transmission	Red
	California sedan, automatic transmission	White
1981	All models	White
1982–1991	All models	Red
	Prelude	
1979	Non-California, manual transmission	Yellow
	Non-California, automatic transmission	Blue
	California, manual transmission	White
	California, automatic transmission	Black
	High-altitude, manual transmission	White
	High-altitude, automatic transmission	Black
1980–1981	All models	White
1982–1991	All models	Red

Table 3-2 Timing Marks for Motors without Colored Marks

Year	Model	Timing Mark
	Civic	
1975	All models	2nd
1976	All models	1st
1977	Non-California	1st
	California sedan	1st
	California wagon, manual transmission	1st
	California wagon, automatic transmission	2nd
	High-altitude, manual transmission	1st
	High-altitude, automatic transmission	2nd
1978–79	California, manual transmission	2nd
	California, automatic transmission	1st
	High-altitude, manual transmission	2nd
	High-altitude, automatic transmission	1st
1980	All models	1st
1981–1991	See FIG. 3-14. The illustration of your model shows the correct timing mark in line with the timing pointer.	
	Accord	
1976–77	All models	1st
1978	Non-California	1st
	California	2nd
	High-altitude	2nd
1979	Non-California, manual transmission	1st
	Non-California, automatic transmission	2nd
	California, manual transmission	2nd
	California, automatic transmission	4th
	High-altitude, manual transmission	2nd
	High-altitude, automatic transmission	4th
1980	All models except for the California sedan	2nd
	California sedan, manual transmission	3rd
	California sedan, automatic transmission	2nd
1981–1991	See FIG. 3-14. The illustration of your model shows the correct timing mark in line with the timing pointer.	
	Prelude	
1979	Non-California, manual transmission	1st
	Non-California, automatic transmission	2nd
	California, manual transmission	2nd
	California, automatic transmission	4th
	High-altitude, manual transmission	2nd
	High-altitude, automatic transmission	4th
1980	All models	2nd
1981–1991	See FIG. 3-14. The illustration of your model shows the correct timing mark in line with the timing pointer.	

marks are used on your motor. If the correct timing mark is directly in line with the timing pointer, your motor is in time.

When comparing your drawing to the appropriate timing chart, if you find the specified timing mark is in line with the timing pointer, your motor is in time. Stop the motor. Disconnect the timing light. If your Honda is a 1988–1991 model and you "jumpered" the timing terminal, remove the jumper wire from the timing terminal and replace the protective rubber cap. If your Honda is a 1988 or 1989 Prelude with a carburetor, reconnect the distributor vacuum tubes. The Second Time Around and Troubleshooting sections can be found at the end of the chapter. From here, chapter 4 on valve adjustment would be your next logical procedure.

Take a minute to read the "For your information" section that appears at the end of this step. This section explains why the motor is in time when the correct timing mark is aligned with the timing pointer.

What to do if the motor is not in time

If the correct timing mark is on the left or right side of the timing pointer, or not visible at all, proceed to STEP 8-1 to time your motor. Before you proceed to STEP 8-1, however, I want to fill you in on a little secret. If you found the correct timing mark to be on the left side of the timing pointer (advanced timing), someone might have timed the motor like this for a reason. This is particularly true if your motor has more than 100,000 miles on it and has never been rebuilt. After you reset the timing in STEP 8-1, you might find your Honda does not run well. For more information, see No. 5 under the Troubleshooting section at the end of this chapter.

Also, before timing your motor, if your schedule permits, take a minute to read the "For your information" section that follows. This section explains why the motor is in time when the correct timing mark is aligned with the timing pointer. You don't have to read this section to time your motor, but I thought you might find it interesting and helpful to know the "why" of what you'll be doing.

For your information

Why is the motor in time when the specified timing mark (on models with more than one timing mark) is aligned with the timing pointer? As you know from the introduction to this chapter, checking the timing of your Honda's motor actually means checking that the spark plugs are sparking when the pistons are the correct distance from the top of the cylinders. To make this check, you connected a timing light into the circuit that sparks the No. 1 spark plug.

Then, with the motor running, you pointed the flashing timing light at the timing marks.

Because the timing light is connected to the circuit that sparks the No. 1 spark plug, it flashes and illuminates the timing marks only when this spark plug sparks. And because the timing marks are positioned in direct relationship to where the No. 1 piston is in its cylinder, you can tell where this piston is in the cylinder when the spark plug sparks by comparing the position of the illuminated timing marks to the timing pointer.

Honda engineers have positioned the timing pointer so that when the No. 1 piston is at the exact top of its cylinder, the TDC timing mark on the spinning wheel will align with the timing pointer. Thus, when the timing light shows the TDC timing mark to be in alignment with the timing pointer, you know that the spark plug is sparking when the piston is at the exact top of the cylinder. Remember: the timing light only lights up and illuminates the timing mark when the spark plug sparks. (The top dead center timing mark is the one with the T next to it in some of the illustrations in FIG. 3-14.) On most models, the timing mark is painted white.

Some Hondas are timed at 5° BTDC, which means the spark plug sparks when the piston is 5 degrees from reaching the top of the cylinder. Some motors are timed at 5° ATDC, which means the spark plug sparks when the piston is 5 degrees into its travel back down the cylinder. And still others are timed at the 6°, 10°, 12°, or more BTDC.

To keep things simple, Honda engineers have placed a series of timing marks on the spinning wheel, each of which, when aligned with the timing pointer, reflects various positions of the piston in the cylinder. To make things even simpler, Honda engineers have also color-coded each timing mark so all you need to do is check if the appropriately colored timing mark is aligned with the timing pointer.

For example, let's say that your particular model has been designed to run at 5° BTDC (spark plug sparks when the piston is 5 degrees before reaching the top of the cylinder). Although I have not given you degree reading information in the timing chart, here is what is happening: You look at the timing chart and see that your motor is in time when the red timing mark is in alignment with the timing pointer. Because the red timing mark is placed on the spinning wheel so that when it is aligned with the timing pointer the piston is 5° from reaching the top of the cylinder, you simply check to see if this red-colored timing mark is aligned with the timing pointer.

Remember that the timing light only lights up and illuminates the timing marks when the spark plug sparks. Thus, when the timing light shows the red timing mark aligned with the timing pointer, you know that the spark plug is sparking when the piston is the correct number of degrees from reaching the top of the cylinder. On various models, this red-colored timing mark is placed on the spinning wheel to reflect different degree readings. And, as you know from the timing chart, some models are in correct time when either the white, blue, yellow, or black timing mark, each of which reflects a different degree reading, is aligned with the timing pointer.

The wheel in which the timing marks are cut is spinning clockwise when viewed from the passenger's side of the vehicle. If the timing mark that is supposed to align with the timing pointer is to the left of the timing pointer, you know that the spark plug is sparking sometime before the piston is the correct distance from the top of the cylinder. If the timing mark that is supposed to be in alignment with the timing pointer is seen to the right of the timing pointer, you know that the spark plug is sparking after the piston has passed the correct distance from the top of the cylinder. In either case, the timing must be adjusted.

STEP 8
How to adjust the timing on all 1981 – 1983 Civics, all 1976 – 1991 Preludes and Accords, and all 1975 – 1980 CVCC Civics with one timing mark

Adjusting the timing is easy. If you found your motor to be out of time, you'll find adjusting the timing fun and easy. All you have to do is loosen what is known as the distributor holding bolt, and slowly turn the distributor until the timing mark is in line with the timing pointer. The motor should not be running when you loosen the distributor holding bolt because, if the wrench slips, you could severely injure your hand on a moving motor part.

Loosen the distributor holding bolt

Stop the motor. Get out your 10 millimeter open- or box-end wrench. Using FIG. 3-16 as a guide, locate and loosen the distributor holding bolt, turning it counterclockwise. Just loosen this bolt a turn or so to allow the distributor to rotate, but don't turn the distributor until you get to the part where you do it with the timing light illuminating the timing marks.

The distributor on your Honda might be in a different location than the one shown in FIG. 3-16 and might even be standing upright.

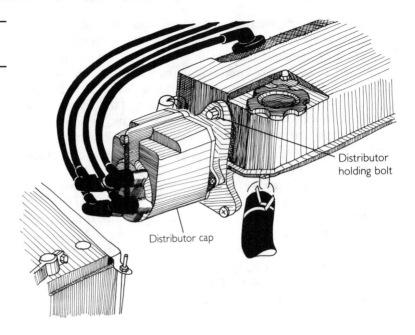

Distributor
holding bolt

Distributor cap

The distributor holding bolt will, however, be in the same place in relation to the distributor as illustrated. Some models have a black rubber cap covering this bolt. Remove the cap to access the bolt.

Which way to turn the distributor

See FIG. 3-17 to learn if your Honda has a side-mounted or end-mounted distributor. On models with a side-mounted distributor, turn the distributor clockwise to move the timing mark to the left (your left). This is called advancing the timing. On all models with an end-mounted distributor, turn the distributor counterclockwise to move the timing mark to the left and advance the timing.

The spark plugs spark sooner when the timing is advanced. By sooner, I mean when the pistons are further from reaching the top of the cylinders. By turning the distributor counterclockwise on models with a side-mounted distributor, the timing mark can be made to move to the right (your right). This is called retarding the timing. On models with an end-mounted distributor, turn the distributor clockwise to move the timing mark to the right and retard the timing.

The spark plugs spark later when the timing is retarded. By later, I mean when the pistons are closer to reaching the top of the cylinder.

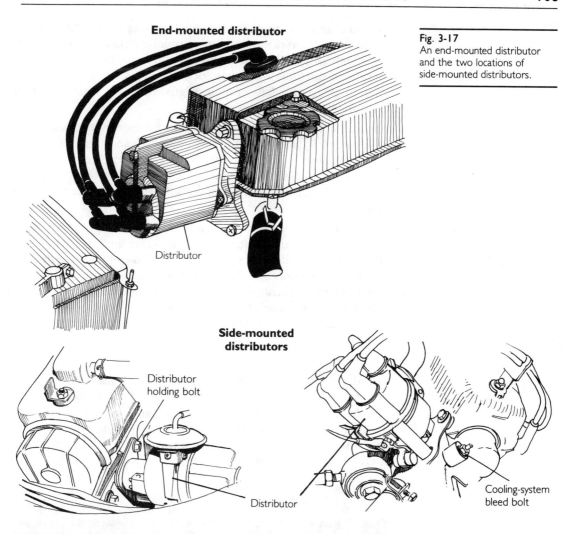

End-mounted distributor

Distributor

Side-mounted distributors

Distributor holding bolt

Distributor

Cooling-system bleed bolt

Why is a side-mounted distributor turned in the opposite direction of an end-mounted distributor to make the same adjustment? Because the distributor shaft turns counterclockwise in a side-mounted distributor and clockwise in an end- mounted distributor.

Examples to help you time your motor

The following examples will help you decide which way to turn the distributor to put your motor into time:

○ If you found your motor to be timed with the timing mark on the right (your right) side of the timing pointer (retarded timing), turn a side-mounted distributor very slowly clockwise or an end-mounted distributor counterclockwise. This will move the timing mark to the left until it aligns with the timing pointer (advancing the timing).

○ If you found your motor to be timed with the timing mark on the left (your left) side of the timing pointer (advanced timing), turn a side-mounted distributor very slowly counterclockwise or an end-mounted distributor clockwise. This will move the timing mark to the right until it aligns with the timing pointer (retarding the timing).

○ If you have so far been unable to see any timing mark, very slowly turn the distributor in one direction and check to see if the timing mark becomes visible. If it doesn't, try turning the distributor in the opposite direction. You will definitely see the timing mark when turning the distributor in one of these directions. Once the timing mark becomes visible, turn the distributor until the timing mark aligns with the timing pointer. See FIG. 3-14.

Start the motor

Flash the timing light on the timing mark, and slowly turn the distributor until the timing mark lines up with the timing pointer. Hondamatics must be in second gear. Put the parking brake on securely! Slowly turn the distributor until the timing mark aligns with the timing pointer. To turn the distributor, grasp the plastic cap, but don't touch the wires, because you might get an electrical shock.

Depending on which direction you are turning the distributor, the motor will either run faster or slower. If the motor should stop running while you're turning the distributor, turn the distributor a little in the opposite direction and then restart the motor.

Danger! If you have a medical condition that makes it particularly dangerous for you to receive an electrical shock, now is the time to be extra careful. The spark plug wires running from the distributor cap, if cracked, can deliver a strong electrical shock. Wear gloves or use a thick rag to grab and turn the distributor. Avoid touching the spark plug wires. If you don't touch the car with your body or free hand while turning the distributor, you won't make a good conductor for electricity and this will reduce any chance of electrical shock.

When the motor is in proper time—when the timing mark is aligned with the timing pointer—carefully retighten (turn clockwise) the distributor holding bolt, keeping hands clear of moving parts. Recheck the timing and if it is still correct, turn off the motor.

Disconnect the timing light and, if necessary, reconnect the spark plug wire. If your Honda is a 1988–1991 model and you "jumpered" the timing terminal, remove the jumper wire and replace the protective rubber cap. If your Honda is a 1988 or 1989 Prelude with a carburetor, reconnect the distributor vacuum tubes. That's it, you're done!

If you just put your motor into "time," you should experience a smoother, more powerful, more fuel-efficient Honda. If you also completed chapters 1 and 2, the difference in your Honda will be so dramatic you'll think you just got yourself a new car! From here, chapter 4, the valve adjusting chapter, would be your next logical procedure.

The Second time around and Troubleshooting sections can be found at the end of the chapter. For an explanation of how turning the distributor puts the motor into time, see "For your information" in STEP 7.

STEP 8-1: How to adjust the timing on all 1981 – 1983 Civics, all 1976 – 1991 Preludes and Accords, and all 1975 – 1980 CVCC Civics with two timing marks

Adjusting the timing is easy. If you found your motor to be out of time, you'll find adjusting the timing fun and easy. All you have to do is loosen what is known as the distributor holding bolt, and slowly turn the distributor until the correct timing mark is in line with the timing pointer. The motor should not be running when you loosen the distributor holding bolt because, if the wrench slips, you could severely injure your hand on a moving motor part.

Loosen the distributor holding bolt

Stop the motor. Get out your 10 millimeter open- or box-end wrench. Using FIG. 3-16 as a guide, locate and loosen the distributor holding bolt; turn it counterclockwise. Just loosen this bolt a turn or so to allow the distributor to rotate—but don't turn the distributor until you get to the part where you do it with the timing light illuminating the timing marks.

Which way to turn the distributor

See FIG. 3-17 to learn if your Honda has a side-mounted or end-mounted distributor. On models with a side-mounted distributor, turn the distributor clockwise to move the timing mark to the left (your left). This is called advancing the timing. On models with an end-mounted distributor, turn the distributor counterclockwise to move the timing marks to the left and advance the timing.

The spark plugs spark sooner when the timing is advanced. Sooner, meaning when the pistons are further from reaching the top of the cylinders.

By turning the distributor counterclockwise on models with a side-mounted distributor, the timing marks can be made to move to the right (your right). This is called retarding the timing. On models with an end-mounted distributor, turn the distributor clockwise to move the timing marks to the right and retard the timing.

The spark plugs spark later when the timing is retarded. By later, I mean when the pistons are closer to reaching the top of the cylinder.

Examples to help you time your motor

The following examples will help you decide which way to turn the distributor to put your motor into time:

○ If you could see the correct timing mark (colored or not) and it was on the right (your right) side of the timing pointer (retarded timing), turn a side-mounted distributor very slowly clockwise or an end-mounted distributor counterclockwise. This will move the timing mark to the left until it aligns with the timing pointer (advancing the timing).

○ If you could see the correct timing mark (colored or not) and it was on the left (your left) side of the timing pointer (advanced timing), turn a side-mounted distributor very slowly counter-clockwise or an end-mounted distributor clockwise. This will move the timing mark to the right until it aligns with the timing pointer (retarding the timing).

○ If you could not see the correct timing mark, but the ones you did see are colored, turn the distributor very slowly clockwise and look for the correctly colored timing mark. See TABLE 3-1. If this timing mark does not appear while turning the distributor clockwise, turn it counterclockwise and look again for the correct colored timing mark. When this timing mark does appear, align it with the timing pointer by turning the distributor as needed.

○ If you could not see all the timing marks and there is no color on those you did see, locate the "first timing mark." This is the timing mark that is the furthest to the right (your right) as seen from the passenger's side of the motor. To locate this first timing mark, simply turn the distributor clockwise and then counterclockwise, and observe the timing marks as you do so. Using FIG. 3-14 as a guide, and some logic, you should have no problem figuring out which timing mark is the first (furthest to the right) timing mark. Once you have figured out which timing mark is the first timing mark, use this timing mark as a reference point. Turn the distributor to the correct timing mark, as designated in TABLE 3-2, in line with the timing pointer.

○ If you have not seen any timing marks as of yet, turn the distributor very slowly clockwise and look for the timing marks. If they do not appear, turn the distributor counterclockwise and look again for the timing marks. They will definitely become visible when turning the distributor in one of these directions. When the timing marks do become visible, if you find them to be colored, refer to TABLE 3-1 and then, by turning the distributor, align the timing mark of the designated color—as shown in the table—with the timing pointer. If, when you find the timing marks, you find that their color is worn off, refer back to Example 4.

Start the motor

Flash the timing light on the timing marks, and slowly turn the distributor until the correct timing mark lines up with the timing pointer.

Hondamatics must be in second gear. Put the parking brake on securely! Slowly turn the distributor until the motor is in proper time. To turn the distributor, grasp the plastic cap, but don't touch the wires. You could receive an electrical shock.

Danger! If you have a medical condition that makes it particularly dangerous for you to receive an electrical shock, now is the time to be extra careful. The spark plug wires running from the distributor cap, if cracked, can deliver a strong electrical shock. Wear gloves or use a thick rag to grab and turn the distributor. Avoid touching the spark plug wires. If you don't touch the car with your body or free hand while turning the distributor, you won't make a good conductor for electricity, and this will reduce any chance of electrical shock.

When the motor is in proper time—when the specified timing mark is in line with the timing pointer—carefully retighten (turn clockwise) the distributor holding bolt, keeping hands clear of moving parts. Recheck the timing. If it hasn't changed, turn off the motor. Disconnect the timing light and, if necessary, reconnect the spark plug wire. If your Honda is a 1988–1991 model and you "jumpered" the timing terminal, remove the jumper wire and replace the protective rubber cap. If your Honda is a 1988 or 1989 Prelude with a carburetor, reconnect the distributor vacuum tubes. That's it, you're done!

If you just put your motor into "time," you're about to experience a smoother, more powerful, more fuel-efficient Honda. If you also completed chapters 1 and 2, the difference in your Honda will be so dramatic, you'll think you just got yourself a new car! From here, chapter 4, the valve adjusting chapter would be your next logical procedure.

The Second Time Around and Troubleshooting sections follow. For an explanation of how turning the distributor puts the motor into time, see the next section, "For your information."

Troubleshooting

If the motor doesn't run as well as it did before you began this chapter, you might have goofed. Ask yourself the following questions:

○ Is it possible my timing light was not connected with the No. 1 terminal in the distributor? This would cause you to put the motor greatly out of time. See STEP 1.

○ Did I remove the spark plug wire from the No. 1 terminal in the distributor? Is this wire plugged back in securely? Did I also remove this spark plug wire from the spark plug? Is it plugged back onto the spark plug?

○ Did I time my motor with the correct timing mark?

○ Did I "jumper" the timing terminal and forget to remove the jumper wire? (All 1988–1991 Civics and fuel-injected Preludes and 1990–1991 Accords.)

○ If your car does not run as well as it did before you began this chapter and you are sure it is timed correctly, this indicates your motor is getting a little "tired."

For older cars with high miles

On older cars, mechanics will sometimes advance the timing a little beyond what the tune-up specifications call for. This, so to speak, makes the old dog do new tricks. Advancing the timing a little beyond the tune-up specifications gives the car more acceleration power.

As you know, to advance the timing, you turn a side-mounted

distributor clockwise and an end-mounted distributor counterclockwise. On models where you stand on the driver's side of the car to see the timing marks, the timing marks move to the right side of the timing pointer as the timing is advanced. On models where you stand on the passenger's side of the car to see the timing marks, the timing mark(s) move to the left side of the timing pointer as the timing is advanced.

If you just set the timing to specifications and the motor feels "tired," advancing the timing mark that belongs in line with the timing pointer 1 to 2 inches from the timing pointer should do it. Do not turn the distributor without the timing light connected and flashing on the timing mark(s).

I should add that this procedure is not legal in states that subscribe to the BAR 90 Smog Program. A car with its timing not set correctly will automatically fail the smog test.

If you advance the timing too far, you will hear pinging, like the sound of marbles being dropped onto a tin roof when you step on the gas to accelerate. You will have to retard the timing a little to get rid of this pinging (turn the distributor in the opposite direction).

Caution! An advance in the timing beyond the tune-up specifications might eventually cause mechanical problems, such as burned valves. So, if you choose to advance the timing beyond the tune-up specifications, you're responsible for whatever happens.

I have worked on older Hondas where the timing had been advanced beyond the tune-up specifications to make them run stronger. Some cars seem to run forever like this while others develop problems. To squeeze a little more "juice" out of a motor, some "hot rodders" advance the timing as a matter of practice. Advancing the timing always increases the idle speed of the motor. Refer to chapter 5, Carburetor and Fuel Injection Adjustment, and turn down the idle speed.

The second time around

This is a condensed version of this chapter to speed you through your next tune-up. If your Honda is a 1975–1978 Accord or Prelude or a 1975–1979 Civic, I suggest you complete chapter 2 before you begin this chapter. All other years and models see chapter 5, and set the idle speed before beginning this chapter. See the beginning of this chapter for more information on both of these requirements.

Tools

☐ timing light

☐ 10 millimeter open-end or box-end wrench

☐ pencil and paper

☐ 1988 and 1989 Preludes with a carburetor (not fuel injected) require a timing light with an advance scale.

Procedures

1. Connect your timing light to the motor.

2. Test your timing light. Is it working?

Numbers 3−5 explain how to check and adjust the timing on all 1984−1991 Civics and all 1975−1979 non-CVCC Civics. For all other years and models, see 6−8.

3. Illuminate the timing marks with the timing light. If you can't see the timing marks, be sure your light is connected to the correct terminal in the distributor cap or with the correct spark plug wire, depending on how you are connected to the circuit. Chalk the timing marks if necessary.

4. Disconnect and plug any vacuum tubes from the distributor on 1975−1977 models. On all 1988−1991 Civics, jumper the timing terminal.

Direct the timing light at the timing pointer and timing mark(s) and check the motor timing. If the correct timing mark is in line with the pointer as shown in FIGS. 3-9A or 3-10A, your motor is in time. Stop the motor and disconnect the timing light. If necessary, reconnect the spark plug wire. Owners of 1975−1977 models, reconnect the vacuum tubes to the distributor. Owners of 1988−1991 models, remove the jumper wire from the timing terminal and replace the protective rubber cap.

5. If the timing must be adjusted, stop the motor and loosen the distributor holding bolt. With the motor running, illuminate the timing marks with the timing light and turn the distributor until the correct timing mark is in line with the timing pointer. Retighten the distributor holding bolt, keeping hands clear of moving parts. Recheck the timing. If it has not changed, stop the motor, disconnect the timing light and if necessary, reconnect the spark plug wire. Owners of 1975−1977 models, reconnect the vacuum tubes to the distributor. Owners of 1988−1991 models, remove the jumper wire from the timing terminal and replace the protective rubber cap.

Numbers 6−8 explain how to check and adjust the timing on all 1981−1983 Civics, all 1976−1991 Preludes and Accords, and all 1975−1980 CVCC Civics.

6. Jumper the timing terminal on all 1988–1991 fuel-injected Preludes and 1990–1991 Accords. On 1988 and 1989 Preludes with a carburetor (not fuel-injected models), disconnect and plug the distributor vacuum tubes.

   Illuminate the timing mark(s) with the timing light. If you can't see the timing marks, be sure you are connected with the correct terminal in the distributor cap or with the correct spark plug wire, depending on how you are connected to the circuit.

7. Check the timing adjustment. If it is correct as shown in TABLE 3-1 or 3-2, stop the motor and disconnect the timing light. If necessary, reconnect the spark plug wire. If your Honda is a 1988–1991 model and you jumpered the timing terminal, remove the jumper wire and replace the protective rubber cap. On a 1988 or 1989 Prelude with a carburetor (not fuel-injected models), reconnect the distributor vacuum hoses.

8. If the timing must be adjusted, stop the motor and loosen the distributor holding bolt. With the motor running, turn the distributor until the correct timing mark is in line with the timing pointer and retighten the distributor holding bolt, keeping hands clear of moving parts. Recheck the timing and, if it hasn't changed, stop the motor, disconnect the timing light and, if necessary, reconnect the spark plug wire. If your Honda is a 1988–1991 model and you jumpered the timing terminal, remove the jumper wire from the timing terminal and replace the protective rubber cap. On a 1988 or 1989 Prelude with a carburetor (not fuel-injected models), reconnect the distributor vacuum hoses.

CHAPTER 4

Valve adjustment

Approximate Completion
Time: 2 hours

*N*ow's the time to forget any intimidating gossip you might have heard about valve adjusting. Why? Because most of what you've heard is probably nothing more than "jabber" from owners of American cars.

Until recently, all American manufacturers built motors with hydraulic valves that never needed adjusting. By contrast, most all German, British, Italian, French, Swedish, and Japanese motors use adjustable (non-hydraulic) valves known as solid lifters.

"Yup," lots of Americans have tinkered with Chevrolets, eaten hot dogs, and gone to ball games, but if they haven't worked on an import car, they have no experience with adjustable valves. And so ugly rumors get started. How did sushi get so popular?

Take a look at FIG. 4-19, which shows you how to check the adjustment of the valves, and FIG. 4-20, which shows you how to adjust the valves. Checking and adjusting the valves is as simple as it looks.

So, now you're wondering why it takes two hours to adjust the valves? Well, it's not the difficulty of the job, but the time-consuming preparation leading to the adjusting procedure. The time estimate at the beginning of this chapter of two hours allows for this being your first valve adjusting experience.

From start to finish a shop mechanic completes the entire valve adjusting job in about 30 minutes. The Honda dealers I called quoted me a price of "about" $79 to adjust the valves on a 1991 Honda. "About" has always meant it's going to cost more money by the time they're done with me.

Something else you'll like about adjusting your Honda's valves is that you're not without your car for the five or six hours the Honda dealer needs it. The valves can only be adjusted when the motor is cold—so your Honda spends the best part of the day just sitting while you ride the bus.

The manufacturer recommends a valve adjustment every 15,000 miles. This interval is far beyond the margin of safety. I strongly recommend a valve adjustment every 6,000–7,000 miles, maximum.

Before you start

Intake valves and exhaust valves are the two types of valves covered in this chapter. Some models have auxiliary intake valves and we'll get to those too. Before you actually begin to adjust valves, I'd like to tell you more about the different types of valves.

Reading this section is completely optional and you won't need to know the things I tell you here to adjust the valves. However, it will be easier for you to adjust the valves if you first learn about the "how" and "why" of the things you'll be doing in this chapter.

What valves do

Intake valves allow the fuel mixture from the carburetor or fuel-injection system to enter the motor. Exhaust valves allow what's left from the combustion of the fuel to exit the motor. Not too difficult. Here's how it all happens:

As the piston moves down the cylinder on the intake stroke seen in FIG. 4-1, the intake valve opens and allows fuel to enter the cylinder. When the piston moves back up the cylinder on the compression stroke, the intake valve closes and seals tightly with the top of the cylinder.

As the piston nears the top of the cylinder, the fuel mixture becomes greatly compressed. At this point, the spark plug sparks and ignites the compressed fuel mixture. The closed valves contain the pressure in the cylinders and thus the full force of the explosion thrusts the piston back down the cylinder on what is known as the power stroke. Whew!!

The force of the piston moving down the cylinder turns the crankshaft, which turns the transmission, which turns the drive shaft, which turns the differential, which in turn, turns the wheels and makes that hoppity Honda go down the road.

Following the explosion of the fuel and the downward thrust of the piston on the power stroke, the piston makes its way back up the cylinder. On this stroke of the piston, known as the exhaust stroke, the exhaust valve opens and allows the by-products and unburned particles from the exploded fuel to leave the cylinder. These

Intake stroke   **Exhaust stroke**

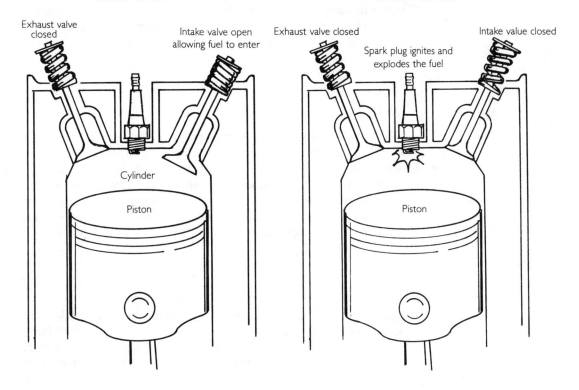

Fig. 4-1
How the valves work.

unburned particles are known as exhaust, and they exit the car through the exhaust pipe.

The next stroke of the piston is the intake stroke and the four-stroke cycle—intake, compression, power and exhaust—begins again. During the four-stroke cycle, the valves and their adjusters are subjected to extreme temperatures. The expansion of the metal from the tremendous heat causes the valves to need periodic adjustment.

A valve can get out of adjustment and become either too tight or too loose. Should the adjustment of a particular valve become too tight, the valve does not completely close during the explosion of the fuel. This exposes the edge of the valve to the explosion of the fuel, the result being a burned valve. A burned valve causes a noticeable loss in motor power because pressure that normally pushes a piston down the cylinder, now escapes past the burned valve.

When the adjustment of a particular valve becomes too loose, the valve opens too late. A late-opening intake valve causes a loss in motor power because it does not leave enough time for the full dose of fuel to enter the cylinder. A late opening exhaust valve affects the motor in a slightly different way, causing the motor to get backed-up with exhaust and slow down. A loose adjustment also permits the valve adjuster to slap against the top of the valve spring, causing increased wear of these parts.

CVCC motors

CVCC motors have an extra valve per cylinder. The initials CVCC stand for Compound Vortex Controlled Combustion. I'll explain this as we go along. The difference between a CVCC motor and a traditional motor is that a CVCC motor not only has intake and exhaust valves, but also auxiliary intake valves. Auxiliary intake valves are smaller in size than normal intake valves, and each one has its own separate chamber, known as a pre-combustion chamber.

The CVCC principle

As a piston moves down its cylinder on the intake stroke, a small quantity of fuel mixture flows past the open auxiliary intake valve and into the pre-combustion chamber. This small quantity of fuel is a gas-heavy, "rich" mixture that is very easy to ignite. While the pre-combustion chamber is taking on fuel, a larger volume of fuel enters the main combustion chamber. This mixture is low in gas and high in air and too "lean" to be ignited by a spark plug alone.

Following the intake stroke, the intake valve and auxiliary intake valve both close and the piston begins its trip back up the cylinder on the compression stroke. The spark plug is positioned in the pre-combustion chamber of the auxiliary intake valve, and it ignites the small, "rich" mixture in the pre-combustion chamber. This explosion flashes through a crossover passage, igniting the larger, leaner mixture being compressed in the main combustion chamber.

The two-stage combustion process allows the CVCC motor to run on a leaner, low-in-gas mixture. Unlike models that require a belt-driven air-injection system to control pollutants, the CVCC motor controls pollutants internally. And, because of the lean fuel mixture used in the main combustion chamber, the CVCC motor gets excellent gas mileage.

All CVCC models do not have the CVCC designation on the body of the car. Many newer Hondas do not have the CVCC designation on the body of the car. But they can have CVCC motors. When you remove the valve cover to adjust the valves, you'll learn if your Honda has a CVCC motor.

12-valve and 16-valve motors

Motors with 12 and 16 valves produce more power than traditional 2-valve-per-cylinder motors. This is because a larger volume of fuel mixture can more quickly enter the cylinders through the additional intake valves. And, more exhaust can quickly exit the motor through two exhaust valves, leaving room for a big fill of fuel.

The advantage of doubling up on valves rather than using bigger valves is this: Opening a big intake valve and a big exhaust valve for a long duration is far less efficient and less manageable than opening two smaller valves for a shorter time period. Plus, two valves can be made to exceed the flow capability of a single valve.

The one difference between adjusting the valves on a 12- or 16-valve motor as compared to a traditional 8-valve motor is that it takes a little more time because there are more valves. Other than that, there's no difference.

What's ahead in this chapter

There are nine steps to adjusting your valves:

STEP 1 How to remove the valve cover.

STEP 2 What you must do and know before you can adjust the valves.

STEP 3 How to close, check, and adjust valve group No. 1.

STEP 4 How to check the valve adjustment.

STEP 5 How to adjust the valves.

STEP 6 How to close, check, and adjust valve group No. 3.

STEP 7 How to close, check, and adjust valve group No. 4.

STEP 8 How to close, check, and adjust valve group No. 2.

STEP 9 How to reassemble the motor.

Note: The valve group closing order of 1, 3, 4, 2 is the normal closing order of the valves while the motor is running. This is why I have followed this order for closing, checking, and adjusting the valves.

Tools

Figure 4-2 illustrates the tools used in this chapter. For a more detailed description of these tools, see chapter 7. You will need:

☐ ratchet wrench with 3/8-inch drive

☐ extension bar with 3-inch drive. A 2-inch or longer extension bar will also work.

Fig. 4-2
Tools used in this chapter.

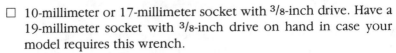

Ratchet wrench with ³/₈" drive

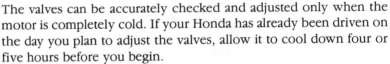

Extension bar with 3" drive

A 10-mm and
17-mm socket
with ³/₈" drive

Medium-size screwdriver

Colored marker

A 10-mm or 12-mm
open-end or box-end
wrench

Feeler gauge

☐ 10-millimeter or 17-millimeter socket with ³/₈-inch drive. Have a 19-millimeter socket with ³/₈-inch drive on hand in case your model requires this wrench.

☐ medium-sized screwdriver

☐ colored marker

☐ 10-millimeter or 12-millimeter open-end or box-end wrench. The required wrench size varies among models.

☐ feeler gauge

STEP 1
How to remove the valve cover

The valves can be accurately checked and adjusted only when the motor is completely cold. If your Honda has already been driven on the day you plan to adjust the valves, allow it to cool down four or five hours before you begin.

See FIGS. 4-3, 4-4, 4-5, and 4-6, and decide which illustration looks the most like your motor. Remove the valve cover from your motor using the upcoming instructions that cover the illustration of your motor.

Remove the valve cover shown in FIG. 4-3

Removing the valve cover is easier than it looks. Removing the valve cover is a simple procedure. Figure 4-3 illustrates this procedure.

○ From the passenger's side of the motor, pull the spark plug wire guide clip free from its support.

○ From the driver's side of the motor, pull cable A free from its rubber holder. On some models, cable A is also secured to the other side of the valve cover by another rubber holder. Free the cable from this holder.

○ With your fingers or pliers, squeeze the spring clip that is holding hose A to the valve cover and pull hose A free from the valve cover.

○ Assemble the ratchet wrench, extension bar, and 10-millimeter socket wrench. Adjust the ratchet wrench to turn counterclockwise. If you need help, see chapter 1, which explains how to set the ratchet wrench to remove the spark plugs. The same wrench setting is used to remove the valve cover.

○ With the ratchet wrench assembly, turn counterclockwise and remove the four 10-millimeter bolts that secure the air filter-box

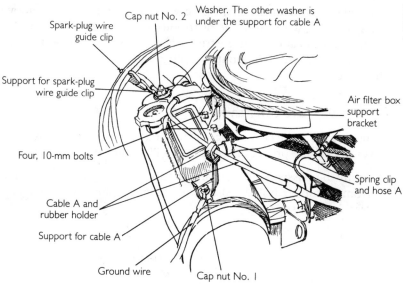

Spark-plug wire guide clip

Cap nut No. 2

Washer. The other washer is under the support for cable A

Support for spark-plug wire guide clip

Air filter box support bracket

Four, 10-mm bolts

Spring clip and hose A

Cable A and rubber holder

Support for cable A

Ground wire

Cap nut No. 1

Fig. 4-3
Removing the valve cover.

support bracket to both the air filter box and the valve cover. Some models have only two bolts. Remove the air filter-box support bracket.

○ From the driver's side of the valve cover, remove the No. 1 cap nut with the ratchet wrench. Remove the ground wire and the support for cable A.

○ From the passenger's side of the valve cover, remove the No. 2 cap nut. Remove the support for the spark plug wire guide clip.

○ With your fingers, remove the two washers from the top of the valve cover. If they are stuck, slip the blade of a screwdriver under each washer and work it free. Do not pry too hard or you could crack the valve cover. Although only one washer is illustrated, there is another one on the opposite side of the valve cover. The rubber beneath the washers is part of the washers.

○ Check for any bracket, cable, or holder I haven't mentioned that needs to be disconnected to remove the valve cover. Be sure to label these parts so you can put them back correctly.

○ With all obstructions out of the way, remove the valve cover using your hands. If it's stuck, a smack on its side with your hand will free it. Put the valve cover in a safe place where it won't get broken and skip to STEP 2.

If the spark plug wires are interfering with removing the valve cover, remove the distributor cap from the distributor and move the distributor cap with the spark plug wires attached. Do not remove the spark plug wires from the distributor cap. See chapter 2 for distributor cap locations and instructions on how to remove the distributor cap. Put the distributor cap back into place after removing the valve cover.

Remove the valve cover shown in FIG. 4-4

Removing the valve cover is easier than it looks. Removing this valve cover is a simple procedure. Figure 4-4 illustrates this procedure:

○ From the passenger's side of the valve cover, pull cable A free from its rubber holder. Also, pull the spark plug wire guide clip free from its support.

Fig. 4-4
Removing the valve cover.

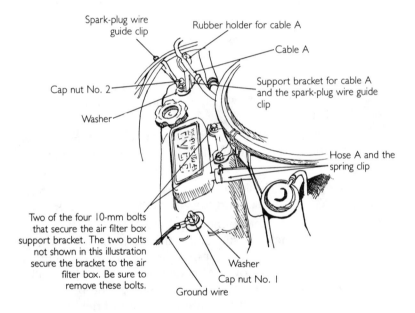

Spark-plug wire guide clip
Rubber holder for cable A
Cable A
Cap nut No. 2
Support bracket for cable A and the spark-plug wire guide clip
Washer
Hose A and the spring clip
Two of the four 10-mm bolts that secure the air filter box support bracket. The two bolts not shown in this illustration secure the bracket to the air filter box. Be sure to remove these bolts.
Washer
Cap nut No. 1
Ground wire

The spark plug wires might interfere with removing the valve cover. In this case, remove the distributor cap from the distributor and move the distributor cap with the spark plug wires intact. Do not remove the spark plug wires from the distributor cap. See chapter 2 for distributor cap locations and instructions on how to remove the distributor cap. Put the distributor cap back into place after removing the valve cover.

○ On the driver's side of the valve cover, use your fingers to squeeze together the spring clip that secures hose A to the valve cover while pulling hose A free from the valve cover.

○ Assemble the ratchet wrench, extension bar, and 10-millimeter socket wrench. Set the ratchet wrench to turn in a counterclockwise direction. For help, see chapter 1, which explains how to set the ratchet wrench to remove the spark plugs. The same wrench setting is needed to remove the valve cover.

○ Turn the ratchet wrench assembly counterclockwise and remove the four 10-millimeter bolts that secure the air filter box support bracket to both the air filter box and valve cover. Some models use only two bolts. Remove the air filter box support bracket.

○ From the driver's side of the valve cover, remove the No. 1 cap nut using the ratchet wrench. Remove the ground wire.

○ From the passenger's side of the valve cover, remove the No. 2 cap nut. Remove the support bracket for cable A and the spark-plug wire guide clip.

○ With your fingers, remove the two washers from the top of the valve cover. If they are stuck, slip the blade of a screwdriver under each washer and work it free. Do not pry too hard or you will crack the valve cover. *Note*: The rubber beneath the washers is part of the washers.

○ Check for any bracket, cable, or holder I haven't mentioned that needs to be disconnected to remove the valve cover. Be sure to label these parts so you can put them back correctly.

○ Now that all obstructions have been removed, remove the valve cover with your hands. If it is stuck, a smack on its side with your hand will free it.

Put the valve cover in a safe place where it won't get broken and skip to STEP 2. If the spark plug wires are interfering with the removal of the valve cover, see the following Pro Tip.

Remove the valve cover shown in FIG. 4-5

Removing the valve cover is easier than it looks. This style valve cover is the easiest to remove. Figure 4-5 illustrates this procedure:

○ With your fingers or pliers, squeeze the spring clip that secures hose A to the valve cover and pull hose A free from the valve cover.

○ Assemble the ratchet wrench, extension bar, and 10-millimeter socket wrench. Set the ratchet wrench to turn counterclockwise.

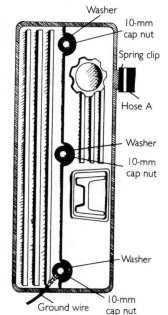

Fig. 4-5
Removing the valve cover.

Washer
10-mm cap nut
Spring clip
Hose A
Washer
10-mm cap nut
Washer
10-mm cap nut
Ground wire

Note: Some models do not secure the valve cover with cap nuts positioned down the center. On these models, nuts are positioned around the valve cover.

For help, see chapter 1, which explains how to set the ratchet wrench to remove the spark plugs. The same wrench setting is needed to remove the valve cover.

○ With the ratchet wrench assembly, turn counterclockwise and remove the three 10-millimeter cap nuts that secure the valve cover. Slip the ground wire free.

○ With your fingers, remove the three washers from the top of the valve cover. If they are stuck, slip the blade of a screwdriver under each washer and work it free. Do not pry too hard or you could crack the valve cover. *Note*: The rubber beneath the washers is part of the washers.

○ Check for a bracket, cable, or holder I haven't mentioned that needs to be disconnected to remove the valve cover from the motor. Be sure to label these parts so you can put them back correctly.

○ Once all obstructions have been removed, remove the valve cover with your hands. If it is stuck, a smack on its side with your hand will free it. Put the valve cover in a safe place where it won't get broken. Skip to STEP 2.

Remove the valve cover shown in FIG. 4-6

Removing the valve cover is easier than it looks. Removing this valve cover is a simple procedure. Figure 4-6 illustrates this procedure:

○ Stand on the driver's side of the motor. The first order of business is to number each of the spark plug wires and then disconnect them from the spark plugs.

Stop! Each spark plug wire is attached to a specific spark plug. The motor will not run unless the spark plug wires are reconnected in the correct order. Label the spark plug wires as follows: From where you are standing on the driver's side of the motor, the spark plug wire closest to you is the No. 1 spark plug wire. As illustrated in FIG. 4-7, spark plug wires 2, 3, and 4 follow in order. Attaching a piece of numbered masking tape to each wire makes a good labeling system. Be sure the tape is on securely. Should you find the spark plug wires are already factory numbered, verify that the numbers correspond to the order of the spark plug wires.

Caution! Do not pull on spark plug wires. This will damage them. Pull only where illustrated in FIG. 4-7. Leave the other end of the spark plug wires connected to the distributor cap.

○ With your fingers or pliers, squeeze together the spring clip that secures hose A to the valve cover and pull hose A free from the valve cover.

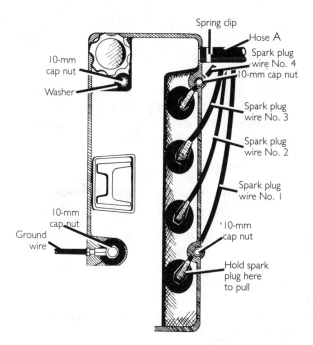

Fig. 4-6
Removing the valve cover.

○ Assemble the ratchet wrench, extension bar, and 10-millimeter socket wrench. Set the ratchet wrench to turn counterclockwise. For help, see chapter 1, which explains how to set the ratchet wrench to remove the spark plugs. The same wrench setting is needed to remove the valve cover.

○ Turn the ratchet wrench counterclockwise and remove the four, 10-millimeter cap nuts that secure the valve cover. Some motors use only two cap nuts. Slip the ground wire free. On 1988–1991 fuel-injected Preludes, 10-millimeter nuts are also positioned around the perimeters of the valve cover. Remove these nuts.

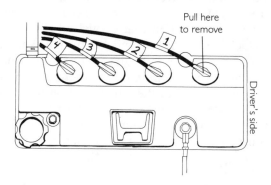

Fig. 4-7
Number the spark plug wires before disconnecting them.

○ Check for any bracket, cable, or holder I haven't mentioned that needs to be disconnected in order to remove the valve cover from the motor. Be sure to label these parts so you can put them back correctly.

○ Now that all obstructions have been removed, remove the valve cover with your hands. If it is stuck, a smack on its side with your hand will free it. Put the valve cover in a safe place where it won't get broken, then go to STEP 2.

STEP 2
What you must do and know
before you can adjust the valves

This is an important step; don't skip it! Every Honda motor has four groups of valves. Some motors have two valves per group, others have three valves per group, and still others have four valves per group. For now, the important thing to know is that your Honda motor has four groups of valves.

The valves can only be checked and adjusted when they are closed. And because of the way a motor operates, only one group of valves is closed at any one time. This means, to adjust all four groups of valves in the motor, each group is closed, checked, and adjusted individually.

In this step, you'll learn about three things you must know and do before you can adjust the valves. First, you'll learn how to turn the motor with a wrench so you can close each group of valves, one group at a time. Next, you'll learn how to identify which group of valves you are closing as you turn the motor. And finally, I'll show you how to know when all the valves of a particular group have completely closed so you can safely check and adjust them.

Locate the 17-millimeter nut used to turn the motor

Start by sitting behind the steering wheel and turning it as far as it will turn to the left. Don't start the motor—oil will shoot everywhere! Turn the ignition key just far enough to allow the steering wheel column lock to release. Remember to turn the key back to the "lock" position when you're through turning the steering wheel.

Leave the steering wheel turned sharp to the left and hop back out of your Honda. Look into the wheel well on the driver's side front wheel and locate the access hole. It's about 3 inches in diameter. Look through the access hole and you'll see the 17-millimeter nut used to turn the motor by hand. I should tell you that some

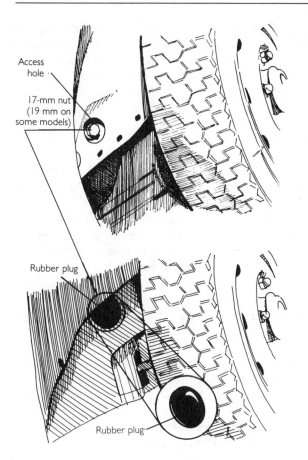

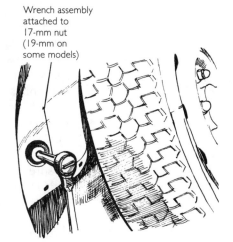

Fig. 4-8
Attach the wrench to turn the motor.

models might use a 19-millimeter nut. Figure 4-8 shows the location of the access hole. As illustrated, the access hole might be covered with a rubber plug. If it is, you need to remove it.

Slip the 17-millimeter wrench over the 17-millimeter nut

Remove the 10-millimeter socket from the extension bar and put the 17-millimeter socket in its place. Slip your wrench assembly over the 17-millimeter nut and just leave it hang there for now.

Stop! Danger! Caution! Only turn the motor counterclockwise. Turning the motor clockwise could totally throw your motor's timing system out of sync.

Now, for the second of the three things you must do and know before you can adjust the valves. You need a way to identify which of the four valve groups is closing as you turn the motor. Mechanics use a simple system to know which group of valves is closing. Let me explain. This is going to take a few minutes, so bear with me. I figure if I first tell you the ''why'' of what you will be doing, the actual job will go quicker and easier when you do it. Plus, it's always nice to know what you're doing. Okay, I'll make it quick!

When you turn the motor to close a group of valves, you'll need a way to know which group of valves inside the motor is, in fact, closing. Remember, you can't see the valves because they are inside the motor as shown in FIG. 4-1. To know which of the four groups of valves is closing as you turn the motor, you will rely on the position of the distributor rotor. For a view of the rotor, skip ahead to FIG. 4-16—but don't remove the distributor cap yet.

While the motor is running, the rotor spins like a top, distributing a spark to each of the four spark plug wire terminals in the distributor cap. As the rotor approaches a spark plug wire terminal, a spark leaps from the rotor to the terminal, travels down the attached spark plug wire, hits the spark plug, and bang!—the fuel in the cylinder ignites.

The key to this example is that a valve group is always closed when the spark plug is igniting the fuel in its cylinder. So, if you manually turn the motor until the rotor points towards the distributor cap terminal connected with the No. 1 spark plug wire, you can be sure the valves in the cylinder of the No. 1 spark plug are closing. This is valve group No. 1. I'll show you how to identify the valve groups when the time comes.

Likewise, if you turn the motor until the rotor points toward the distributor cap terminal for spark plug wire No. 3, you can be sure all the valves in the cylinder of the No. 3 spark plug are closing. This is valve group No. 3. The same holds true for the other two terminals in the distributor cap.

Unfortunately, you can't see the rotor through the distributor cap. So, to know which spark plug wire terminal the rotor is pointing towards while you turn the motor, you will first mark and number the body of the distributor to show the position of each spark plug wire terminal in the distributor cap. Then, you'll remove the distributor cap so you can see which of your marks the rotor is pointing toward as you turn the motor. I use a child's brightly colored marking pen for marking the distributor.

Mark and number the distributor body

To correctly mark and number the distributor body, locate the distributor cap on your motor. It's the plastic object with four or five thick wires running from it. Figure 4-9 shows the various types of

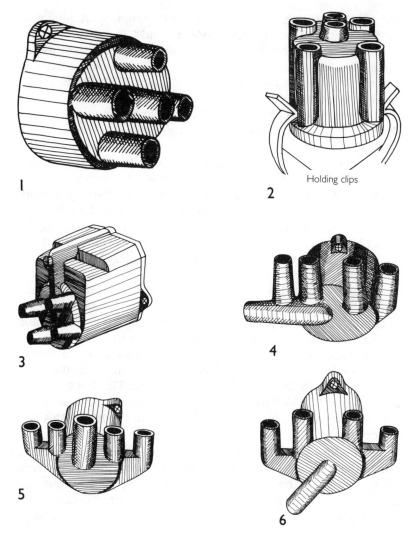

1

2

Holding clips

3

4

5

6

distributor caps found on Hondas. If your distributor cap is similar in design to distributor caps 4, 5, or 6 shown in FIG. 4-9, a special procedure is required to mark and number the position of the spark plug wire terminals. Skip to the procedure that explains how to mark your distributor cap.

Fig. 4-9
Distributor caps found in a variety of models.

Marking distributor caps 1, 2, and 3

These instructions are for marking distributor caps 1, 2, and 3, which are shown in FIG. 4-9. Skip to the next procedure for models with distributor cap 4, 5, or 6. Stand on the driver's side of your Honda. The spark plug closest to where you are standing is spark

Fig. 4-10
Mark the distributor on models
with distributor caps 1, 2, or 3,
shown in Fig. 4-9.

Mark.

plug No. 1. The wire attached to this spark plug is spark plug wire
No. 1. If in doubt, see chapter 1, FIGS. 1-3 and 1-4.

Put your finger on this spark plug wire and follow it to its distributor cap terminal. Mark the body of the distributor directly in
line with this distributor cap terminal. Figure 4-10 illustrates this
marking procedure. Write the number 1 next to this mark.

Okay, now for the next mark. Put your finger on the next spark
plug wire in the lineup. This is spark plug wire No. 2. Follow it back
to the distributor cap. Mark the metal body of the distributor
directly in line with this spark plug wire terminal. Write the number
2 next to this mark. Are you starting to see what's happening?

Repeat this marking process for spark plug wire No. 3 and spark
plug wire No. 4, one at a time. When you have finished marking the
distributor, remove the distributor cap and, without removing the
spark plug wires from the cap, move the cap clear of the rotor. If you
need help removing the distributor, see chapter 2, FIG. 2-19 for
instructions.

Double check that you have accurately followed each spark
plug wire back to the distributor cap. Incorrectly numbering a mark
on the distributor body will turn out to be disastrous to your motor.

Starting with the mark you numbered 1 on the distributor, follow the numbered marks around the distributor and you should
find the order to be 1, 3, 4, 2. This is the order in which the spark
plugs are sparked. It is called the *firing order*. The firing order is
also the order in which the four individual valve groups close. You'll
be closing, checking, and adjusting the four valve groups in this 1, 3,
4, 2 order.

If you find your number order to be 1, 2, 4, 3, you're reading
around the distributor in the wrong direction. No problem, just read
the numbers moving in the other direction. If your number sequence still does not agree with this 1, 3, 4, 2 order (for example: 1,
4, 3, 2), you have mislabeled a mark and must correct the mistake.

Marking distributor caps 4, 5, and 6

To mark distributor caps 4, 5, and 6 as shown in FIG. 4-9, remove the
distributor cap from the distributor. To do this, use a Phillips screwdriver and unscrew the two mounting screws. If a clip with wires is
attached to a mounting screw, completely remove this screw and
slip the clip free. Do not pull on any wires and do not remove the
wires from the distributor cap. For help, see chapter 2, FIG. 2-19.

Look into the distributor cap and notice the four metal pegs
illustrated in FIG. 4-11. These four metal pegs pick up the spark from
the rotor. Notice that metal peg A and metal peg B are directly
beneath their related spark plug wire terminals. Metal pegs C and D,

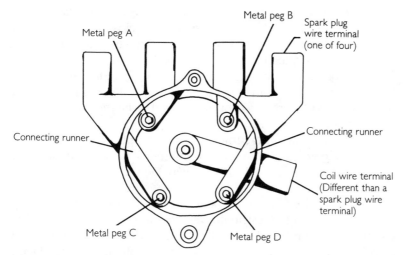

Metal peg B
Spark plug
wire terminal
(one of four)

Metal peg A

Connecting runner

Connecting runner

Coil wire terminal
(Different than a
spark plug wire
terminal)

Metal peg C

Metal peg D

Fig. 4-11
The offset position of the metal pegs inside the distributor cap. For models with distributor caps 4, 5, or 6, shown in Fig. 4-9.

however, are "offset" from their related spark plug wire terminals but are connected with runners to their related spark plug wire terminals. Here's what you do next:

Begin by marking the outside of the distributor cap directly above each metal peg. Figure 4-12 illustrates this procedure. Your marks might not be in the exact location as illustrated. To get each mark right above a metal peg, I put one fingertip on a metal peg and another fingertip on top of the distributor cap. When I feel I've got the "on top" finger directly above the "inside" finger, I make a mark right under the finger that's on top. Go ahead and mark the position of all four pegs.

As shown in FIG. 4-12, after marking the peg positions, draw a line from the two offset peg marks to their related spark plug wire terminal. Use the connective runners inside the distributor cap as a guide.

Fig. 4-12
Mark the position of the metal pegs on top of distributor caps 4, 5, or 6, shown in Fig. 4-9.

Draw a line across the distributor cap, connecting this "offset" peg mark with its related spark plug wire terminal.

Draw a line across the distributor cap, connecting this "offset" peg mark with its related spark plug wire terminal.

Your four marks directly above the four metal pegs inside the distributor cap.

Now you're going to correctly number each mark. Stand on the driver's side of your Honda. The spark plug closest to you is spark plug No. 1. Spark plug wire No. 1 is connected to this spark plug. If in doubt, see chapter 1, FIGS. 1-3 and 1-4.

Put your finger on spark plug wire No. 1 and follow it back to its distributor cap terminal. Follow this terminal down to its related mark you made on the distributor cap and write the number 1 next to this mark.

Repeat this procedure for the next spark plug wire in line. This is spark plug wire No. 2. Write the number 2 next to the mark you made for this peg on the distributor cap. Do the same for spark plug wires No. 3 and 4.

When you're finished numbering your marks, put the distributor cap back onto the distributor and line it up as if you were going to screw it down. Hold it in place and mark the distributor body directly in line with the four marks on the distributor cap. Figure 4-13 illustrates this procedure. Give each mark the same number it has on the distributor cap. Notice that in FIG. 4-13 there are two more marks to draw and number.

Fig. 4-13
Marking and numbering a distributor that uses distributor caps 4, 5, or 6, shown in Fig. 4-9.

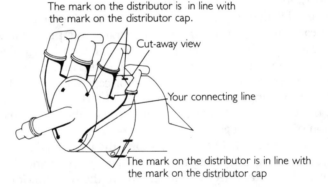

The mark on the distributor is in line with the mark on the distributor cap.

Cut-away view

Your connecting line

The mark on the distributor is in line with the mark on the distributor cap

Double check that you have accurately followed each spark plug wire back to the distributor cap

Incorrectly numbering a mark on the distributor body will turn out to be disastrous to your motor. Starting with your mark numbered 1 on the distributor, follow the numbered marks around the distributor and you should find the order to be 1, 3, 4, and 2. This order is the order in which the spark plugs are sparked. This is called the *firing order*. The firing order is also the order in which the four individual valve groups close. You'll be closing, checking, and adjusting the four valve groups in this 1, 3, 4, and 2 order.

If you find your number order to be 1, 2, 4, 3, you're reading around the distributor in the wrong direction. No problem, just read the numbers moving in the other direction. If your number

There are a couple of directions you can take to get from the mark on the cap to the distributor body. Draw two lines from the mark on the top of the distributor cap down to the body of the distributor. Make these lines 90 degrees to each other, then mark the body of the distributor between these two lines. See FIG. 4-14.

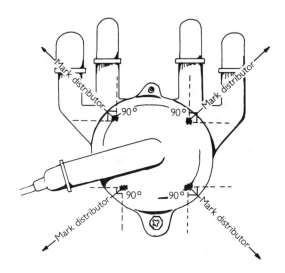

Fig. 4-14
Using 90-degree lines to accurately mark a distributor that uses distributor caps 4, 5, or 6, shown in Fig. 4-9.

sequence still does not agree with this 1, 3, 4, 2 order (for example: 1, 4, 3, 2), you have mislabeled a mark and must correct the mistake.

How to know when all the valves in a group are closed

At last, the third thing you must do and learn before you can adjust the valves. I'll bet by now you forgot that there's a third thing to do before you actually adjust the valves. This takes just a minute.

When you actually turn the motor to close the first group of valves to be checked and adjusted (valve group No. 1), the rotor will point to the number on the distributor that shows you which group of valves you are closing. The timing belt pulley marks, which you are about to locate, will show you exactly when all the valves of the group are completely closed and in position to be checked and adjusted.

Figure 4-15 illustrates the timing belt pulley used on your model. The timing belt pulley is positioned on the passenger's side of the valve train as shown in the illustration of your model in FIG. 4-15.

Fig. 4-15
The timing belt pulley marks.

Civic
1975 – 1979 1200 Models

The timing belt pulley marks can be seen from the passenger's side of the motor. Remove the timing belt pulley cover. The first four illustrations below show the positions for checking and adjusting the valve groups.

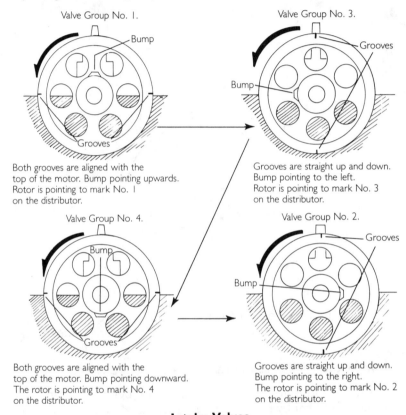

Valve Group No. 1.

Both grooves are aligned with the top of the motor. Bump pointing upwards. Rotor is pointing to mark No. 1 on the distributor.

Valve Group No. 3.

Grooves are straight up and down. Bump pointing to the left. Rotor is pointing to mark No. 3 on the distributor.

Valve Group No. 4.

Both grooves are aligned with the top of the motor. Bump pointing downward. The rotor is pointing to mark No. 4 on the distributor.

Valve Group No. 2.

Grooves are straight up and down. Bump pointing to the right. The rotor is pointing to mark No. 2 on the distributor.

Intake Valves

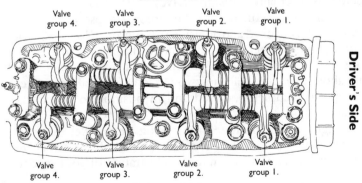

Valve group 4.   Valve group 3.   Valve group 2.   Valve group 1.

Valve group 4.   Valve group 3.   Valve group 2.   Valve group 1.

Driver's Side

Exhaust Valves

Civic
1975 – 1979 1200 Models

Fig. 4-15.
Continued.

The timing belt pulley marks can be seen from the passenger's side of the motor. Remove the timing belt pulley cover. These illustrations show the position for checking and adjusting the valve groups. See page 137 for valve group illustration.

1975
(Except 1200 Models)

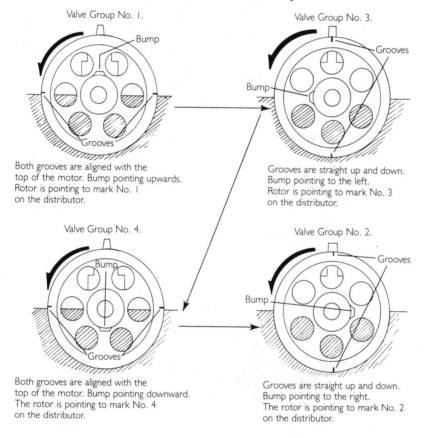

Valve Group No. 1.

Both grooves are aligned with the top of the motor. Bump pointing upwards. Rotor is pointing to mark No. 1 on the distributor.

Valve Group No. 3.

Grooves are straight up and down. Bump pointing to the left. Rotor is pointing to mark No. 3 on the distributor.

Valve Group No. 4.

Both grooves are aligned with the top of the motor. Bump pointing downward. The rotor is pointing to mark No. 4 on the distributor.

Valve Group No. 2.

Grooves are straight up and down. Bump pointing to the right. The rotor is pointing to mark No. 2 on the distributor.

Fig. 4-15.
Continued.

Civic
1976 – 1979
(Except 1200 Models)

The timing belt pulley marks can be seen from the passenger's side of the motor. Remove the timing belt pulley cover. The four illustrations below show the positions for checking and adjusting the valve groups. See page 137 for valve group illustration.

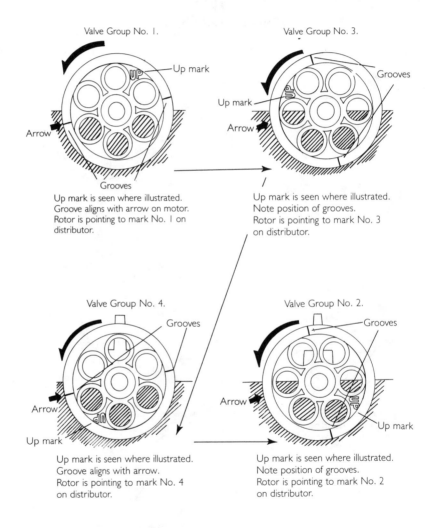

Valve Group No. 1.

Up mark

Arrow

Grooves

Up mark is seen where illustrated.
Groove aligns with arrow on motor.
Rotor is pointing to mark No. 1 on
distributor.

Valve Group No. 3.

Grooves

Up mark

Arrow

Up mark is seen where illustrated.
Note position of grooves.
Rotor is pointing to mark No. 3
on distributor.

Valve Group No. 4.

Grooves

Arrow

Up mark

Up mark is seen where illustrated.
Groove aligns with arrow.
Rotor is pointing to mark No. 4
on distributor.

Valve Group No. 2.

Grooves

Arrow

Up mark

Up mark is seen where illustrated.
Note position of grooves.
Rotor is pointing to mark No. 2
on distributor.

Civic
1980 – 1982
(Except 1200 Models)

Fig. 4-15.
Continued.

The timing belt pulley marks can be seen from the passenger's side of the motor. Remove the timing belt pulley cover. The four illustrations below show the position for checking and adjusting the valve groups. See page 137 for valve group illustration.

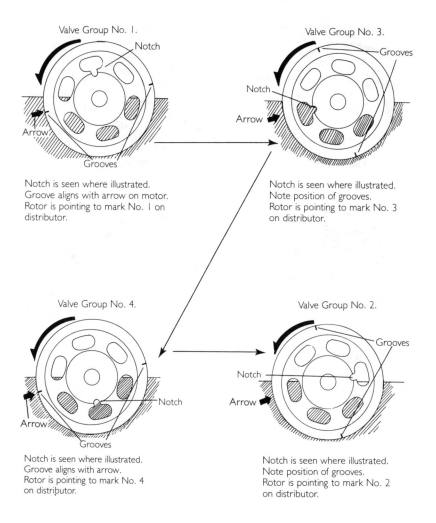

Valve Group No. 1.

Notch is seen where illustrated.
Groove aligns with arrow on motor.
Rotor is pointing to mark No. 1 on distributor.

Valve Group No. 3.

Notch is seen where illustrated.
Note position of grooves.
Rotor is pointing to mark No. 3 on distributor.

Valve Group No. 4.

Notch is seen where illustrated.
Groove aligns with arrow.
Rotor is pointing to mark No. 4 on distributor.

Valve Group No. 2.

Notch is seen where illustrated.
Note position of grooves.
Rotor is pointing to mark No. 2 on distributor.

Fig. 4-15.
Continued.

Civic
1983
(Except 1200 Models)

Timing belt pulley marks can be seen from the passenger's side of the motor. Remove the timing belt pulley cover. The illustrations below show the positions for checking and adjusting the valve groups.

Valve Group No. 1.

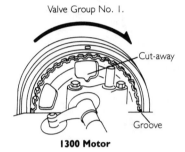

1300 Motor

Valve Group No. 3.

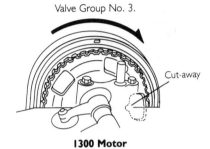

1300 Motor

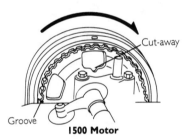

1500 Motor

Cut-away at top. Groove aligned with top of motor as illustrated. Rotor is pointing to mark No. 1 on distributor.

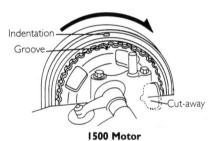

1500 Motor

Cut-away is on right side as illustrated. Groove on 1300 motor not visible. Groove on 1500 motor aligned with indentation. Rotor is pointing to mark No. 3 on distributor.

Fig. 4-15.
Continued.

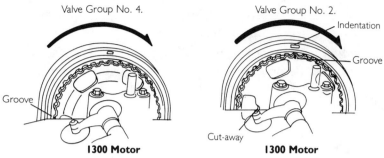

Valve Group No. 4.

Valve Group No. 2.

Indentation

Groove

Groove

1300 Motor

Cut-away

1300 Motor

Cut-away on left side as illustrated.
On 1300 motor groove is aligned with
indentation. On 1500 motor groove is
at bottom and not seen. Rotor is pointing
to mark No. 2 on distributor.

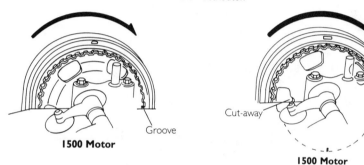

Groove

1500 Motor

Cut-away

1500 Motor

Cut-away on bottom and not seen.
Groove aligned with top of motor as
illustrated. Rotor is pointing to
mark No. 4 on distributor.

1975 – 1983
(Except 1200 Models)

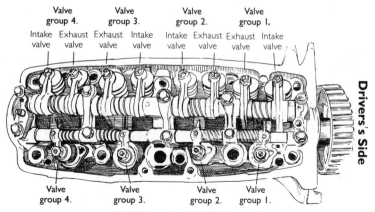

Valve group 4.

Valve group 3.

Valve group 2.

Valve group 1.

Intake valve — Exhaust valve — Exhaust valve — Intake valve — Intake valve — Exhaust valve — Exhaust valve — Intake valve

Driver's Side

Valve group 4.

Valve group 3.

Valve group 2.

Valve group 1.

Auxiliary Intake Valves

Fig. 4-15.
Continued.

Civic
1984 – 1987

Timing belt pulley marks can be seen from the passenger's side of the motor. Remove the timing belt pulley cover. The illustrations below show the positions for checking and adjusting the valve groups.

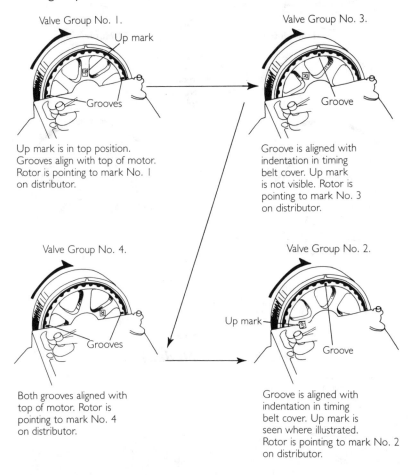

Valve Group No. 1.

Up mark

Grooves

Up mark is in top position. Grooves align with top of motor. Rotor is pointing to mark No. 1 on distributor.

Valve Group No. 3.

Groove

Groove is aligned with indentation in timing belt cover. Up mark is not visible. Rotor is pointing to mark No. 3 on distributor.

Valve Group No. 4.

Grooves

Both grooves aligned with top of motor. Rotor is pointing to mark No. 4 on distributor.

Valve Group No. 2.

Up mark

Groove

Groove is aligned with indentation in timing belt cover. Up mark is seen where illustrated. Rotor is pointing to mark No. 2 on distributor.

Civic
1984 – 1987
(Except HF Model)

Intake Valves

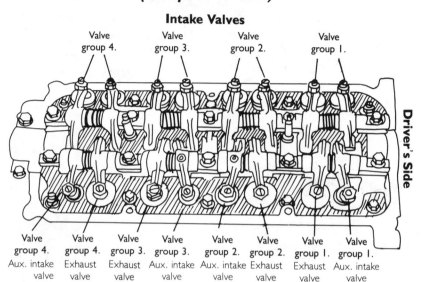

Valve group 4.
Valve group 3.
Valve group 2.
Valve group 1.

Driver's Side

| Valve group 4. | Valve group 4. | Valve group 3. | Valve group 3. | Valve group 2. | Valve group 2. | Valve group 1. | Valve group 1. |
| Aux. intake valve | Exhaust valve | Exhaust valve | Aux. intake valve | Aux. intake valve | Exhaust valve | Exhaust valve | Aux. intake valve |

Civic
1984 – 1987
(HF Model)

Intake Valves

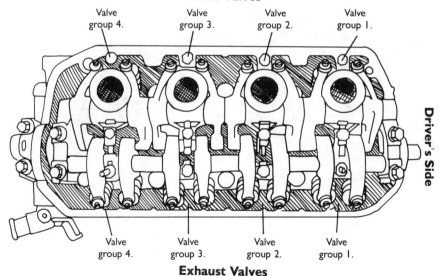

Valve group 4.
Valve group 3.
Valve group 2.
Valve group 1.

Driver's Side

Valve group 4.
Valve group 3.
Valve group 2.
Valve group 1.

Exhaust Valves

Fig. 4-15.
Continued.

Fig. 4-15.
Continued.

Civic
1988 – 1991
(All Except Si, 4-WD, and 1.6 Models)

The timing belt pulley marks can be seen from the passenger's side of the motor. Remove the timing belt pulley cover. The position for checking and adjusting the valve groups are shown in the illustrations below. See page 142 for valve group illustration.

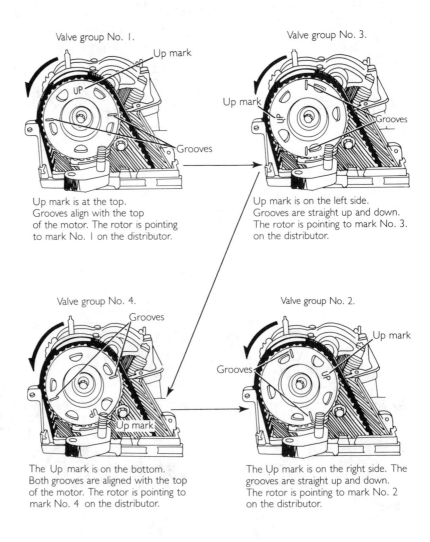

Valve group No. 1.

Up mark is at the top.
Grooves align with the top
of the motor. The rotor is pointing
to mark No. 1 on the distributor.

Valve group No. 3.

Up mark is on the left side.
Grooves are straight up and down.
The rotor is pointing to mark No. 3.
on the distributor.

Valve group No. 4.

The Up mark is on the bottom.
Both grooves are aligned with the top
of the motor. The rotor is pointing to
mark No. 4 on the distributor.

Valve group No. 2.

The Up mark is on the right side. The
grooves are straight up and down.
The rotor is pointing to mark No. 2
on the distributor.

Civic
1988 – 1991
(Si, 4-WD, and 1.6 Models are shown below)

The timing belt pulley marks can be seen from the passenger's side of the motor. The positions for checking and adjusting the valve groups are shown in the illustrations below. See page 142 for valve group illustration.

Fig. 4-15.
Continued.

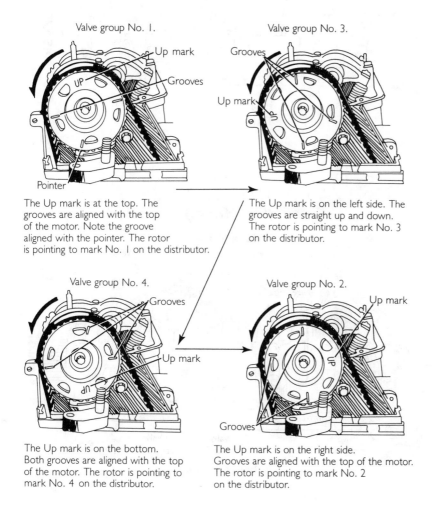

Valve group No. 1.

The Up mark is at the top. The grooves are aligned with the top of the motor. Note the groove aligned with the pointer. The rotor is pointing to mark No. 1 on the distributor.

Valve group No. 3.

The Up mark is on the left side. The grooves are straight up and down. The rotor is pointing to mark No. 3 on the distributor.

Valve group No. 4.

The Up mark is on the bottom. Both grooves are aligned with the top of the motor. The rotor is pointing to mark No. 4 on the distributor.

Valve group No. 2.

The Up mark is on the right side. Grooves are aligned with the top of the motor. The rotor is pointing to mark No. 2 on the distributor.

Fig. 4-15.
Continued.

Civic
1988 – 1991
(Except HF Model)

Intake Valves

Valve group 4. Valve group 3. Valve group 2. Valve group 1.

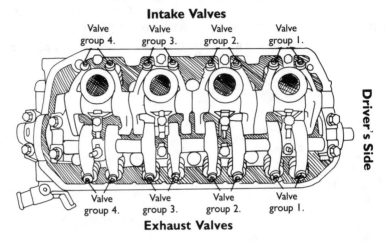

Driver's Side

Valve group 4. Valve group 3. Valve group 2. Valve group 1.

Exhaust Valves

Civic
1988 – 1991
(HF Model)

Intake Valves

Valve group 4. Valve group 3. Valve group 2. Valve group 1.

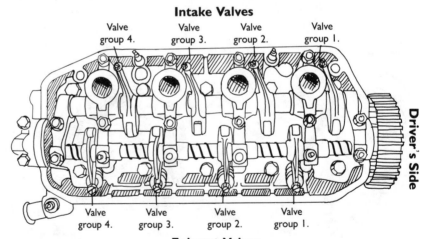

Driver's Side

Valve group 4. Valve group 3. Valve group 2. Valve group 1.

Exhaust Valves

Accord
1976 – 1979

Fig. 4-15.
Continued.

The timing belt pulley marks can be seen from the passenger's side of the motor. Remove the timing belt pulley cover. The positions for checking and adjusting the valve groups are shown in the illustrations below. See page 146 for valve group illustration.

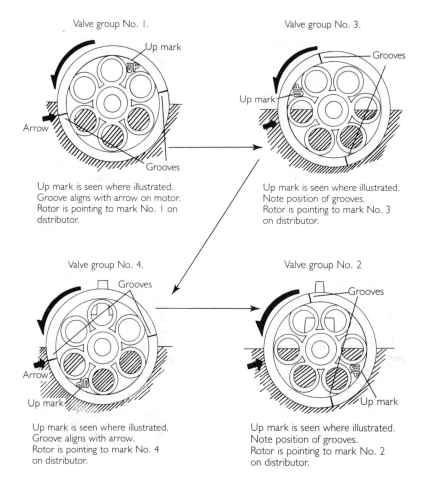

Valve group No. 1.

Up mark is seen where illustrated. Groove aligns with arrow on motor. Rotor is pointing to mark No. 1 on distributor.

Valve group No. 3.

Up mark is seen where illustrated. Note position of grooves. Rotor is pointing to mark No. 3 on distributor.

Valve group No. 4.

Up mark is seen where illustrated. Groove aligns with arrow. Rotor is pointing to mark No. 4 on distributor.

Valve group No. 2

Up mark is seen where illustrated. Note position of grooves. Rotor is pointing to mark No. 2 on distributor.

Fig. 4-15.
Continued.

Accord
1980 – 1982

The timing belt pulley marks can be seen from the passenger's side of the motor. Remove the timing belt pulley cover. The positions for checking and adjusting the valve groups are shown in the illustrations below. See page 146 for valve group illustration.

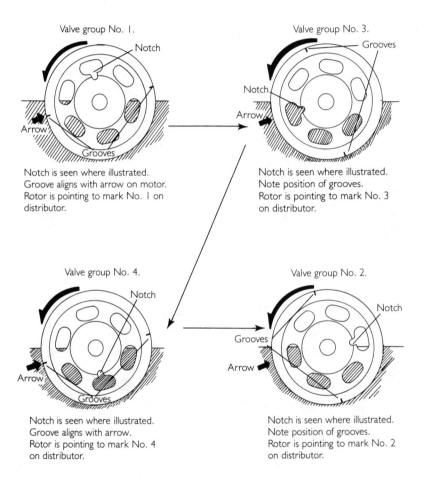

Valve group No. 1.

Notch is seen where illustrated.
Groove aligns with arrow on motor.
Rotor is pointing to mark No. 1 on distributor.

Valve group No. 3.

Notch is seen where illustrated.
Note position of grooves.
Rotor is pointing to mark No. 3 on distributor.

Valve group No. 4.

Notch is seen where illustrated.
Groove aligns with arrow.
Rotor is pointing to mark No. 4 on distributor.

Valve group No. 2.

Notch is seen where illustrated.
Note position of grooves.
Rotor is pointing to mark No. 2 on distributor.

Accord
1983

Fig. 4-15.
Continued.

The timing belt pulley marks can be seen from the passenger's side of the motor. Remove the timing belt pulley cover. The positions for checking and adjusting the valve groups are shown in the illustrations below. See page 146 for valve group illustration.

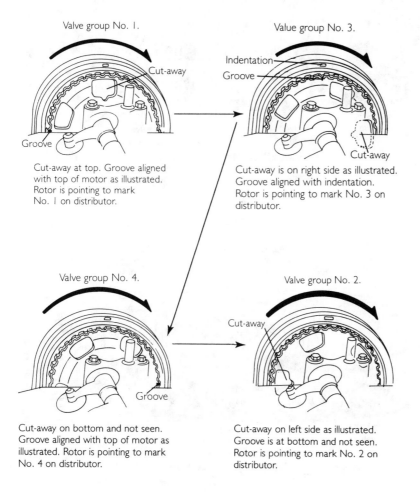

Valve group No. 1.

Cut-away at top. Groove aligned with top of motor as illustrated. Rotor is pointing to mark No. 1 on distributor.

Value group No. 3.

Cut-away is on right side as illustrated. Groove aligned with indentation. Rotor is pointing to mark No. 3 on distributor.

Valve group No. 4.

Cut-away on bottom and not seen. Groove aligned with top of motor as illustrated. Rotor is pointing to mark No. 4 on distributor.

Valve group No. 2.

Cut-away on left side as illustrated. Groove is at bottom and not seen. Rotor is pointing to mark No. 2 on distributor.

Fig. 4-15.
Continued.

Accord
1976 – 1981

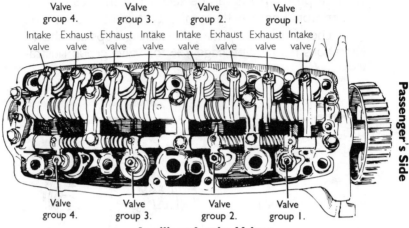

Auxiliary Intake Valves

Accord
1982 – 1983

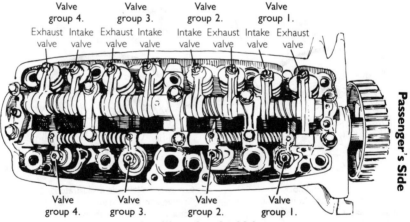

Auxiliary Intake Valves

Accord
1984 – 1989

Fig. 4-15.
Continued.

The timing belt pulley marks can be seen from the passenger's side of the motor. Remove the timing belt pulley cover. The positions for checking and adjusting the valve groups are shown in the illustrations below. See page 148 for valve group illustration. NOTE: Instead of a hole, the word Up is found on some models.

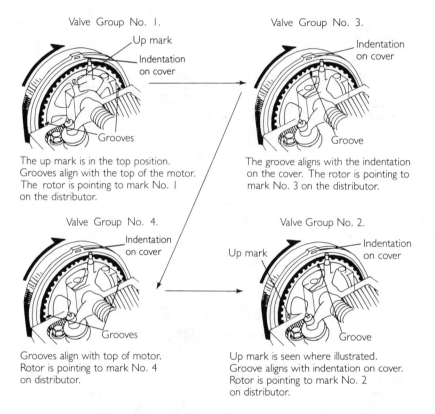

Valve Group No. 1.

The up mark is in the top position. Grooves align with the top of the motor. The rotor is pointing to mark No. 1 on the distributor.

Valve Group No. 3.

The groove aligns with the indentation on the cover. The rotor is pointing to mark No. 3 on the distributor.

Valve Group No. 4.

Grooves align with top of motor. Rotor is pointing to mark No. 4 on distributor.

Valve Group No. 2.

Up mark is seen where illustrated. Groove aligns with indentation on cover. Rotor is pointing to mark No. 2 on distributor.

Fig. 4-15.
Continued.

Accord
1984 – 1986

Intake Valves

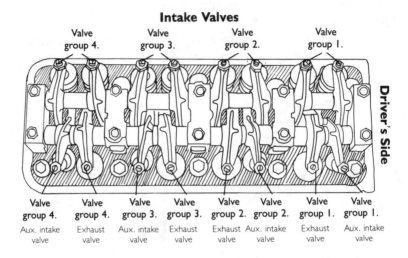

Valve group 4.   Valve group 3.   Valve group 2.   Valve group 1.

Driver's Side

Valve group 4.	Valve group 4.	Valve group 3.	Valve group 3.	Valve group 2.	Valve group 2.	Valve group 1.	Valve group 1.
Aux. intake valve	Exhaust valve	Aux. intake valve	Exhaust valve	Exhaust valve	Aux. intake valve	Exhaust valve	Aux. intake valve

Accord
1987 – 1989

Intake Valves

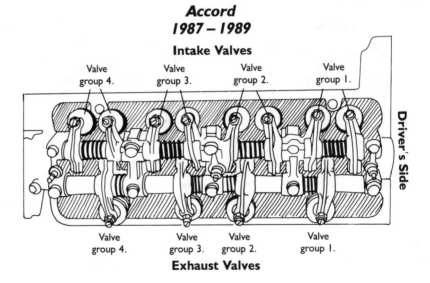

Valve group 4.   Valve group 3.   Valve group 2.   Valve group 1.

Driver's Side

Valve group 4.   Valve group 3.   Valve group 2.   Valve group 1.

Exhaust Valves

Accord
1990 – 1991

Fig. 4-15.
Continued.

Timing belt pulley marks can be seen from the passenger's side of the motor. Remove the timing belt pulley cover. The first four illustrations below show the positions for checking and adjusting the valve groups.

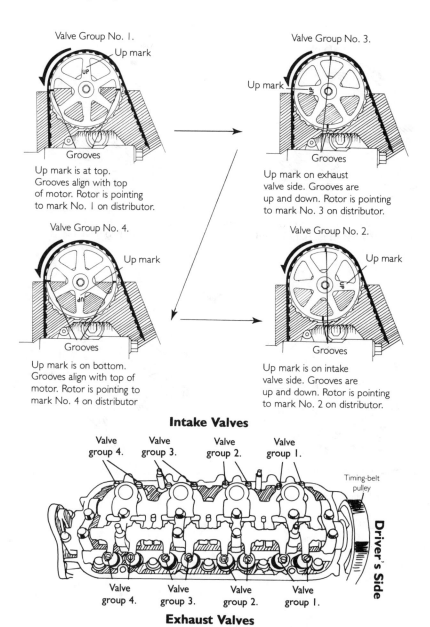

Valve Group No. 1.
Up mark

Grooves

Up mark is at top.
Grooves align with top
of motor. Rotor is pointing
to mark No. 1 on distributor.

Valve Group No. 3.
Up mark

Grooves

Up mark on exhaust
valve side. Grooves are
up and down. Rotor is pointing
to mark No. 3 on distributor.

Valve Group No. 4.
Up mark

Grooves

Up mark is on bottom.
Grooves align with top of
motor. Rotor is pointing to
mark No. 4 on distributor

Valve Group No. 2.
Up mark

Grooves

Up mark is on intake
valve side. Grooves are
up and down. Rotor is pointing
to mark No. 2 on distributor.

Intake Valves

Valve group 4. Valve group 3. Valve group 2. Valve group 1.

Timing-belt
pulley

Driver's Side

Valve group 4. Valve group 3. Valve group 2. Valve group 1.

Exhaust Valves

Fig. 4-15.
Continued.

Prelude
1979 – 1982

Timing belt pulley marks can be seen from the passenger's side of the motor. Remove the timing belt pulley cover. The positions for checking and adjusting the valve groups are illustrated below.

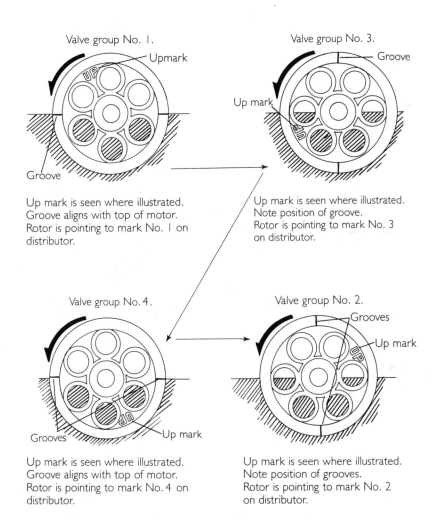

Valve group No. 1.

Up mark is seen where illustrated.
Groove aligns with top of motor.
Rotor is pointing to mark No. 1 on distributor.

Valve group No. 3.

Up mark is seen where illustrated.
Note position of groove.
Rotor is pointing to mark No. 3 on distributor.

Valve group No. 4.

Up mark is seen where illustrated.
Groove aligns with top of motor.
Rotor is pointing to mark No. 4 on distributor.

Valve group No. 2.

Up mark is seen where illustrated.
Note position of grooves.
Rotor is pointing to mark No. 2 on distributor.

Prelude
1979 – 1981

Fig. 4-15.
Continued.

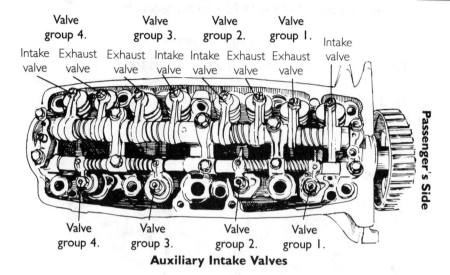

Valve group 4.   Valve group 3.   Valve group 2.   Valve group 1.

Intake valve   Exhaust valve   Exhaust valve   Intake valve   Intake valve   Exhaust valve   Exhaust valve   Intake valve

Passenger's Side

Valve group 4.   Valve group 3.   Valve group 2.   Valve group 1.

Auxiliary Intake Valves

Prelude
1982

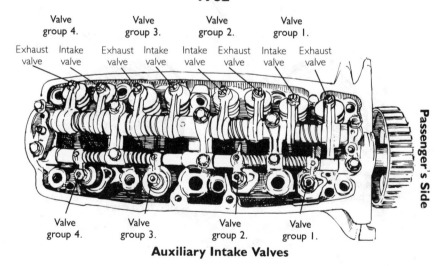

Valve group 4.   Valve group 3.   Valve group 2.   Valve group 1.

Exhaust valve   Intake valve   Exhaust valve   Intake valve   Intake valve   Exhaust valve   Intake valve   Exhaust valve

Passenger's Side

Valve group 4.   Valve group 3.   Valve group 2.   Valve group 1.

Auxiliary Intake Valves

Fig. 4-15.
Continued.

Prelude
1983 – 1987 Carbureted and Fuel-Injected
Models and 1988 – 1990 Carbureted Models Only

1983 – 1987

Timing belt pulley marks can be seen from the passenger's side of the motor. Remove the timing belt pulley cover. The positions for checking and adjusting the valve groups are illustrated below. NOTE: Instead of a hole, the word Up is found on some models

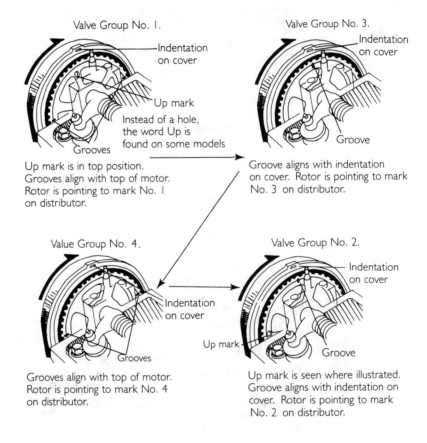

Valve Group No. 1.

Indentation on cover

Up mark
Instead of a hole, the word Up is found on some models

Grooves

Up mark is in top position. Grooves align with top of motor. Rotor is pointing to mark No. 1 on distributor.

Valve Group No. 3.

Indentation on cover

Groove

Groove aligns with indentation on cover. Rotor is pointing to mark No. 3 on distributor.

Value Group No. 4.

Indentation on cover

Grooves

Grooves align with top of motor. Rotor is pointing to mark No. 4 on distributor.

Valve Group No. 2.

Indentation on cover

Up mark

Groove

Up mark is seen where illustrated. Groove aligns with indentation on cover. Rotor is pointing to mark No. 2 on distributor.

Prelude
1988 – 1990

Fig. 4-15.
Continued.

Remove the timing belt pulley cover. Timing marks can be seen from the passenger's side of the motor. The positions for checking and adjusting the valve groups are shown below. See page 154 for valve group illustrations.

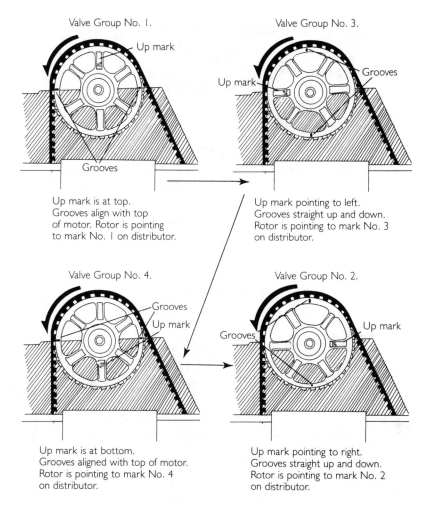

Valve Group No. 1.

Up mark

Grooves

Up mark is at top.
Grooves align with top
of motor. Rotor is pointing
to mark No. 1 on distributor.

Valve Group No. 3.

Up mark

Grooves

Up mark pointing to left.
Grooves straight up and down.
Rotor is pointing to mark No. 3
on distributor.

Valve Group No. 4.

Grooves

Up mark

Up mark is at bottom.
Grooves aligned with top of motor.
Rotor is pointing to mark No. 4
on distributor.

Valve Group No. 2.

Grooves

Up mark

Up mark pointing to right.
Grooves straight up and down.
Rotor is pointing to mark No. 2
on distributor.

Fig. 4-15.
Continued.

Prelude
1983 – 1987 Carbureted and Fuel-Injected Models and 1988 – 1990 Carbureted Models Only Continued

1983

Intake Valves

Valve group 4.   Valve group 3.   Valve group 2.   Valve group 1.

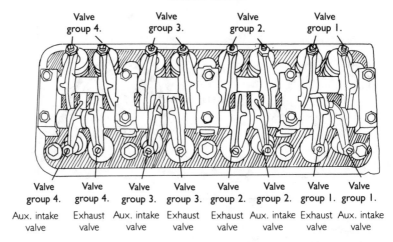

Valve group 4.	Valve group 4.	Valve group 3.	Valve group 3.	Valve group 2.	Valve group 2.	Valve group 1.	Valve group 1.
Aux. intake valve	Exhaust valve	Aux. intake valve	Exhaust valve	Exhaust valve	Aux. intake valve	Exhaust valve	Aux. intake valve

Prelude
1984 – 1990

Intake Valves

Valve group 4.   Valve group 3.   Valve group 2.   Valve group 1.

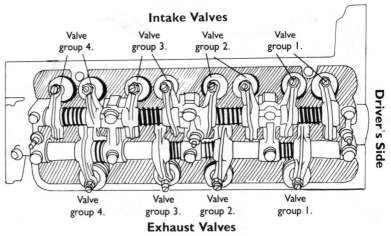

Driver's Side

Valve group 4.   Valve group 3.   Valve group 2.   Valve group 1.

Exhaust Valves

Prelude
1988 – 1991 Fuel Injected Models

Fig. 4-15.
Continued.

Timing belt pulley marks can be seen from the passenger's side of the motor. Remove the timing belt pulley cover. See page 156 for valve group illustrations.

Valve Group No. 1.

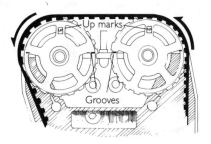

Up marks are at top. Grooves on back side of pulley align with top of motor. Rotor is pointing to mark No. 1 on distributor.

Valve Group No. 3.

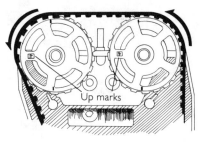

Up marks are on exhaust valve side. Grooves on Rotor are pointing to mark No. 3 on distributor.

Valve Group No. 4.

Up marks are at bottom. Rotor is pointing to mark No. 4 on distributor.

Valve Group No. 2.

Up marks are on intake valve side. Rotor is pointing to mark No. 2 on distributor.

Fig. 4-15.
Continued.

Prelude
1988 – 1991 Fuel-Injected Models Continued

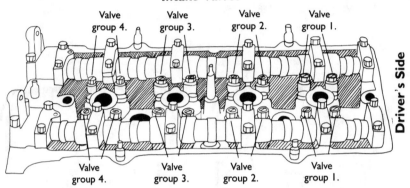

Intake Valves

Valve group 4.   Valve group 3.   Valve group 2.   Valve group 1.

Driver's Side

Valve group 4.   Valve group 3.   Valve group 2.   Valve group 1.

Exhaust Valves

Depending on which side your timing belt pulley is marked, you might have to remove the timing belt pulley cover to see the marks on the timing belt pulley. Locate the illustration of your model in FIG. 4-15. If it is necessary to remove the timing belt pulley cover, the illustration instructs you to do so. To remove a timing belt pulley cover, remove the two or three 10-millimeter bolts that secure it.

I'll tell you about positioning the timing belt pulley marks when the time comes. For now, you just need to know these marks exist. The timing belt pulley is driven by the timing belt, and together, they turn the cam shaft that opens and closes the valves. So, it stands to reason that this pulley can be positioned to completely close a group of valves.

Fig. 4-16
This rotor has a metal-tipped end and a plastic end. Your distributor might look different, however.

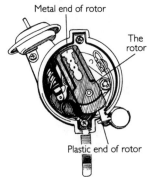

Metal end of rotor

The rotor

Plastic end of rotor

STEP 3
How to close, check, and adjust valve group No. 1

The one rule to remember while turning the motor is that you can only turn the motor counterclockwise. If you turn too far and pass the spot where the timing belt pulley marks are in the correct position, you can't turn the motor back. You have to keep turning counterclockwise until you get a second chance to put everything into alignment.

Caution! Turning the motor clockwise can throw the timing system out of sync and damage the motor.

Okay, turn the motor counterclockwise until the metal-tipped end of the rotor is within an inch of pointing to your No. 1 mark on the distributor. The metal-tipped end of the rotor is shown in FIG. 4-16.

If you're finding it hard to turn the motor, remove the spark plugs. This will allow all internal pressure to escape from the motor, making it easy to turn. To remove the spark plugs, see chapter 1. Before removing the spark plug wires from the spark plugs, be sure to number each spark plug wire, beginning with No. 1 and continuing through No. 4. You must do this because the spark plug wires must be reconnected in the same order. The No. 1 spark plug wire is the wire closest to you when you are standing on the driver's side of the motor. See FIG. 4-7 for an example of how to label the spark plug wires using masking tape for labels.

Continue to turn the motor very slowly. When the timing belt pulley marks begin to get close to where you want them (FIG. 4-15), you can nudge the wrench with your hand to turn the motor ever so slightly.

I want to remind you never to turn the motor clockwise because this could damage it. Should you turn too far and pass the spot where the timing belt pulley marks are positioned for checking and adjusting valve group No. 1, continue to turn the motor counterclockwise until you get a second chance to correctly position the marks. One time around should do it.

Double check the position of the distributor rotor and timing belt pulley marks. At this point, the metal-tipped end of the rotor should be pointing to the No. 1 mark on the distributor body and the timing belt pulley marks should be positioned for adjusting valve group No. 1 as shown in FIG. 4-15.

When you start turning the rotor, you might not be able to see all the timing belt pulley marks shown in the illustration of your model. This is okay because they will become visible as you turn the motor.

Caution! Repeat this step. Do not go on to STEP 4 if the:

○ plastic end of the rotor (not the metal-tipped end) is pointing to the No. 1 mark on the distributor.

○ metal-tipped end of the rotor is pointing to any mark other than the No. 1 mark.

○ metal-tipped end of the rotor is pointing to the No. 1 mark on the distributor but the timing belt pulley marks are not aligned for valve group No. 1 as shown in FIG. 4-15.

STEP 4
How to check the valve adjustment

As usual, I am going to tell you a little about what you'll be doing in this step before you actually do it. I'll keep it short. With STEP 3 completed, all the valves in valve group No. 1 are closed inside the motor and in position to be checked and adjusted.

Have a look at the parts of the motor you couldn't see before removing the valve cover. Using FIG. 4-17 as a guide, you'll see that your motor has two rows of rocker arms and that each rocker arm has an adjusting screw on one end. Beneath this adjusting screw end of the rocker is a valve spring. Beneath the other end of the rocker arm is a cam lobe. All these parts are shown in FIG. 4-17.

The valves themselves, as you have already learned, are located

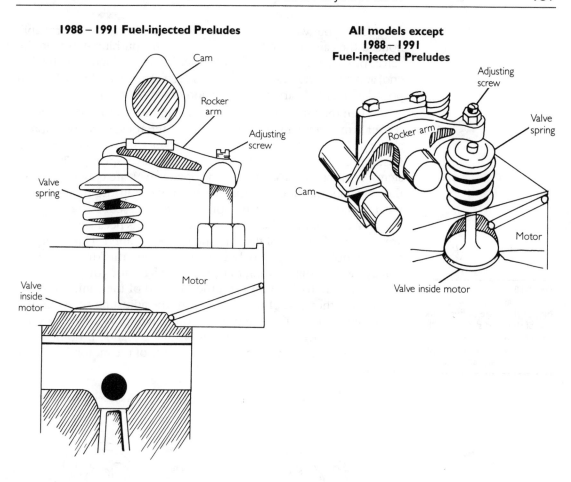

1988 – 1991 Fuel-injected Preludes

Cam

Rocker arm

Adjusting screw

Valve spring

Valve inside motor

Motor

All models except 1988 – 1991 Fuel-injected Preludes

Adjusting screw

Valve spring

Rocker arm

Cam

Motor

Valve inside motor

Fig. 4-17
The cam, rocker arm, valve spring, and adjusting screw.

inside the motor and out of sight. Each valve, however, has a corresponding rocker arm with adjusting screw, valve spring, and cam lobe. When mechanics talk about adjusting valves, they are actually speaking of adjusting the small space between each rocker arm and valve spring. The space between these two parts exists only when the corresponding valve in the motor is closed, which is why you just went through the ordeal of closing the valves.

Take a few minutes and read the ''For your information'' section that follows. It will help you understand what's happening and make the upcoming procedures easy for you.

For your information

Fuel-injected 1988 – 1991 Preludes are set up a little differently than the models described in this explanation. The principle of operation is, however, identical.

While you were turning the motor in STEP 3, you probably noticed the cams turning and the rocker arms pushing down on the valve springs. As shown in FIG. 4-18, each cam has a high end (the thin end) and a low end (the thick end). As each cam turns, the rocker arm positioned directly above rides up and down on its lobes.

When the high (pointed) end of a cam turns into contact with a rocker arm, it actually lifts up the end of the rocker arm positioned above it. In turn, the other end of the rocker arm rotates downward, pushing down on and compressing the valve spring. The valve stems, as shown in FIG. 4-18 (see the open valve), are connected with the valve springs and, for this reason, a valve in the motor opens when its corresponding valve spring is compressed.

In FIG. 4-18, the other valve is closed. This is because the rocker arm is on the low end of the cam and not being lifted. This is the key to the whole concept, so button down your thinking cap, here comes the part that's going to turn on the light for you!

Fig. 4-18
An open and closed valve. Notice the space between the top of the valve spring and the rocker arm on the closed valve. It is this space that is checked and, if necessary, adjusted.

When the rocker arm is on the low end of the cam, not being lifted, the other end of the rocker arm (the adjusting screw end) is not pushing down and compressing the valve spring. When a valve spring is not being compressed, it is fully expanded, holding the valve closed, up against the top of the inside of the motor. The valve is closed!

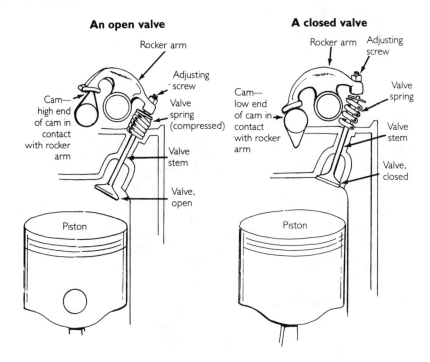

An open valve

Rocker arm

Adjusting screw

Cam—high end of cam in contact with rocker arm

Valve spring (compressed)

Valve stem

Valve, open

Piston

A closed valve

Rocker arm   Adjusting screw

Valve spring

Cam—low end of cam in contact with rocker arm

Valve stem

Valve, closed

Piston

On the closed valve in FIG. 4-18, look for the space between the top of the valve spring and the rocker arm. It is the width of this space that gets checked and adjusted when you adjust the valves. This space does not exist when the valve is being pushed open, which is why the valves have to be closed before they can be checked and adjusted.

Checking the valve adjustment on all models except 1988 – 1991 fuel-injected Preludes

To check the valve adjustment on all models except the 1988–1991 fuel-injected Prelude, a feeler gauge blade is inserted between the rocker arm and the top of the valve spring. This is shown in the top illustration of FIG. 4-19. I'll tell you which feeler gauge blade to use in just a minute, just be sure not to insert the blade at an angle, or you will get a false reading.

Fig. 4-19
Check the valve adjustment with a feeler gauge blade.

All models except 1988 – 1991 Fuel-injected Preludes

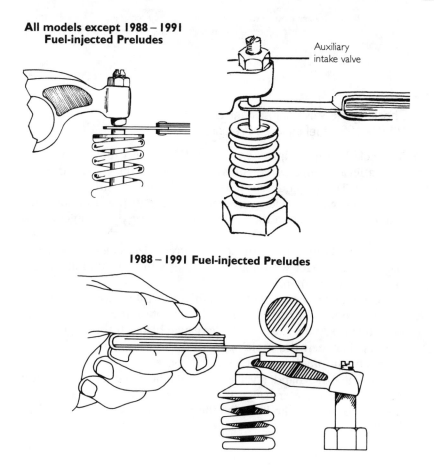

Auxiliary intake valve

1988 – 1991 Fuel-injected Preludes

A valve is in adjustment if the correct size feeler gauge blade makes light contact with both the rocker arm and the top of the valve spring as it is slipped between them.

If the feeler gauge blade slips in very easily—not making contact with both the rocker arm and the top of the valve spring—the valve is out of adjustment. Try the next feeler gauge blade size. If this larger-size blade will slip between the rocker arm and the top of the valve spring, the valve is definitely out of adjustment—it is too loose.

On the other hand, a valve is out of adjustment and too tight if the correct-size feeler gauge blade will not slip in, or if force is required to make it slip between the rocker arm and the top of the valve spring.

If you're finding it hard to turn the motor, remove the spark plugs. This will allow all internal pressure to escape from the motor, making it easy to turn. To remove the spark plugs, see chapter 1.

Checking the valve adjustment on 1988 – 1991 fuel-injected Preludes

To check the valve adjustment on the 1988 – 1991 fuel-injected Prelude, a feeler gauge blade is inserted between the rocker arm and cam lobe. This procedure is illustrated on the right side in FIG. 4-19. I'll tell you which feeler gauge blade to use in just a minute, just remember not to insert the blade at an angle, or you will get a false reading.

A valve is in adjustment if the correct size feeler gauge blade makes light contact with both the rocker arm and cam lobe as it is slipped between them.

If the feeler gauge blade slips in very easily—not making contact with both the rocker arm and cam lobe—the valve is out of adjustment. Try the next size feeler gauge blade. If this larger blade will slip between the rocker arm and the cam lobe, the valve is definitely out of adjustment—it is too loose.

On the other hand, a valve is out of adjustment and too tight if the correct-size feeler gauge blade will not slip in, or if force is required to make it slip between the rocker arm and the cam lobe.

When checking valve adjustment, accuracy is the key. If a valve feels even the slightest bit out of adjustment, don't leave it that way and figure you'll get to it next time.

Which feeler gauge blade(s) to use

Notice in the illustration of your model in FIG. 4-15, that some valves are called intake valves and other valves are called exhaust valves. In addition, some motors also have auxiliary intake valves—these are the CVCC motors I talked about in the introduction to this chapter.

On 1975−1977 CVCC Civics, one size feeler gauge blade is used to check both the intake, auxiliary intake, and exhaust valves. For all other models, two different size feeler gauge blades are required, one to check the intake valves and another, larger size, to check the exhaust valves.

See TABLE 4-1 and get out the feeler gauge blade or blades

Table 4-1 Feeler Gauge Blade Size

Model and Year	*Size (inches)*
Civic	
1975−1977	.006
1978−1979 (1200 model only)	.006
1978−1983	
(except 1200 model)	.006 and .008
1984−1987	.008 and .010
1988−1989	
Civic	.008 and .010
CRX HF	.006 and .008
CRX Std	.008 and .010
CRX Si	.008 and .010
1990	
Civic	.008 and .010
CRX HF	.006 and .008
CRX DX	.008 and .010
CRX Si	.008 and .010
1991	
Civic	.008 and .010
CRX DX	.008 and .010
CRX Si	.008 and .010
Accord	
1976−1978	.006 and .008
1979−1989	.006 and .011
1990−1991	.010 and .012
Prelude	
1979−1987	.006 and .011
1988−1991	.006 and .011
Twin-cam models	.004 and .007

needed for your particular model. Fold the remaining blades back into the handle of the tool. Just in case you find these decimal numbers confusing, the .004-inch blade is thinner than the .007-inch blade. The .008-inch blade is thinner than the .010-inch blade. And the .010-inch blade is thinner than the .012-inch blade. That's not too difficult.

Check the adjustment of the valves in valve group No. 1

As shown in FIG 4-15, check the adjustment of all the valves in valve group No. 1. If two different size feeler gauge blades are required for your motor, the one thing you absolutely must remember is to use the smaller size feeler gauge blade to check the intake valves and the larger size feeler gauge blade to check the exhaust valves. If your motor also has auxiliary intake valves, check these valves using the same small blade used to check the intake valves.

Go ahead and actually check the space between the rocker arms and valve springs of the valves in valve group No. 1 as shown in the illustration of your model in FIG. 4-15. On 1988–1991 fuel-injected Preludes, you'll be checking the space between the rocker arms and cam lobes of the valves in valve group No. 1.

Caution! Remember to use only the smaller size feeler gauge blade on the intake valves and the larger size feeler gauge blade on exhaust valves. Failure to do this will result in big motor trouble.

If you found all the valves in valve group No. 1 to be in adjustment, proceed to STEP 6. If you found any valves in valve group No. 1 to be out of adjustment, proceed to STEP 5 and adjust only the valves that are out of adjustment in valve group No 1. That's it! You can only work with the valves in valve group No. 1 at this time. After completing STEP 5, you'll turn the motor again and check and adjust the next group of valves.

When checking valve adjustment, accuracy is the key. If a valve feels even the slightest bit out of adjustment, don't leave it that way and figure you'll get at it next time.

STEP 5
How to adjust the valves

Follow this step to adjust only the valves you found to be out of adjustment in STEP 4.

Loosen the adjusting screw holding nut

With a 10-millimeter or 12-millimeter open or box-end wrench, loosen the adjusting screw holding nut shown in FIG. 4-20. Turn it about two full turns counterclockwise. Turn the adjusting screw with a screwdriver to adjust the valve. Turning the adjusting screw counterclockwise makes the adjustment looser.

Check the space between the rocker arm and the valve spring

The valve is in adjustment when the feeler gauge blade (the same one you used for checking the adjustment) makes light contact with both the rocker arm and the top of the valve spring as it is slipped between them. On 1988–1991 fuel-injected Preludes, the feeler gauge will make light contact with the rocker arm and cam lobe for the valve to be in correct adjustment.

Fig. 4-20
Loosen the adjusting screw holding nut and turn the adjusting screw to adjust the valve.

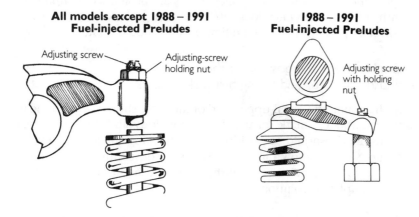

All models except 1988 – 1991 Fuel-injected Preludes

Adjusting screw

Adjusting-screw holding nut

1988 – 1991 Fuel-injected Preludes

Adjusting screw with holding nut

Retighten the adjusting screw holding nut

Hold the adjusting screw with the screwdriver and tighten the holding nut to secure the adjustment. When the valve is in correct adjustment, hold the adjusting screw with the screwdriver and don't allow it to turn while you retighten the adjusting-screw holding nut securely. Recheck the adjustment. If the adjustment has changed, repeat.

Caution! Adjust only those valves you found to be out of adjustment in STEP 4. Remember: On motors that require two different-sized feeler gauge blades, the smaller-size blade is used for the intake and auxiliary intake valves and the larger size blade is used for the exhaust valves.

STEP 6
How to close, check, and adjust valve group No. 3

Valve group No. 3 is the next group of valves you will check and adjust. This group of valves automatically closes next when you continue to turn the motor counterclockwise.

Turn the motor

Turn the motor a little less than a half turn counterclockwise with the wrench assembly. Then, turn a little more until the metal end of the rotor is pointing to your 3 mark on the distributor and the timing belt pulley marks are positioned for checking and adjusting valve group No. 3 (shown in FIG. 4-15).

I want to remind you never to turn the motor clockwise, because this could damage the motor. Should you turn too far and pass the spot where the timing belt pulley marks are positioned, continue to turn the motor counterclockwise until you get a second chance to correctly position marks. One time around should do it.

Double check the position of the distributor rotor and timing belt pulley marks

At this point, the metal-tipped end of the rotor should be pointing to your number 3 mark on the distributor body and the timing belt pulley marks should be positioned for checking and adjusting valve group No. 3 as shown in FIG. 4-15. If it's not, continue turning the motor counterclockwise until they align. It might take as much as one complete revolution.

Check the space between the rocker arms and valve springs

You're now ready to check the adjustment of the valves in valve group No. 3 as shown in FIG. 4-15. If two different size feeler gauge blades are required for your motor, the one thing you absolutely must remember is to use the smaller feeler gauge blade to check the intake valves and the larger feeler gauge blade to check the exhaust valves. If your motor has auxiliary intake valves, use the same small blade used to check the intake valves.

Check the space between the rocker arms and valve springs of the valves as shown in the illustration of your model in FIG. 4-15. If you find any of the valves in this group to be out of adjustment, see STEP 5 for adjustment procedures. If you find all the valves in this group to be in adjustment, proceed to STEP 7.

Caution! Remember to use only the smaller feeler gauge blade on the intake valves and the larger feeler gauge blade on the exhaust valves. Failure to do this will result in big motor trouble.

STEP 7
How to close, check, and adjust valve group No. 4

The next group of valves you will check and adjust is valve group No. 4. This group of valves automatically closes next when you continue to turn the motor counterclockwise.

Turn the motor

Turn the motor a little less than half a turn counterclockwise with the wrench assembly. Then, turn a little more until the metal end of the rotor is pointing to your 4 mark on the distributor and the timing belt pulley marks are positioned for checking and adjusting valve group 4 (shown in FIG. 4-15).

I want to remind you to never turn the motor clockwise because this could damage the motor. Should you turn too far and pass the spot where the timing belt pulley marks are positioned, continue to turn the motor counterclockwise until you get a second chance to correctly position the marks. One time around should do it.

Double check the position of the distributor rotor and timing belt pulley marks

Double check the position of the distributor rotor and timing belt pulley mark(s). At this point, the metal-tipped end of the rotor should be pointing to the number 4 mark on the distributor body and the timing belt pulley marks should be positioned for checking and adjusting valve group No. 4 as shown in FIG. 4-15. If they are not positioned correctly, continue turning the motor counterclockwise until they are aligned.

Check the space between the rocker arms and valve springs

You're now ready to check the adjustment of the valves in valve group No. 4 shown in FIG. 4-15. If two different-size feeler gauge blades are required for your motor, the one thing you absolutely must remember is to use the smaller feeler gauge blade to check the intake valves and the larger feeler gauge blade to check the exhaust valves. If your motor has auxiliary intake valves, use the same small blade to check the intake valves.

As shown in the illustration of your model in FIG. 4-15, check the space between the rocker arms and valve springs of the valves in valve group No. 4 only. If any of the valves in this group are out of adjustment, adjust them at this time. If you find all the valves in this group to be in adjustment, proceed to STEP 7.

Caution! Remember to use only the smaller feeler gauge blade on the intake valves and the larger feeler gauge blade on the exhaust valves. Failure to do this will result in big motor trouble.

STEP 8
How to close, check, and adjust valve group No. 2

The next, and last, group of valves you will check and adjust is valve group No. 2. This group of valves automatically closes next when you continue to turn the motor counterclockwise.

Turn the motor

Turn the motor a little less than half a turn counterclockwise with the wrench assembly. Then, turn a little more until the metal end of the rotor is pointing to your 2 mark on the distributor and the timing belt pulley marks are positioned for checking and adjusting valve group No. 3 (shown in FIG. 4-15).

I want to remind you once again never to turn the motor clockwise because this could damage the motor. Should you turn too far and pass the spot where the timing belt pulley marks are positioned, continue to turn the motor counterclockwise until you get a second chance to correctly position the marks. One time around should do it.

Double check the position of the rotor and timing belt pulley

Double check the position of the distributor rotor and timing belt pulley indicator and grooves. At this point, the metal-tipped end of the rotor should be pointing to the number 2 mark on the distributor body and the timing belt pulley marks should be positioned for checking and adjusting valve group No. 2 as shown in FIG. 4-15. If they are not positioned correctly, continue turning the motor counterclockwise until they are aligned.

Check the adjustment of valve group No. 2

Check the adjustment of the valves in valve group No. 2 as shown in FIG. 4-15. If two different size feeler gauge blades are required for your motor, use the smaller feeler gauge blade to check the intake valves and the larger feeler gauge blade to check the exhaust valves.

If your motor has auxiliary intake valves, use the same small blade used to check the intake valves.

As shown in the illustration of your model in FIG. 4-15, check the space between the rocker arms and valve springs of the valves in valve group No. 2 only. If any of the valves in this group are out of adjustment, adjust them at this time. If you find all the valves in this group to be in adjustment, proceed to STEP 9.

Caution! Remember to use only the smaller size feeler gauge blade on the intake valves and the larger size feeler gauge blade on the exhaust valves. Failure to do this will result in big motor trouble.

STEP 9
How to reassemble the motor

Check the condition of the valve cover gasket

The valve cover gasket is the black gasket that fits between the valve cover and the motor (the valve cover gasket is located in the valve cover). Never run the motor without a valve cover gasket. The valve cover gasket should not be excessively worn or torn. If it is, replace it with a new one.

To replace a valve cover gasket, first remove all traces of the old gasket. This might involve scraping off parts of the old gasket with a sharp knife. Next, coat the side that will contact the motor with clean motor oil to ensure a tight seal. There is no need to use gasket cement.

Put the valve cover back into place. As you put the valve cover back onto the motor, make sure the valve cover gasket does not slip free from the valve cover. Once the valve cover is in place, check around the entire perimeter of the valve cover to ensure the valve cover gasket is correctly in place.

Put the washers back

Put the washers into place on top of the valve cover and push them down until their rubber bottoms fit into the holes provided for them in the valve cover.

Mount parts back onto the valve cover

Loosely mount all removed parts back onto the valve cover—any brackets, holders, hoses, or wires attached to the top of the valve cover. Refer to the illustration of your particular model. Finger-tighten the nuts and bolts that hold these parts in place. Use pliers to slide holding clips into place for hoses. Don't overtighten the nuts that hold the valve cover in place, it will crack the valve cover. The next procedure explains what to do.

Tighten the cap nuts

Tighten the cap nuts alternately, a little at a time. With the 10-millimeter socket wrench, extension bar, and ratchet wrench, turn each cap nut a little at a time until each is evenly snugged down—tightened enough so that it will not loosen with engine vibration. This allows the valve cover to settle evenly onto the engine. Don't overtighten the cap nuts because you can easily crack the valve cover.

On 1988–1991 fuel-injected Preludes, valve cover mounting nuts are also positioned around the perimeter of the valve cover. Start with the nuts at the middle and crisscross back and forth across the valve cover, working your way out to the ends of the valve cover. The idea is to move the tension from the center of the valve cover to the ends, rather than from the ends of the valve cover to the center, which might crack it.

Tighten all remaining bolts and nuts used to mount brackets and holders to the valve cover. As with the valve cover mounting nuts, do not overtighten nuts and bolts.

Replace the distributor cap

Put the distributor cap back into place on top of the distributor and reattach the holding clips or tighten the mounting screws, whichever method is used to keep the cap in place. If you can't get the holding clips back into place with your fingers, use a pair of pliers.

Reconnect the spark plug wires

On the models shown in FIG 4-16, spark plug wires were removed from the spark plugs before the valve cover was removed. Be sure to reconnect each wire in the order it was removed. The motor will not run if the spark plug wires are out of order.

That's it, you're done! Congratulations, you have just saved yourself some real dollars and completed a sophisticated mechanical procedure. Your Honda should run smoother, stronger, and get better mileage with the valves in adjustment.

Troubleshooting

If the motor doesn't run as well as it did before you began this chapter, you might have goofed. Ask yourself the following questions:

○ Does the motor start but run poorly? If yes, ensure that no wires were pulled free from the distributor cap or spark plugs when you removed the distributor cap. Also, make sure hose A has been reconnected to the valve cover. See FIGS. 4-3, 4-4, 4-5, or 4-6, whichever illustrates how to remove the valve cover from your motor.

○ While the motor is idling, do you hear a rather loud tick . . . tick . . . tick sound? If yes, this indicates one (or more) of the valves you adjusted is too loose. Redo this chapter and find the one (or more) valves that are too loose and correctly adjust them.

○ While checking the valve adjustment, I find no space between a rocker arm and valve spring (or, as in the case of 1988–1991 fuel-injected Preludes, between the rocker arm and cam)? If yes, it is possible that the corresponding valve is burnt. This is because when the space between the rocker arm and the valve spring (rocker arm and cam on 1990–1991 twin-cam Prelude) becomes extremely out of adjustment and too tight, the rocker arm presses on the valve spring and holds the valve open when it should be closed. A valve that remains open during the explosion of the fuel in the cylinder will become burnt around the edges.

If the motor continues to lack power after completing the other tune-up chapters in this manual, consult a professional mechanic. One or more valves might be burnt.

The second time around

This section is a condensed version of this chapter to speed you through your next tune-up. Do not attempt to adjust the valves on your Honda unless the motor is completely cold.

Tools

☐ ratchet wrench
☐ 10-millimeter socket wrench
☐ 17 or 19-millimeter socket wrench
☐ 3-inch extension bar with $3/8$-inch drive
☐ 12-millimeter open or box-end wrench
☐ feeler gauge
☐ medium-size screwdriver
☐ bright marker

Procedure

There are nine steps to adjusting valves:

1. Remove the valve cover.

2. Mark and correctly number the distributor to reflect the position of the spark plug wire terminals in the distributor cap. Locate the timing belt pulley mark(s) for your particular model in FIG. 4-15. Remove the distributor cap if you have not yet done so.

3. Turn the motor and position the rotor and timing belt pulley marks(s) so that the valves in valve group No. 1 will be closed. See FIG. 4-15.

4. Check the valve adjustment of the valves in valve group No. 1 only. See TABLE 4-1 for the correct feeler gauge blade(s). If two blades are used, the larger blade is used on the exhaust valve and the smaller blade on the intake valves, including auxiliary intake valves.

5. Adjust the valves in need of adjustment in valve group No. 1 only.

6. Turn the motor and close valve group No. 3, and check and adjust these valves.

7. Turn the motor and close valve group No. 4, and check and adjust these valves.

8. Turn the motor and close valve group No. 2, and check and adjust these valves.

9. Reassemble the motor.

CHAPTER 5

Carburetors & fuel injection

Approximate Completion
Times: 20 minutes or less.
Listed with each procedure.

*A*ll Hondas through 1984 are equipped with carburetors. The CRX Si and Accord SEi 1985 models are fuel injected—all other models have carburetors. The 1986 and 1987 fuel-injected models are the CRX Si, Accord SEi, and the Prelude Si—all others are carbureted.

Beginning in 1988 and continuing through 1989, every model became fuel injected except the Accord DX/LX and the non-Si Prelude. By 1990, all models became fuel injected except the non-Si Prelude. All 1991 models are equipped with fuel injection.

Some models are not covered in this chapter, such as fuel-injected models and some 1980 and newer carbureted models. These Hondas were left out for a variety of reasons. Let me explain about the fuel-injected models first.

The majority of fuel-injected models rely on an onboard computer to control the fuel-injection system, making adjustment rarely necessary. Shop manuals recommend not adjusting the system unless a problem is obvious. In addition, adjusting the fuel-injection system requires expensive specialty tools. Although fuel-injected Hondas are not covered in this chapter, I have included procedures to help you determine if adjustment is necessary.

The reason why various carbureted models are not covered is because, beginning in 1980, many carbureted models became either computer controlled or required special propane gas equipment to adjust. The cost of this equipment is too expensive to be a worthwhile investment for home use. In addition, most 1980 and newer carbureted models require that the carburetor be completely removed from the motor in order to access the mixture adjusting screw. Definitely a job for a professional.

Fortunately, these particular carbureted models rarely require adjustment because of their onboard computer system. You'll find many 1980–1990 carbureted models covered in this chapter. If your model is not included, however, there are still procedures to help you determine if adjustment is necessary.

When to make adjustments

The carburetor is normally adjusted as the last phase of a tune-up. Replacing worn spark plugs and ignition parts, adjusting the valves, and setting the ignition timing change a motor's fuel requirements. Therefore, a compatible fuel system adjustment is needed following the completion of these procedures. For this reason, it's best to complete this chapter as the last phase of your tune-up.

If your motor is running poorly and you believe the carburetor is the cause, it's okay to adjust the carburetor right now. After completing the other phases of your tune-up, return to this chapter and again complete the adjustment procedures.

Danger! If you have a medical condition that makes it particularly dangerous for you to receive an electrical shock, be careful not to touch any under-hood wires or objects while running the motor in this chapter. Although the chance of receiving an electrical shock is extremely small, it pays to be careful.

Before you start

Reading this section is completely optional. If you have the time, do take a few minutes and find about the "how" and "why" of the things you'll be doing in this chapter.

The carburetor mixes air from the atmosphere with gas from the fuel tank (FIG. 5-1). It then delivers this mixture to the motor. Inside the motor, this air/gas mixture is pressurized and, as shown in FIG. 3-1 of chapter 3, ignited by the spark plugs.

To ensure maximum motor efficiency, power, and good gas mileage, the mixture of air and gasoline entering the motor must be combined in the correct proportions. The ideal mixture is 14.7 parts of air to 1 part gasoline. No problem here, you won't have to measure this mixture!

If there is an excess of gas in the air/gas mixture, the carburetor is running too rich. This causes gas to be wasted and the motor not to run up to par. If there is an excess of air in the mixture, the carburetor is running too lean. A very lean mixture can burn hot enough to severely damage a motor.

A screw sticking out from the side of the carburetor, known as the air/gas adjusting screw, is used to adjust the mixture. Carburetor

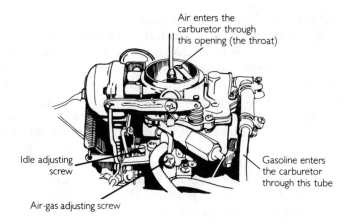

Air enters the carburetor through this opening (the throat)

Idle adjusting screw

Gasoline enters the carburetor through this tube

Air-gas adjusting screw

Fig. 5-1
The not-so-mysterious carburetor.

adjusting is simple and logical, so forget any of those unfounded rumors you might have heard about the "mysterious" carburetor.

What is the difference between carburetion and fuel injection? The major difference between carburetion and fuel injection is that fuel injection injects gas into the motor in proportion to the volume of air being drawn in. Injecting a precisely metered amount of gas permits a fuel-injected motor to closely maintain a 14.7 to 1 fuel ratio in a variety of driving situations.

A carburetor is not as sophisticated and relies completely on the internal vacuum of the motor to suck in both fuel and air. For this reason, a carburetor is unable to fully respond to varied driving conditions and thus, a ratio of 14.7 to 1 is merely an average of the many mixtures that occur throughout a typical driving day. On newer carbureted models, a computer-controlled carburetor, known as a *feedback* carburetor takes the place of the traditional carburetor. A computer-controlled carburetor runs much closer to a 14.7 to 1 ratio.

Fuel-injected Hondas and those with feedback carburetors that adhere closely to a 14.7 to 1 mixture get excellent gas mileage and have more power. And because they are more efficient, they produce less smog than traditionally carbureted models. Being under control of the computer also means these systems rarely require adjusting.

Carburetors and fuel-injection systems also control the idle speed. In addition to controlling the air/gas mixture entering the motor, the carburetor or fuel-injection system also controls the speed of the motor when the driver's foot is not pressing on the accelerator. The speed of the motor when it's running by itself is known as the *idle speed*.

If your motor idles too slow, it might feel as though it is going to stop running each time you approach a red light. Too low an idle speed might also make your Honda feel rough and bumpy at a stop.

In contrast to a low idle speed, a high idle speed will cause an automatic transmission Honda to creep forward at red lights unless the brake is firmly applied. On manual transmission models, a high idle speed is easily recognized because the motor will be racing.

The speed of the motor is figured in revolutions per minute (RPM), which is the number of complete revolutions the motor makes in one minute. If you counted the number of times you spun in a circle for one minute, besides being dizzy, you would know your RPM. A tachometer counts RPM and is a useful tool for adjusting idle speed. The idle speed is adjusted by turning the idle adjusting screw, which is discussed later in the chapter.

Spray cleaning the carburetor and a quick check of the carburetor choke valve is advisable. A strong spray of carburetor cleaner down the throat of a carburetor washes away built-up black soot. The change this simple procedure can make in a motor is often incredible. I have seen a number of carburetors that would not go into adjustment until a shot of carburetor cleaner was applied.

While spray cleaning the carburetor, you'll see the choke valve right at the top of the carburetor. This valve cuts off a portion of the air entering the carburetor when a motor is cold. The result is a very rich (gas-heavy) mixture that a motor needs when it is cold. Once a motor warms up, it needs a far leaner (less gas and more air) mixture to run efficiently and well.

In this chapter, you'll also check the choke valve to ensure it opens and allows air to flow freely into the carburetor. A nonoperable choke valve, or one that is out of adjustment, can cause hard starting, poor gas mileage, and a tremendous loss of motor power.

What's ahead in this chapter

This chapter is divided into four separate procedures, as opposed to a sequence of steps. The reason for this layout is because each procedure in this chapter can be completed on an individual basis, unlike a series of steps that are all completed during one work session. The four procedures are:

1. How to check the choke valve on all Hondas equipped with a carburetor.

2. How to spray-clean the carburetor.

3. How to check and adjust the idle speed.

4. How to adjust the air/gas mixture.

Tools

Figure 5-2 illustrates the tools you'll use in this chapter. For a more complete description of these tools, see chapter 7. You will need:

Fig. 5-2
The tools used in this chapter.

Screwdriver

- [ ] screwdriver. A medium-size screwdriver will work fine for all covered models except 1975–1979 Preludes, Accords, and CVCC Civics. These models require a screwdriver with a combined handle and blade length not to exceed 5 inches.

- [ ] tachometer (optional). The unit pictured in FIG. 5-2 is a combination tach-dwell meter. When using a combination meter, be certain the selector switch is in the "tach" position when checking RPM.

Tachometer

- [ ] spray-type carburetor cleaner (optional). **Caution!** All 1986 and newer carbureted models must be spray cleaned with O2 Sensor Safe carburetor spray. Using regular spray will damage the O2 sensor and may harm the computer system controlling the carburetor. Be sure the carburetor spray you purchase states clearly on the can that it is O2 sensor safe.

Note: For 1990–1991 Accords and 1988–1991 Civics, in order to connect a tachometer to your motor, your meter must have an inductive pick-up. An inductive pick-up allows you to connect your meter by simply clipping a lead on to a spark plug wire as opposed to connecting it to the coil, which is not accessible on your model.

Carburetor cleaner

How to check the choke valve on all carbureted Hondas

This procedure takes about 15 minutes to complete and covers all carbureted models except 1983 and newer-carbureted Preludes. On these model, you cannot see the choke valve.

Caution! Firmly apply the parking brake. A manual transmission must be in neutral. An automatic transmission must be in park.

The choke valve restricts the flow of air to the carburetor. This is very important when the engine is cold because a decrease in the flow of air to the carburetor causes the fuel mixture to become very rich. It is this rich (gas-laden) mixture that is essential for easy starts when the engine is cold. It is equally important, however, for the choke valve to cease restricting the flow of air once the engine has warmed up. In its straight up and down position, the choke valve is not obstructing the throat of the carburetor and, therefore, does not decrease the amount of air entering the carburetor. If the choke valve does not assume the straight up and down position once the engine has warmed up, the fuel mixture will be greatly out of balance and the choke valve must be adjusted.

Warm up the motor

Warm up the motor until the temperature gauge reaches normal operating temperature. If your Honda has an automatic choke—does not have a choke control knob on the dashboard—depress the accelerator pedal periodically during the warm-up period until you hear the motor slow down to its normal idle speed.

If your Honda has a manually controlled choke, warm up the motor and then push the control knob all the way to the dashboard to disengage the choke valve. Figure 5-4 explains the purpose of the choke valve and the necessity for checking it.

On models with an automatic choke, it's important to depress the accelerator pedal during warm-up. The action of the accelerator pedal combined with the heat from the motor disengages the automatic choke valve on many models. Because you will be checking if the choke valve disengages, you definitely want to follow this warm-up routine.

Remove the top from the air filter box

Stop the motor, open the hood, and stand on the driver's side of your Honda. Big as day, you'll see a large, round object with a long snout sticking out from it. This is the air filter box (see FIG. 5-3). It is mounted on top of the carburetor. The choke valve is inside the carburetor, which can be seen after removing the top of the air filter box.

To disassemble, remove the wing nut and wing nut washer by hand. Turn the wing nut counterclockwise. The wing nut washer might be glued into place. If so, leave it alone, and it will come off with the top of the air filter box. If there are holding clips, flip up the levers on the holding clips and then remove the top of the air filter box.

To reassemble, put the top of the air filter box back into place, and replace the wing nut washer and the wing nut. Turn the wing nut clockwise and tighten by hand. If there are holding clips, reattach the holding clips to the top of the air filter box and push down on the levers to secure the clips.

Locate the choke valve

Using FIG. 5-4 as a guide, look down the throat of the carburetor and locate the choke valve. This valve is really just a flap of metal that

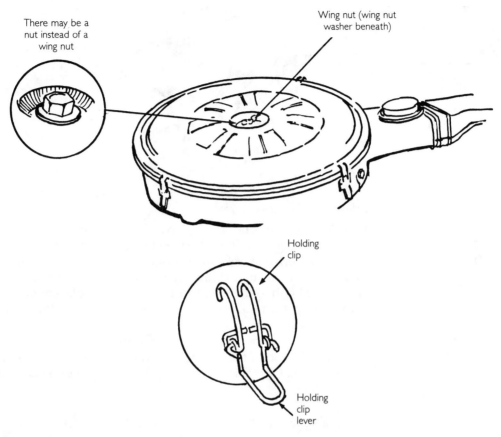

There may be a
nut instead of a
wing nut

Wing nut (wing nut
washer beneath)

Holding
clip

Holding
clip
lever

swings over to cover one side of the carburetor when the motor is cold. To see how the automatic choke valve covers the throat of the carburetor, touch the top of the choke valve with your finger and move it. On models with a manually controlled choke, pull the choke knob out an inch or two to see the choke valve move. Note that on some models, a screen covers the throat of the carburetor. This screen makes it a bit difficult to see the choke valve clearly. Use a flashlight if the car is not in bright light.

With the motor running, the choke valve should be vertical, as shown in FIG. 5-4.

If your Honda has an automatic choke (no control knob on the dashboard) and the choke valve is not in a straight up-and-down position, be sure you have warmed up the motor as explained earlier. If it's still not straight up and down, it needs adjustment. Manually controlled chokes must have the control knob pushed to the dashboard during testing. If the choke valve is not in a vertical position, adjustment is needed.

Fig. 5-3
Removing the top from the air filter box on carbureted models.

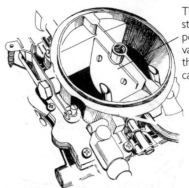

The choke valve in a straight up-and-down position. The choke valve is located inside the throat of the carburetor.

Adjusting the choke valve

Adjusting an automatic choke valve is an easy operation, but so many factors enter into the adjustment that you are better off having a qualified mechanic make the adjustment. You can adjust a manual choke yourself. To adjust a manual choke, turn off the motor. Push the control knob to the dashboard. Follow the choke control cable to the carburetor until you reach the screws that hold it in place. Loosen these screws. Hold the choke valve in the vertical position and tighten the screws. That's all there is to it!

Leave the top of the air filter box off if you plan to spray clean the carburetor. Otherwise, see FIG. 5-3 for instructions to reassemble the air filter box.

How to spray clean the carburetor

This procedure takes about 15 minutes to complete. You'll need an assistant to sit inside the car during this procedure while you "play" with the carburetor. All carbureted models are covered in this procedure. **Caution!** All 1986 and newer carbureted models must be spray cleaned with "O2 Sensor Safe" carburetor spray. Using a carburetor spray not designated O2 sensor safe will damage the O2 sensor and might harm the computer system controlling the carburetor.

Warm up the motor

If you haven't done so, warm up the motor until the temperature gauge reaches normal operating temperature. If your Honda has an automatic choke—does not have a choke control knob on the dashboard—depress the accelerator pedal periodically during the warm-up period until you hear the motor slow down to its normal idle speed.

If your Honda has a manually controlled choke, warm up the motor and then push the control knob all the way to the dashboard to disengage the choke valve. Have your friend sit in the car and race the motor while you spray the cleaner. With the motor warmed up and the top of the air filter box removed, have a friend start the motor while you stand to one side—not in front—of your Honda.

About 30 seconds of spraying the carburetor should do it. Spray the carburetor cleaner directly into the carburetor. Wash black carbon deposits from the walls and get into all those little corners and accessible parts. The motor will attempt to stop running as you spray. Have your friend in the car work the accelerator pedal to keep the motor running. If the motor stops, you stop. Continue spraying after your friend restarts the motor. Figure 5-3 illustrates how to reassemble the air filter box.

Caution! Do not get your face over the top of the carburetor. The motor can blow the cleaner right back out through the top of the carburetor.

How to check and adjust the idle speed

This procedure takes about 20 minutes and covers 1976–1985 carbureted Accords, 1975–1985 carbureted Civics (CVCC and non-CVCC), and 1979–1990 carbureted Preludes. If your model is not covered here, as I mentioned at the start of the chapter, it is because it is computer-controlled and requires expensive equipment to adjust. Also, some carbureted models and all fuel-injected models are not covered. If you do own a model for which adjustment is not covered, you can, however, learn if adjustment is needed.

For instructions on how to determine if adjustment is necessary, see the subhead "Checking and adjusting the idle speed with a tachometer," or "Checking and adjusting the idle speed without a tachometer." Should you determine adjustment is necessary, have a licensed smog station make the actual adjustment.

What to do if you just turned
here from the middle of chapter 3

If you're adjusting the idle speed to complete chapter 3, and adjustment procedures for your model are not included, there are some things you can do, even if adjustment is needed. First, determine if adjustment is needed. To do this, warm up the motor as explained in the following section and then check the idle speed under the subhead "Checking and adjusting the idle speed with a tachometer," or "Checking and adjusting the idle speed without a tachometer."

If you find the idle speed is too high, turn on the headlamps. This should lower the idle speed considerably. Next, turn on the defroster, the windshield wipers, etc. As each accessory is turned on, a larger load will be placed on the alternator. This will, in turn, slow down the motor as it begins to work harder.

Turning on the right combination of accessories will get you the idle speed you need for checking and adjusting the timing. Turning on the air conditioning will not slow down the motor because there is a system that compensates for the air conditioner and maintains a constant idle speed.

If the idle speed is too low, I don't know of any such way to raise the idle speed. You'll probably find it will increase once the timing is set correctly. Set the timing and recheck the idle speed and chances are, it will be right on the money.

Checking and adjusting the idle speed with a tachometer

If you're not using a tachometer, skip to the next section on page 188.

Connect the tachometer to the motor

A tachometer is connected to the motor exactly like a dwell meter. To connect your tachometer, see chapter 2, page 47. "How to adjust

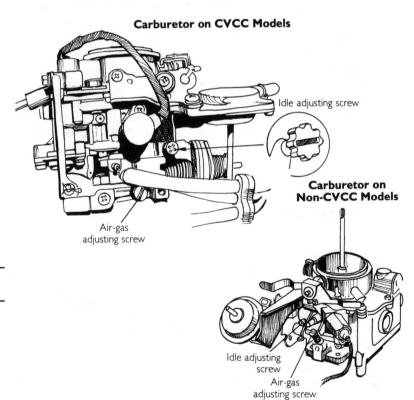

Carburetor on CVCC Models

Idle adjusting screw

Air-gas adjusting screw

Carburetor on Non-CVCC Models

Idle adjusting screw

Air-gas adjusting screw

Fig. 5-5
Honda carburetors.

the points with a dwell meter.'' Connect your tachometer to the motor as if it were a dwell meter and then turn back to this chapter.

Special note: If you own a 1990−1991 Accord or 1988−1991 Civic, I hope you read the blurb in the tool section of this chapter about getting a tachometer with an inductive pick-up. You need an inductive pick-up to connect a tachometer to your model.

Warm up the motor

If you haven't done so, warm up the motor until the temperature gauge reaches normal operating temperature. If your Honda has an

Twin Carburetors on 1983 − 1990 Prelude

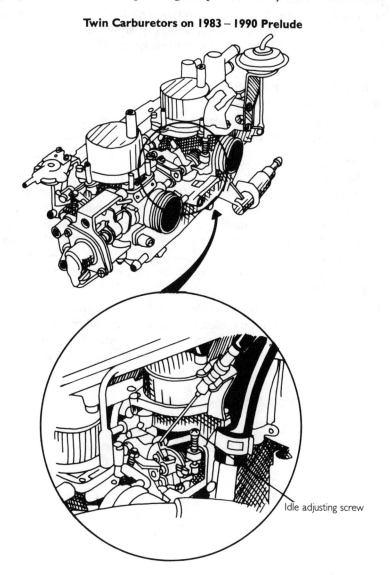

Idle adjusting screw

Fig. 5-5
Continued.

automatic choke—does not have a choke control knob on the dashboard—depress the accelerator pedal periodically during the warm-up period until you hear the motor slow down to its normal idle speed. For a manually controlled choke, warm up the motor and then push the control knob all the way to the dashboard to disengage the choke valve.

Locate the idle speed adjusting screw

Turn off the motor. See FIG. 5-5 and select the illustration that covers your model. Locate the idle adjusting screw in the illustration and on your carburetor. For CVCC carbureted models, the idle adjusting screw might be fitted with the plastic cap shown in the encircled illustration. In this case, you can turn it by hand or with a screwdriver.

Getting the motor ready for
an accurate idle speed reading

The following must be completed with the motor not running. The motor is restarted when it is time to check the idle speed.

1. See the Idle Speed Chart in TABLE 5-1 and find the posted idle speed for your motor. Depending on your model Honda, various electrical accessories must be either on or off while checking and adjusting the idle speed. Also, some models with an automatic transmission are to have the gear selector in a specified gear. Before checking the idle speed, see "Getting ready to check the idle speed with a tachometer" further in the chapter. Follow the preparation instructions listed in TABLE 5-1 that pertain to your particular model.

Fig. 5-6
The fan leads and how to disconnect them.

2. All 1975–1979 non-CVCC Civics and every Honda 1980, 1981, and 1985, turn off the radiator cooling fan and all other electrical accessories. To temporarily disable the cooling fan, disconnect the fan leads shown in FIG. 5-6. To disconnect the fan leads, sepa-

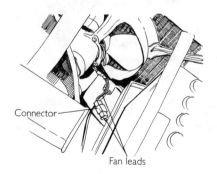

Connector

Fan leads

Table 5-1 ʼIdle Speeds

Year	Model	RPM
	Civic (non-CVCC)	
1975−1978	Manual transmission	750−850
	Automatic transmission	700−800
	(in first gear)	
1979	Manual transmission	650−750
	Automatic transmission	650−750
	(in first gear)	
	Civic (CVCC)	
1975−78	Manual transmission	800−900
	Automatic transmission	700−800
	(in second gear)	
1979	Manual transmission	650−750
	Automatic transmission	600−700
	(in second gear)	
	All Civics	
1980	Manual transmission	700−800
	Automatic transmission	700−800
1981	Manual transmission	700−800
	Automatic transmission	700−800
1982−1985	Automatic transmission	650−750
	Manual transmission	650−750
1986−1987	Except CRX Si, automatic transmission	650−750
	Manual transmission	650−750
	CRX Si manual transmission	700−800
1988	Except CRX HF, manual transmission	700−800
	Automatic transmission	700−800
	CRX HF manual transmission	600−700
	Automatic transmission	700−800
	California and high-altitude only	600−700
1989−1991	Civic (wagon)	700−800
	CRX	700−800
	CRX HF	550−650
	CRX Si	700−800
	California and high-altitude only	600−700
	Accord	
1976−78	Manual transmission	800−900
	Automatic transmission	700−800
	(in second gear)	
1979	Manual transmission	650−750
	Automatic transmission	650−750
	(in second gear)	
1980−1982	Manual transmission	750−850
	Automatic transmission	750−850
1983−1984	Manual transmission	700−800
	Automatic transmission	650−750

Table 5-1 Continued.			
1985–1987	Except LXi manual transmission	700–800
	Automatic transmission	650–750
	LXi manual transmission	700–800
	Automatic transmission	700–800
1988	Except LXi manual transmission	800–850
	Automatic transmission	700–800
	LXi manual transmission	750–800
	Automatic transmission	750–800
1989	All Accords, manual transmission	750–850
	Automatic transmission	680–780
1990–1991	All Accords, manual and auto transmission	700–800

Prelude

1979	Manual transmission	650–750
	Automatic transmission (in second gear)	650–750
1980–1981	Manual transmission	750–850
	Automatic transmission	750–850
1982	Manual transmission	700–800
	Automatic transmission	700–800
1983	Manual transmission	750–850
	Automatic transmission	700–800
1984–1985	Manual transmission	750–850
	Automatic transmission	750–850
1986–1987	Except Si, manual transmission	750–850
	Automatic transmission	750–850
	Si manual transmission	700–800
	Automatic transmission	700–800
1988	Except Si, manual transmission	800–850
	Automatic transmission	750–800
	Si manual transmission	750–800
	Automatic transmission	750–800
1989	Low-altitude manual and auto transmission	700–800
	High-altitude manual transmission	750–850
	Automatic transmission	700–800
1990–1991	All Preludes, Manual transmission	700–800
	Automatic transmission	700–800

*If the tune-up decal under the hood shows different specifications than this table, use the specifications on the tune-up decal.

rate the connector into two parts. Depress the small clip and pull the unit in half. Do not pull on the fan leads! If you prefer, you can leave the fan leads connected and check and adjust the idle speed during the "off" cycles of the fan.

Caution! When you start the motor, be careful not to run it any longer than necessary with the fan leads disconnected; it will overheat.

3. On all 1975–1979 models, turn on the headlights. This is the one exception to turning off the electrical accessories. On these models, turning on the headlights puts a drag on the alternator, which, in turn, puts a small drag on the motor, slowing it down. This drag on the motor needs to be present during the adjustment procedure so that it can be compensated for in the adjustment.

4. On 1980–1985 models, remove the black vacuum tube from the air control diaphragm as illustrated in FIG. 5-7. Plug the end of the tube with something you're sure you can easily get back out again. The pointed end of a pencil works well, but break off the lead to safeguard against it breaking off in the tube and getting sucked into the motor.

5. If your car is equipped with a manual choke, push the choke control knob to the dashboard.

6. Apply the parking brake!

Reading the tachometer

Finally, you're ready to check the idle speed. Start the motor and put an automatic transmission into drive. Put a manual transmission into neutral. Set the cylinder selector knob on your tachometer to the 4-cylinder position. Set the high/low knob to the low position.

Compare the reading on the tachometer with TABLE 5-1. Remember: If your Honda is a 1982–1984 model, the radiator fan should be running while checking the idle speed.

Disconnect here

Air diaphragm tube

Fig. 5-7
Locating and disconnecting the air diaphragm tube.

If the tachometer reading is lower or higher than the posted reading, the idle speed is out of adjustment. If the idle speed is within the specified range, there's nothing more for you to do in this procedure.

Adjusting the idle speed using a tachometer

To adjust the idle speed using a tachometer:

1. Turn the idle adjusting screw clockwise to increase the motor speed and counterclockwise to lower the motor speed. On 1982–1984 models, the radiator fan should be running while adjusting the idle speed. Pause during the adjustment procedure when the fan cycle is off.

Whenever you turn any adjusting screw, count the exact number of turns you move it. If you find you accidentally turned the wrong screw or made a mistake, you can turn the screw back to its original position.

2. When the idle speed is set correctly, turn off the motor. Turn off the headlights on non-CVCC Civics. Reconnect the black vacuum tube to the air control diaphragm on 1980–1985 models. If you're planning to set the timing or adjust the carburetor air/gas mixture, leave the tachometer connected; otherwise, disconnect it. Reconnect the radiator fan leads if necessary.

If the motor is not running smoothly at the correct RPM reading, it could be an incorrect air/gas mixture or an incorrect timing adjustment. See chapter 3.

Checking and adjusting the idle speed without a tachometer

Warm up the motor

If you haven't done so, warm up the motor until the temperature gauge reaches normal operating temperature. If your Honda has an automatic choke, depress the accelerator pedal periodically during the warm-up period until you hear the motor slow down to its normal idle speed. For Hondas with a manually controlled choke, warm up the motor and then push the control knob all the way to the dashboard to disengage the choke valve.

Locate the idle speed adjusting screw

Turn off the motor. See FIG. 5-5 and select the illustration that covers your model. Locate the idle adjusting screw in the illustration and on your carburetor.

Getting the motor ready
for an accurate idle speed reading

Firmly apply the parking brake and start the motor. Turn on the headlights on all 1975–1979 non-CVCC Civics. This puts a drag on the alternator which, in turn, puts a small drag on the motor, slowing it down. This drag on the motor needs to be present during the adjustment procedure so that it can be compensated for in the adjustment.

Put an automatic transmission into drive. Hondas with a manual transmission must be in neutral. If your car has a manual choke, push the control knob to the dashboard.

Checking the idle speed using your senses

Sit in the driver's seat. How does your Honda feel? Is it rough and bumpy? Are you being shaken around in the driver's seat? Is the steering wheel vibrating in your hands? Is the shift lever flopping about? Does the motor stop running if you don't keep your foot lightly on the accelerator pedal? When the electric radiator cooling fan turns on, does this make the motor idle rough? If your Honda displays any or all of these traits, it's safe to assume the idle speed is too low.

An automatic transmission model with a motor that idles too high requires that your foot be firmly on the brake to keep the car standing still when the transmission is in gear and the parking brake is off.

A manual transmission model idles too high if, when idling in neutral, the engine sounds like it is going fast enough to move the car about 10 to 15 miles per hour if it were in first gear. If you're not sure, drive to a level place where there is no traffic and see how fast your car goes in first gear without your foot on the accelerator pedal. About three miles per hour is fine; any faster indicates that the idle is too high. To slow down the idle speed, turn the idle screw counterclockwise.

Adjusting the idle speed using your senses

To increase the idle speed, turn the idle adjusting screw clockwise and counterclockwise to decrease the idle speed. When you feel the idle speed is set correctly, turn off the motor. Remember to turn off the headlights on 1975–1979 non-CVCC Civics.

Whenever you turn any adjusting screw, count the exact number of turns you move it. If you find you accidentally turned the wrong screw or made a mistake, you can turn the screw back to its original position.

If the motor is not running smoothly at the correct RPM reading, it could be an incorrect air/gas mixture or an incorrect timing adjustment. See chapter 3.

How to adjust the air/gas mixture

This procedure takes about 20 minutes to complete. This procedure covers 1990−1991 Accords, 1975−1985 carbureted Civics (CVCC and non-CVCC), and 1975−1990 carbureted Preludes.

If your model is not covered here, as I mentioned at the start of this chapter, adjustment procedures on fuel-injected models and some 1980 and newer carbureted models are not covered. In this section, no 1980 or newer models are covered. See the introduction to this chapter for an explanation.

Although the mixture adjustment on fuel-injected models and 1980 and newer carbureted models should be made by a qualified smog station, you can determine if adjustment is needed. To do this, see chapter 1, STEP 4. If the light brown deposits mentioned in this step are found on your spark plugs, the air/gas adjustment is okay and no adjustment is necessary.

If the spark plugs are covered with black deposits, see the section "How to spray clean the carburetor" earlier in this chapter to check the operation of the choke valve on carbureted models. A stuck or out-of-adjustment choke valve can cause black deposits because it prevents the air from flowing freely into the mixture, resulting in a rich (gas-heavy) mixture.

A dirty air filter can also cause the plugs to be coated with a black deposit. This, too, is because a dirty air cleaner blocks air from flowing freely into the mixture. If you replace a dirty air cleaner as discussed in chapter 6, clean the spark plugs and drive the car for a few days. Then, recheck the spark plugs. Chances are they will look good.

Pre-1980 models

For pre-1980 models, there are three important things to do before adjusting the air/gas mixture:

1. Ensure that the choke valve is working correctly.

2. Fully assemble the air filter box as explained in FIG. 5-3.

3. Set the idle speed correctly.

    Spray cleaning the caburetor is optional, but I recommend it before adjusting the air/gas mixture.

Warm up the motor and then turn it off

Warm up the motor until the temperature gauge reaches normal operating temperature. If your Honda has an automatic choke, depress the accelerator pedal periodically during the warm-up period until you hear the motor slow down to its normal idle speed.

    A Honda with a manually operated choke valve need not be accelerated while the motor is warming up. The choke valve, however, should be in the disengaged position—choke control knob pushed to the dashboard—before proceeding to adjust the idle speed.

Locate the air/gas mixture adjusting screw

See FIG. 5-5. Using the illustration of your model as a guide, locate the air/gas adjusting screw on your carburetor. Is there a limiter cap on top of the mixture adjusting screw? If there is a limiter cap like the one shown in FIG. 5-8, remove it from the adjusting screw. The easiest way to remove it is to pry it off with a screwdriver. If you are not sure whether a limiter cap is in use, you'll find out when you turn the air/gas screw. A limiter will limit this screw to one turn.

Setting the air gas mixture with a tachometer

If you're not using a tachometer, see the section "Adjusting the air/gas mixture without a tachometer" for adjustment procedures. The

Fig. 5-8
The limiter cap.

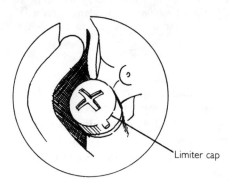

Limiter cap

following procedures will guide you through setting the idle speed with a tachometer. I'm assuming your tachometer is already connected because you should have already completed the section "How to check and adjust the idle speed." To adjust the air/gas mixture with a tachometer:

1. Apply the parking brake and start the motor.

2. Put an automatic transmission into first gear and a manual transmission into neutral.

3. Turn on the headlights. This puts a drag on the alternator, which in turn puts a small drag on the motor that slows it down. This drag on the motor needs to be present during the adjustment procedure so it can be compensated for in the adjustment.

4. For all non-CVCC Civics, make sure that the radiator cooling fan is not operating. To turn off the cooling fan, unplug the fan leads shown in FIG. 5-7. If you prefer not to disconnect the fan leads, adjust during the "off" cycles of the fan.

Caution! Do not run the motor any longer than necessary with the fan leads disconnected; it will overheat.

Making the adjustment

To adjust the air/gas mixture:

1. Place the screwdriver into the head of the air/gas adjusting screw. Keep your eyes on the tachometer and slowly turn the air/gas adjusting screw clockwise until the tachometer shows a noticeable drop in the RPM reading. If no drop in RPM occurs, see the Troubleshooting section at the end of this chapter.

Whenever you turn an adjusting screw of any kind, count the exact number of turns you moved it. Should you find you accidentally turned the wrong screw or made a mistake, you can turn the screw back to its original position.

2. After a considerable drop in the RPM reading, turn the air/gas adjusting screw in the opposite direction until the highest, steady RPM reading is reached. Repeat this procedure a second time so as not to turn the screw past the point where the highest steady RPM reading is reached. The idea is to turn the screw no further than necessary.

3. On non-CVCC Civics only, after the highest steady RPM reading is reached, use the idle speed screw to reset the idle speed as follows. This is a different setting than the one shown in TABLE 5-1.

  1975–1978 Models

| With manual transmission | 870 RPM |
| With automatic transmission | 770 RPM |

  1979 Models

| With manual transmission | 800 RPM |
| With automatic transmission | 750 RPM |

4. On CVCC Civics, Preludes, and Accords only, after the highest steady RPM reading is reached, use the idle speed screw to reset the idle speed as follows. This is a different setting than the one shown in TABLE 5-1.

  1975–1978 Models

| With manual transmission | 910 RPM |
| With automatic transmission | 800 RPM |

  1979 Civics

| With manual transmission | 730 RPM |
| With automatic transmission | 730 RPM |

  High-Altitude Models

  (except at sea level)

| With manual transmission | 910 RPM |
| With automatic transmission | 780 RPM |

  1979 Preludes and Accords

| Manual transmission | 750 RPM |
| Automatic transmission | 750 RPM |

  High-altitude models

  (except at sea level)

| With manual transmission | 880 RPM |
| With automatic transmission | 750 RPM |

5. With the idle speed set to the preceding RPM reading, turn the air/gas screw clockwise as slow as possible until the tachometer shows the following drop in the RPM reading:

  1978 Non-CVCC Civic

| Manual transmissions | 800 RPM |
| Automatic transmissions | 750 RPM |

1979 CVCC Civic
    Manual transmissions   700 RPM
    Automatic transmissions   700 RPM

1978 CVCC Civic, Prelude, and Accord
    Manual transmissions   850 RPM
    Automatic transmissions   750 RPM

1979 Civics
    Manual transmissions   700 RPM
    Automatic transmissions   650 RPM

1979 Preludes and Accords
    Manual transmissions   700 RPM
    Automatic transmissions   700 RPM

6. On all models, once the RPM drop has occurred, the air/gas mixture is correct. Turn off the motor, turn off the headlights, reconnect the fan leads, and disconnect the tachometer. That's it, you're done!

With the idle speed and air/gas mixture in adjustment, your motor will squeeze some extra mileage out of each tank of gas. Plus, you'll have peace of mind knowing you're environmentally correct. If you've already completed all the other phases of your tune-up, your Honda should be feeling like new.

Adjusting the air/gas mixture without a tachometer

To adjust the air/gas mixture without a tachometer:

O Apply the parking brake and start the motor.

O Put an automatic transmission into first gear and a manual transmission into neutral.

O Turn on the headlights. This puts a drag on the alternator, which, in turn, puts a small drag on the motor that slows it down. This drag on the motor needs to be present during the adjustment procedure.

Adjusting the air/gas mixture

To adjust the air/gas mixture:

O Slowly turn the air/gas screw clockwise until the engine begins to run rough. If there is no change in the way the motor runs, see the Troubleshooting section at the end of this chapter.

O With the motor now running rough, turn the air/gas screw counterclockwise until the engine sounds smooth.

Whenever you turn an adjusting screw of any kind, count the exact number of turns you moved it. Should you find you accidentally turned the wrong screw or made a mistake, you can turn the screw back to its original position.

○ Once again, slowly turn the air/gas screw clockwise until the engine begins to run rough, then slowly turn the air/gas screw counterclockwise again until the engine again sounds smooth. This time, use the least amount of turns possible to "smooth out" the motor. Do not turn the air/gas screw counterclockwise any further than necessary.

That's all there is to it. You've just used your ear to adjust the carburetor. Turn off the motor and the headlights. That's it, you're done! With the idle speed and air/gas mixture in adjustment, your motor will squeeze some extra mileage out of each tank of gas. Plus, you'll have peace of mind knowing you're environmentally correct. If you have already completed all the other phases of your tune-up, your Honda should be feeling like new.

Troubleshooting

Here's what to do if you goofed and your car does not run well:

1. If you have adjusted the air/gas screw and the car does not run as well as it did before the adjustment, repeat the section on the air/gas mixture adjustment. The same applies to idle adjustment.

2. If you did not see a decrease in the RPM reading while turning the air/gas screw clockwise, spray clean the carburetor as explained in the beginning of the chapter. You might also consider adding a carburetor cleaner to the gas tank. On 1986 and newer models, be sure to use only O2 sensor safe cleaner.

If doing these things doesn't decrease the RPM when turning the air/gas adjusting screw, your Honda has a carburetor problem. If the car runs well and the spark plugs aren't covered with black soot, I suggest you drive it the way it is, particularly if it will pass its smog test.

The second time around

This section is a condensed version of this chapter to speed you through your next tune-up.

Tools

☐ screwdriver—non-CVCC Civics require a medium-sized screwdriver. CVCC Civics, Preludes, and Accords require a screwdriver that has a blade and handle length of no more than 5 inches.

☐ tachometer (optional)

Procedures

1. Check the choke valve. Warm up the motor and then turn it off. Remove the top of the air filter box. Start the motor, and check that the choke valve is in the vertical position shown in FIG. 5-4.

2. Spray-clean the carburetor, keeping your face clear of the top of the carburetor. Carburetor cleaning is optional but recommended. Replace the cover to the air cleaner box.

3. Adjust the idle speed on pre-1986 models to the specifications in TABLE 5-1. The motor must be warmed up to make this adjustment.

4. Adjust the air/gas mixture on pre-1980 models. Warm up the motor. If you're not using a tachometer, adjust the air/gas screw for a smooth idle. If you're using a tachometer, turn the air/gas screw to find the highest steady idle speed, then drop the idle as specified in the text.

Periodic maintenance

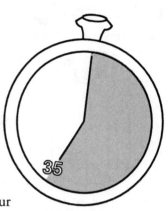

*K*eeping up with oil changes and periodic maintenance is the best thing you can do for your Honda. The simple procedures in this chapter do more to prevent costly repairs and maintain your Honda's integrity than any other chapter in this handbook.

Approximate Completion Time: 35 minutes for oil change. Maintenance procedures vary.

Before you start

Motor oil, transmission fluid, radiator coolant, brake fluid, and clutch fluid are the lifeblood of your Honda. Keeping these fluids at the required levels ensures your Honda the lubrication, cooling capacity, and hydraulic pressures it needs to operate smoothly and without suffering accelerated or excessive wear. Plus, when it comes to brakes, your safety is at stake too.

I strongly advise changing your Honda's oil and oil filter every 3,000 miles or every three months, whichever comes first. After 3,000 miles of driving, oil is already dirty, thin, and full of gases and other wastes that occur as a by-product of burning gasoline. Worn, dirty oil ruins a motor in no time.

Although your owner's manual recommends an oil change at twice this mileage or more, this is stretching things too far. Most car enthusiasts change their oil every 2,500 miles like clockwork. I do!

The maintenance section of this chapter is as important as any other chapter in this handbook. You'll find it's the simple little things that keep your Honda feeling like it did when it was new.

What's ahead in this chapter

This chapter is divided into two sections. The first section explains how to change the oil and oil filter. The next section covers periodic maintenance, including:

Fig. 6-1
Tools used to change the oil
and oil filter.

Ratchet wrench with ³/₈″ drive

17-mm
socket with ³/₈″ drive

Oil filter wrench

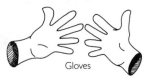

Oil drain pan

Gloves

A container for
transporting used oil

○ Checking the air filter element.

○ Checking the battery water.

○ Lubricating the chassis.

○ Checking the clutch and brake fluid.

○ Inspecting the exhaust and evaporative emission control systems.

○ Checking the fan belt(s).

○ Lubricating the doors, trunk, hood, and hood release.

○ Lubricating the locks.

○ Checking the motor oil level.

○ Inspecting the oxygen (O2) sensor.

○ Checking the power steering fluid.

○ Checking the radiator coolant.

○ Inspecting the radiator hoses.

○ Inspecting the timing belt.

○ Inspecting the tires.

○ Checking the transmission fluid.

○ Checking 4-WD rear differential fluid.

○ Other miscellaneous checks and inspection.

Tools

Figure 6-1 illustrates the tools you'll use to change the oil and oil filter. The tools for the periodic maintenance of your Honda are listed with each procedure. You will need:

☐ ratchet wrench with ³/₈-inch drive. The ³/₈-inch refers to the size of the drive peg.

☐ 17-millimeter socket with ³/₈-inch drive.

☐ oil filter wrench. Note that these come in different sizes, so when you purchase a new oil filter, purchase a wrench to fit it.

☐ oil drain pan. Anything low enough to slide under the car and collect 5 quarts of oil.

☐ gloves. The oil drain plug and filter are going to be hot. Also, the Environmental Protection Agency now tells us used motor oil can be harmful, and even cancer causing, to exposed skin.

☐ container for transporting used oil. After you drain the oil, you'll want to dump it at your local gas station or parts store that accepts used oil.

How to change the oil and oil filter

Depending on the year and model, your Honda holds between 3.2 and 3.8 quarts of oil. This includes the oil required to refill the oil filter. I suggest you purchase five quarts of oil and carry the extra in the trunk. This way, you can avoid high-priced gas station oil when you're on the road, and also stick with the same brand.

Oil is available in different thicknesses. The thickness of an oil is referred to as viscosity rating or weight (W). To select the correct weight oil for your Honda, see CHART 6-1 and find the arrow that best reflects the temperature of where you drive. Purchase oil of the weight shown on your temperature arrow. The weight of the oil is stamped on the can or bottle. If in doubt, show CHART 6-1 to the parts person where you buy your oil.

In addition to coming in various weights, oil, like everything else, is manufactured to meet different quality standards. Your Honda requires high-quality oil. Use API grade SE or SF rated oil. This rating, along with the oil weight, is stamped on the can or bottle. Don't settle for less.

Many discount parts stores do sell name brand oil filters, while others might sell only their own brand. If the off-brand oil filters are anything like the poorly made off-brand motor parts, you don't want one of these filters on your Honda.

Better oil filters have an integral bypass. Be sure the oil filter you purchase has one. In the event the oil filter becomes clogged, the by-pass allows oil to by-pass the filter and continue to flow through the motor.

Chart 6-1
Choosing the correct weight motor oil for your Honda.

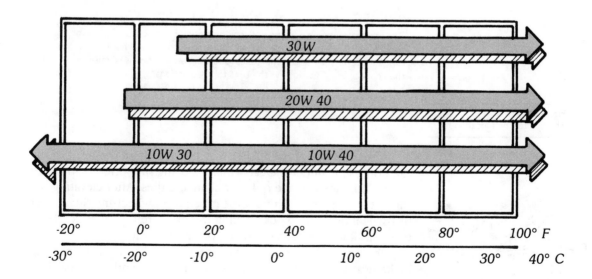

Chances are, you are not going to need a new gasket for the oil drain bolt; but just in case you do, you'll want to have a spare on hand. Occasionally, an oil drain bolt gasket will tear when the drain bolt is removed. If you don't use the new drain bolt gasket this oil change, you'll use it someday and be very happy you have it on hand. A Honda dealer is the best place to get the correct gasket.

Warm up the motor

Before draining the oil from the motor, warm up the motor until the temperature gauge reaches normal operating temperature. Then turn off the motor. Warming up the motor circulates the oil and allows it to pick up dirt and gases you want to exit the motor when you drain the oil.

Caution! Put an automatic transmission into park and apply the parking brake. Put a manual transmission into first gear and apply the parking brake. The car should be on a level surface with the wheels blocked.

Locate the oil drain bolt

Attach the 17-millimeter socket to the ratchet wrench. Flip the adjusting lever on the wrench so that the wrench can turn the socket counterclockwise, the direction to turn the oil drain bolt to remove it. If in doubt, see chapter 1. With wrench in hand, slide on your back under the car, just behind the front wheels. From this position, you'll have no trouble locating the oil drain bolt shown in FIG. 6-2.

Are you having trouble fitting under your Honda because it's too low or you're too wide? I have this problem myself and choose to believe that Hondas are too low. Whatever the reason, the easiest and quickest solution is to raise the car off the ground. See **Caution**! in the text for instructions.

Fig. 6-2
The oil drain bolt location.

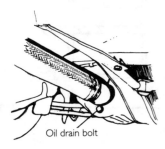

Oil drain bolt

Caution! If you use the spare tire jack to raise the front of the car, don't slide under the car while it's being supported by the jack alone. This jack is made only for changing tires. After elevating the car, put wooden blocks under the raised front wheel and then lower this wheel onto the blocks, taking the pressure off the jack. Never trust a jack to support a car while you're under it.

To prevent the car from rolling off the blocks, apply the parking brake. Put an automatic transmission into park and a manual into first gear. As an extra safety precaution, put a large rock behind the back wheels. Once you have the car supported, push it from side to side, back to front, and front to back. Be positive it is not going to fall!

Loosen the oil drain bolt

With the wrench assembly, unscrew the oil drain bolt a couple of turns. The oil drain bolt can be stubborn, and you might have to use some strength to loosen it—don't remove it, just loosen it.

Caution! After you begin draining the oil, do not start the motor until it is again filled with oil to the correct level. Starting a motor while it is low on oil, or drained of oil, will destroy it in a matter of seconds!

While laying on your back and looking up at the oil drain bolt, it is easy to become confused about which way to turn your wrench to loosen this bolt. No problem—you already set your ratchet wrench to turn counterclockwise.

Position the oil drain pan

Now that you have loosened the oil drain bolt, slide the oil drain pan into position to catch the oil that's about to exit the motor. I usually put a few newspapers under the oil drain pan to catch any spills.

Remove the oil drain bolt. Watch out, it's hot! The oil that's about to pour out of the motor is hot, and so is the oil drain bolt. If it's too hot to handle, allow it to drop into the oil drain pan where you can find it later as you pour this used oil into a disposal container.

Caution! The Environmental Protection Agency (EPA) now warns us that prolonged contact with used engine oil might cause skin problems, including cancer. The EPA recommends you wear protective rubber gloves and minimize your exposure to used motor oil. Wash your hands and other exposed skin as soon as possible after exposure.

Remove the oil filler cap

Removing the oil filler cap will help the oil flow from the motor. Figure 6-5 illustrates the oil filler cap location.

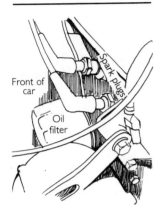

Locate the oil filter

While the oil is draining, it is a good time to change the oil filter. The oil filter is mounted on the front side of the motor just below the spark plugs or on the other side of the motor (the side that faces the passenger's compartment). If the oil filter is just below the spark plugs, you can reach it from a standing position. If the oil filter is not visible below the spark plugs, it is on the other side of the motor, and to reach it, you must slide under the car. See FIG. 6-3. The oil filter on your model might be on the other side of the motor on the passenger's compartment side. You will have to slide under the car to access these oil filters.

Loosen the oil filter

With the oil filter wrench, loosen the oil filter by turning it counter-clockwise about a half turn. Figure 6-4 shows how to use an oil filter wrench.

Slide the drain pan under the oil filter

By now, the oil has all drained from the motor. If not, wait until all dripping stops and then slide the drain pan under the oil filter. With the oil filter loose, grab it with a rag and remove it by hand. Watch out! It's hot!

Lubricate the new oil filter gasket

Important! As you know, the new oil filter comes with a gasket. If the gasket from the old oil filter is stuck to the motor, remove it.

Before installing the new oil filter, completely coat its rubber gasket with a light layer of clean motor oil. This rubber gasket seals the oil filter to the motor and failure to lubricate it can result in a poor seal, causing oil to shoot out from between the oil filter and the motor. Also, wipe the surface of the motor where the oil filter gasket will contact with a clean rag.

Install the new oil filter

Turn the new oil filter clockwise by hand until the gasket just contacts the mounting surface. Then, to complete the tightening of the oil filter, carefully follow the directions that come with the new oil filter.

Check the condition of the oil drain bolt gasket

Before you replace the drain bolt, check the condition of the drain bolt gasket. If it is torn or worn excessively, you should replace it. You will find the drain bolt gasket either around the drain bolt itself or stuck to the motor. If it's stuck to the motor, leave it there.

Reinstall the drain bolt

Spread new motor oil on the oil drain bolt gasket to help it seal. Begin by turning the drain bolt with your hand. When you are absolutely sure it is going in correctly, flip the lever on your ratchet wrench and continue tightening the drain bolt securely into the motor. Use a little muscle to ensure it is in tight.

Are you having trouble fitting under your Honda because it's too low or you're too wide? I have this problem myself and choose to believe that Hondas are too low. Whatever the reason, the easiest and quickest solution is to raise the car off the ground. See **Caution**! in the text for instructions.

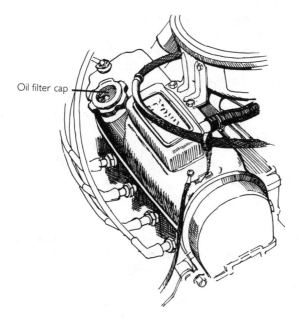

Oil filter cap

Fig. 6-5
The oil filter cap.

Be absolutely sure the drain bolt is going in correctly and not cross-threading before you use the ratchet wrench. If you just can't get the drain bolt started back into the motor correctly, you'll have to remove the gasket from the motor. If you're careful, you won't ruin the gasket.

Carefully remove the gasket from the motor by slipping the blade of a sharp knife or single-edged razor blade under it. Once the gasket is removed, scrape the mounting surface clean and inspect it. If it's not ruined, you can reuse it. With this gasket, or a new one in place around the drain bolt, you'll have no problem starting the drain bolt back into the motor.

Don't pour any oil into the motor until you read this!

You will not need all the oil you have purchased. Pouring too much oil into a motor can cause excess crankcase pressure, which usually results in blown or leaking gaskets. Begin by pouring 2 quarts of oil into the motor. Then check the oil level on the oil dipstick. See the "Checking the motor oil level" section in this chapter and FIG. 6-11 for locating and reading the oil dipstick—there's a special procedure for reading the oil dipstick. If the level on the dipstick reads full, or close to full, you're all set to move on to the next procedure. If 2 quarts are not enough to bring the oil level to the full line, add more oil. It takes 1 quart to bring the level from the low line to the full line. Do not overfill.

When the oil level is at the full line, replace the oil dipstick and oil filler cap. Start the motor and let it idle for a few minutes. This allows the oil filter to fill with oil. Stop the motor and check the oil level again. Turn off the motor and recheck the oil level on the dipstick. Because about a quart of oil is now in the oil filter, the reading on the dipstick will show the oil level to be low. Add the necessary amount of oil to bring the level up to the full position. Be extra careful not to add too much oil.

Once the oil level is correct, replace the dipstick and the oil filler cap. Start the motor and check that no oil is leaking from the oil filter or oil drain bolt!

Let's talk!

I'd feel guilty if I didn't remind you to avoid pouring the old oil from your motor down the sewer, or into a dumpster. Putting oil in small cans and hiding it among your normal trash is something else to avoid. Most gas stations and many auto parts stores will accept your used oil. A couple of phone calls is all it takes to find a safe place to dump used oil and do something positive for the planet.

Periodic maintenance

Checking the air filter element

The air filter element should be replaced every 15,000 miles or more often if you drive in dusty conditions.

Fig. 6-6
Clean the air filter element
from the inside out.

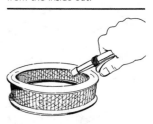

Locate the air filter element on carbureted models

On models with a carburetor, remove the top of the air filter box to find the air filter. See FIG. 5-3 in chapter 5 and follow the accompanying instructions. Once the top of the air filter box is removed, you can't miss the air filter element (FIG. 6-6).

*Inspect and replace the air filter
element on carbureted models*

If the air filter element has been used for 15,000 miles or is brown with dust or caked with dirt, replace it. If you're not sure replacement is necessary, hold the air filter up to the sun and look through it from the inside out. If you cannot see light through the ribs of the element, it's dirty and needs replacing. Never drive without an air filter element.

Locating the air filter element on fuel-injected models

To find the air filter, you must first remove the top of the air filter box. Figure 6-7 illustrates the different air filter box locations. Select the illustration that most closely shows the air filter box used on your model. Follow the instructions to remove the top from the air filter box and find the air filter element. Early models use bolts to hold the cover on the air filter box, while later models use clips that can be flipped free with your fingers. See illustrations C and D. If the air filter box is behind the motor next to the passenger's compartment like the one shown in (C), it's easy to access. Flip the four or five clips free with your fingers and remove the top. If your air filter is like the one shown in A, B, or D, remove the bolts holding the cover and then remove the cover and the tubular air filter. Once the top of the air filter box has been removed, you can't miss the air filter element—it's that ribbed thing. You can remove it with your hands.

*Inspecting and replacing the air filter
element on fuel-injected models*

If the air filter element has been used for 15,000 miles or is brown with dust or caked with dirt, replace it. If you're not sure replacement is necessary, hold the ribbed side of the air filter element up to the sun and look through it from the flat side. If you cannot see light through the ribs of the element, it's dirty and needs replacing. Never drive without an air filter element.

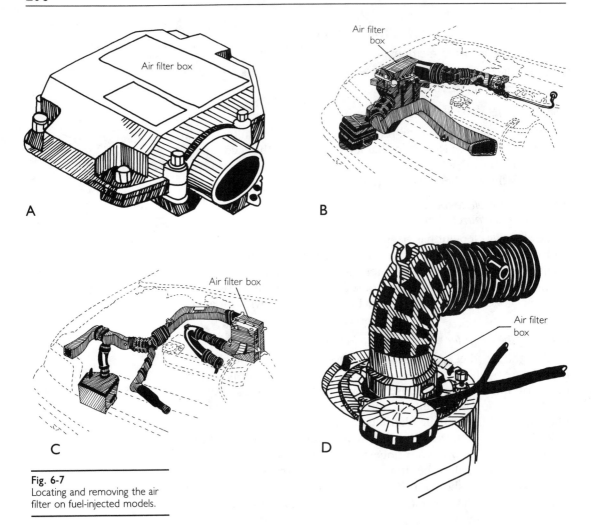

Fig. 6-7
Locating and removing the air filter on fuel-injected models.

Checking the battery water

Some batteries never need servicing. If your Honda has this type of battery, it will say so somewhere on the battery. Maintenance-free is the term usually used. You cannot add water to a maintenance-free battery.

If your battery is the serviceable type, remove the caps on top of the battery once a week and check the fluid level. Some caps must be unscrewed, while others just pull off. See FIG. 6-8. Some batteries have upper- and lower-level lines marked on the battery itself. If your battery is this type, add distilled water until the fluid level is

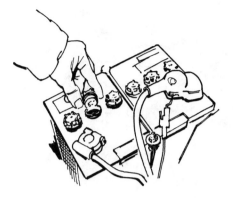

Fig. 6-8
Check the water level in the battery.

between the two lines. If your battery does not have upper- and lower-level lines, add the distilled water only until the fluid level reaches the bottom of the filler wells.

Do not overfill the battery. Should you notice any dirt or fluffy beige material accumulating around the battery terminals, remove it with a rag or non-metal brush. A solution of water and baking soda works very well. Because the battery starts your car, you'd do well to be good to it.

Lubricating the chassis

I suggest you take your Honda to a service station and pay the few dollars to have a lube job done. Because this needs to be done only once every 24,000 miles, you will spend about the same for four lube jobs as you would for a grease gun plus grease, not to mention having to slide around on your back under the car on a Saturday morning.

Checking the clutch and brake fluid

Check the clutch and brake fluid each time you buy gas—it only takes a second. Figure 6-9 shows the location of the brake and clutch fluid reservoirs. On the outside of each reservoir you'll see a "high" and "low" level line. Maintain the fluid at the high line. Use only Department of Transportation DOT 3 or DOT 4 brake fluid. Some early 1970 models have only one brake fluid reservoir.

Some models do not have the clutch fluid reservoir shown in FIG. 6-8. This is because these models have a cable-controlled clutch and do not require fluid to operate.

Important: Do not use a lesser-rated fluid. This could cause brake failure. Do not mix different brands of brake fluid. Pour fluid

Fig. 6-9
Clutch and brake fluid
reservoirs.

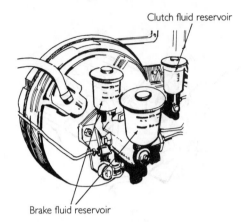

Clutch fluid reservoir

Brake fluid reservoir

There's usually no need to remove the caps from the reservoirs to check the
fluid levels. Just give the car a nudge. As the fluid moves in the reservoir, you'll be
able to see how its level relates to the level lines.

slowly from the container to ensure that no air bubbles form in the
reservoir.

Often, a fan belt that is loose and slipping will produce a squeaky, screaming
sound when you press on the accelerator pedal.

Changing the brake fluid

Change the brake fluid once a year. Brake fluid absorbs the moisture
that eventually corrodes metal brake lines and other brake parts.
The result is an expensive repair bill. The best way to change the
brake fluid is to take your Honda to a brake station and have them do
it with a power bleeder. It shouldn't cost much and it takes all of
about 15 minutes. I take my cars in for this service and find it well
worth it.

Inspecting the exhaust and evaporative
emission control systems

Your Honda is equipped with two types of emission control systems. It has an exhaust emission control system and an evaporative
emission control system. The exhaust system reduces pollutants that

would otherwise spew from the tail pipe. Today's exhaust emission systems are very well designed and are keeping pollutants to a minimum. Honda recommends inspecting the exhaust emissions system every 15,000 miles on 1975–1980 models and every 60,000 miles on newer models. The actual checking and serving of this system is, however, beyond the focus of this book.

The evaporative system traps gas fumes trying to evaporate into the atmosphere from the gas tank and carburetor. These trapped fumes are stored and eventually burned in the motor. Honda recommends inspecting the evaporative emissions system every 30,000 miles on 1975–1980 models and every two years or 60,000 miles, whichever comes first, on newer models. The actual checking and serving of this system is, however, beyond the focus of this handbook.

You will be glad to know a federal mandate makes the manufacturer of the vehicle responsible for the working condition of these systems for five years or 50,000 miles, whichever comes first. This means, if your car fails its smog test, take it up with the dealer that sold you the car.

Checking the fan belt(s)

Inspect the fan belt(s) for cracks, fraying, and excessive wear. A defective belt must be replaced. Inspect the outside surface of the fan belts as well as the inside surface that rides in the pulleys.

Next, check the fan belt tension. Press on the fan belt at its midpoint. Give it a firm push. You should feel the fan belt deflect 1/2 inch. If the belt moves further than 1/2 inch, it is too loose; if it moves less than this, it is too tight.

It's important to maintain correct fan belt tension. A loose fan belt will slip and not drive the alternator, which supplies the electricity to run your motor. An excessively tight fan belt puts extra pressure on the alternator bearings, causing them to wear out.

Adjusting fan belt tension

To adjust fan belt tension, use a 14-millimeter open or box-end wrench to loosen the holding bolt shown in FIG. 6-10. Turn the bolt counterclockwise. You can now move the alternator back and forth along the slotted bar. With a strong stick or metal bar, pry on the alternator while you check the fan belt tension with the thumb of your other hand. Tighten the holding bolt when the belt will deflect 1/2 inch only.

Fig. 6-10
Adjusting the fan belt tension.

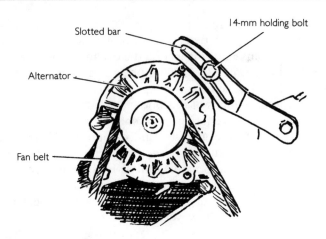

Slotted bar

14-mm holding bolt

Alternator

Fan belt

Lubricating the doors, trunk, hood, and hood release

I'm big on this simple procedure because sagging doors and squeaky trunks or hoods can easily be prevented. A quick shot of spray lubricant to all the hinges and a little petroleum jelly or grease to the latching points will do the trick.

There's a number of excellent spray lubricants now available. Ask a mechanic or the parts person at a professional (not a discount) parts store to recommend one. Again, I am suggesting you stay with a professional store because they deal mostly with shops, receiving reliable feedback on which products do the job and which products aren't worth stocking.

Okay, here we go. Open the doors one at a time and look for the hinges they swing on. There's a top hinge and a bottom hinge. Give these hinges a good spray of lubricant. Do the same with the trunk and hood, spraying anything that pivots to permit opening and closing. If you get lubricant on the paint, wipe it off immediately with a wet rag.

Have a look at the latching side of each door. Spray a little lubricant on the latching mechanisms. Next, slowly close the doors and look for the metal pegs they latch with on the body of the car. Put a light coat of petroleum jelly or grease on these pegs.

Do the same with the trunk and hood. Spray the trunk and hood latching mechanism with lubricant and put a light coat of petroleum jelly or grease on the surface of the object they latch with when closed. If the object the hood or trunk latches with is attached to moving parts, spray lubricate these parts.

All Hondas have a hood latch that is released from inside the car. Prop the hood open and have a friend pull and push the operating lever from inside the car. You'll see the release mechanism moving right where the hood latches to the body of the car. Spray lubricate these parts.

Lubricating the locks

Graphite makes an excellent lubricant for every lock on your car. It's sold in spray cans and squeeze tubes. Push the spray nozzle of the squeeze tube lightly into each lock and give it a small blast. Do the doors, trunk, ignition, and glove box locks.

Checking the motor oil level

Oil is the lifeblood of your motor. Running a motor low on oil will destroy it in short order. Next to regular oil changes, checking and maintaining the oil level is the most important thing you can do to protect your Honda's mechanical condition.

Check the oil every time you buy gas. Better yet! Check the oil level in the morning before starting the motor. This will give you a more accurate reading. In addition, check the oil when the car is on a level surface. If it's on a slant, you'll get a false reading.

The location of the oil dipstick varies between models. Figure 6-11 illustrates the various locations of the oil dipstick. To check the motor oil level, stop the motor and:

1. Pull the oil dipstick from the motor, wipe it clean with a rag, and reinsert it into the motor.

2. Pull the dipstick again from the motor. Check the oil level, which should be at the full (F) mark or at least between the full mark

Fig. 6-11
Two possible oil dipstick locations.

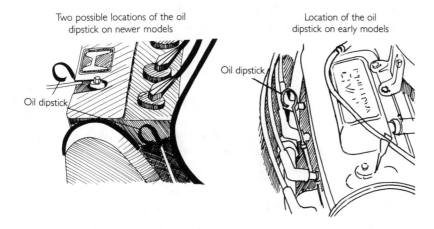

Two possible locations of the oil dipstick on newer models

Location of the oil dipstick on early models

Oil dipstick

Oil dipstick

Oil dipstick

Fig. 6-12
Replacing the O2 sensor.

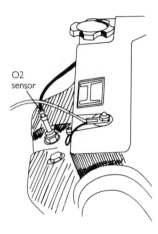

O2
sensor

and the low (L) mark. Some dipsticks have an upper and lower hole instead of level lines. Never run the motor when the oil level is below the low mark.

3. Add oil, if necessary. Chart 6-1 lists which oil to use. Try to stay with the same brand oil. Oil companies use different additives and you don't want to take a chance on these additives clashing with each other, especially in your motor.

Inspecting the oxygen (O2) sensor

The O2 sensor is screwed into the exhaust system as illustrated in FIG. 6-12. The O2 sensor is sometimes located further down the pipe it is mounted in. In this case, follow the pipe toward the bottom of the motor to locate it. Its function is to sample exhaust gases and send an electrical signal to the computer, telling it to fatten up the air/gas mixture (add gas) or lean it out (send less gas and more air).

When the "check engine" light illuminates the dash, black smoke pours from the exhaust pipe, or your gas mileage decreases, the O2 sensor is often the culprit.

To remove the O2 sensor, you will need an O2 sensor socket wrench. Turn the sensor counterclockwise to remove it. You must paint the threads of the new sensor with anti-seize compound before installing it. Failure to do this will cause the sensor to weld itself into the pipe, making it impossible to remove.

Checking the power steering fluid

Power steering relies on hydraulic pressure to make turning the steering wheel easy. About once a month, check the power steering fluid reservoir level with the front wheels of your Honda pointing straight ahead. The motor should not be running.

Figure 6-13 shows the location of the power steering reservoir. On 1988 and newer models, this reservoir is translucent and you can see the fluid level without removing the reservoir cap. Keep the fluid level between the two level lines.

On 1987 and earlier models, remove the reservoir cap with its attached dipstick. The dipstick shows a hot level (to be used after driving the car) and a cold level (for checking the level when the motor is cold). Use only Honda power steering fluid, which can be purchased from a Honda dealer.

Checking the radiator coolant

It is important to check the coolant level. See FIG. 6-14 and decide if your Honda has an open or closed cooling system. Check the radia-

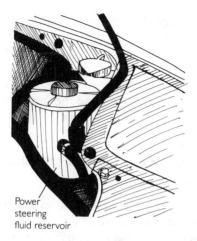

Fig. 6-13
Checking the power steering
fluid level.

Power
steering
fluid reservoir

tor coolant in an open system at least once a week, when the engine is cold. Remove the radiator cap and check the level of the coolant. Push down on the radiator cap and turn counterclockwise to remove it. The coolant level should be about $3/4$ inch below the bottom of the filler neck. If the level is too low, use distilled water to refill the radiator. See FIG. 6-14.

All radiators have an overflow tube. On a closed system, the overflow tube is connected to a thermal expansion tank. As shown in FIG. 6-14, closed radiator systems have an overflow tube that runs from the filler neck on the radiator to a semi-clear plastic tank known as a thermal expansion tank. On models with a thermal expansion tank, remove the radiator cap only to clean and drain the

Fig. 6-14
Checking and draining the
radiator coolant of opened and
closed systems.

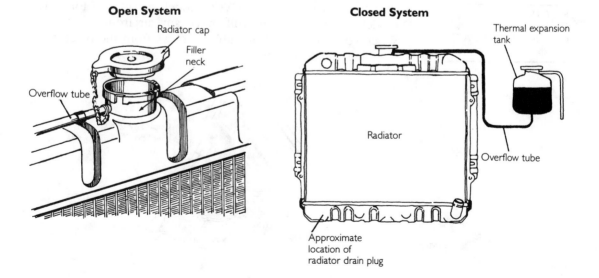

Open System

Radiator cap

Filler
neck

Overflow tube

Closed System

Thermal expansion
tank

Radiator

Overflow tube

Approximate
location of
radiator drain plug

cooling system. Check the level of coolant in the system by checking the level in the thermal expansion tank. The coolant should be up to the full line on the tank. Use coolant made for an aluminum motor.

Caution! Never add water to a hot, overheating motor. This will damage the cooling system and the motor. The motor must be running when adding water to a warm motor.

Changing the coolant

Change the coolant every 30,000 miles. To change the coolant:

1. Remove the radiator cap.

2. Put a pan under the radiator and loosen the drain bolt at the bottom of the radiator as shown in FIG. 6-14. Turn this bolt counterclockwise using your fingers or pliers. Often, this bolt has "ears" on it to help you grip it. If this bolt does not loosen when you turn it counterclockwise, turn it clockwise. Some radiator drain bolts are reverse-threaded and tighten and loosen in the opposite direction of a normal bolt.

3. Drain the coolant from the thermal expansion tank.

4. Mix a solution of 50 percent antifreeze and 50 percent water. Be sure to use antifreeze designed for use in aluminum motors. Tighten the radiator drain bolt and fill the radiator to the filler neck. The radiator takes about 4.2 quarts. **Caution!** After refilling the radiator, you must bleed the system as described in numbers 5 and 6.

5. Start the motor and let it idle. With a 12-millimeter wrench, loosen (turn counterclockwise) the cooling system bleed bolt shown in FIG. 6-15 for non-CVCC models or FIG. 6-16 for CVCC models. This procedure will purge any air from the system. When coolant, free of air bubbles, flows from the bleed bolt, retighten the bleed bolt.

Fig. 6-15
Cooling system bleed bolt on 1975 – 1979 non-CVCC models.

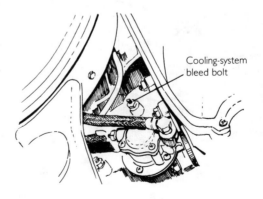

Cooling-system bleed bolt

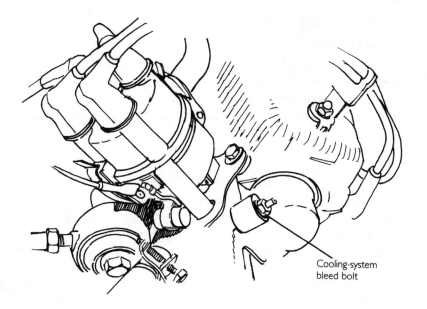

Fig. 6-16
Cooling system bleed bolt
on 1975 – 1979 CVCC
models and all 1980 and
newer models.

Cooling-system
bleed bolt

6. It might be necessary to purge additional air trapped in the system. Carefully loosen the radiator cap and put the heater control
in the HOT position. Once the motor reaches normal operating
temperature, refill the radiator, keeping an eye on the water level
until it stabilizes. Next, fill the thermal expansion tank to the full
mark and retighten the radiator cap.

Inspecting the radiator hoses

See FIG. 6-17 to locate the radiator hoses. There might also be a few
additional smaller hoses under the hood which, like the radiator
hoses, also carry coolant to, and around, the motor. To learn which
hoses these are, warm-up the motor with the heater ON and the air
conditioner (if so equipped) OFF. Then turn off the motor. Feel the
hoses with your fingers. Hoses carrying coolant are warm or hot.
Don't burn yourself!

Inspect the radiator hoses and the smaller hoses that carry coolant for the following problem areas:

   ○ Chaffing or burning

   ○ Swelling

   ○ Hardening

   ○ Softening

Fig. 6-17
Inspecting the radiator hoses.

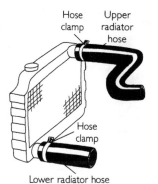

Hose   Upper
clamp   radiator
              hose

Hose
clamp

Lower radiator hose

○ Oil-soaked

○ Gas-soaked

Any of these six conditions is a sign that hose failure is near. Should a hose "blow" while you're out on the road, you could be left stranded. Running a motor that is low on coolant, or without coolant, will ruin it. In addition, an automatic transmission is cooled by a separate chamber connected to the radiator. Losing the coolant from the radiator can overheat the transmission and ruin it, too.

Removing and replacing radiator hoses

The large upper and lower radiator hoses can be purchased at an auto parts store. Now, more than ever, you want to stay away from the discount stores and get a top-quality hose. The smaller hoses with the funny bends in them will have to be purchased from the dealer.

To remove the desired hose, use a screwdriver to loosen the clamp on each end of the hose. It's a good idea to use new clamps when installing the new hose. If the hose is stuck, cut it with a razor blade or knife. You can also slide a screwdriver under the end of the hose and gently work it free. Before moving the bottom radiator hose, see the following section "Changing the bottom radiator hose."

Caution! After refilling the radiator to replace any lost coolant, you must bleed the system. See numbers 5 and 6, under "Changing the coolant," in the section titled "Checking the radiator coolant."

Danger! If your Honda is equipped with air conditioning (AC), do not disconnect any AC system hoses by yourself. If an AC system hose appears worn and in need of replacement, have a qualified AC shop do the job. This system is under tremendous pressure and personal injury will result if you attempt to loosen these hoses without first relieving system pressure.

If in doubt as to which hoses are AC system hoses, warm up the motor with the heater ON and the AC system OFF. Then, stop the motor and feel the hoses. The warm or hot hoses will have coolant in them from the radiator and the others will be filled with refrigerant for the AC unit. Leave the AC hoses alone!

Changing the bottom radiator hose

Before you can change the bottom radiator hose, you have to first drain the radiator. Find something clean to drain the radiator coolant into. Coolant is expensive and getting more so all the time. You can reuse coolant if it's not brown and rusty. To drain the coolant, see the "Checking the radiator coolant" section and follow the instructions under "Changing the coolant."

Caution! After refilling the radiator, you must bleed the system. See numbers 5 and 6, under ''Changing the coolant,'' in the section titled ''Checking the radiator coolant.''

Inspecting the timing belt

In Hondas, timing belts are a serious subject. Should the timing belt on your Honda slip or break, extreme damage to the motor might instantly occur. What is a timing belt? A timing belt is a rubber belt that runs between the crankshaft and the camshaft. The crankshaft is turned by piston power and the timing belt transfers this power to the camshaft, which operate the valves. See FIG. 6-18.

Although you can't see the timing belt because it is behind the timing belt cover, it looks somewhat like the belt that runs the alternator and air conditioning compressor. But, unlike a typical alternator belt, a timing belt is notched on its underside. These notches fit into the notches on the crankshaft and camshaft pulleys, ensuring that the timing belt does not slip.

What happens when a timing belt slips or breaks? When a timing belt slips or breaks, the movement of the pistons and the valves are no longer in sync. This means there's a good chance of the

Fig. 6-18
The timing belt and related parts.

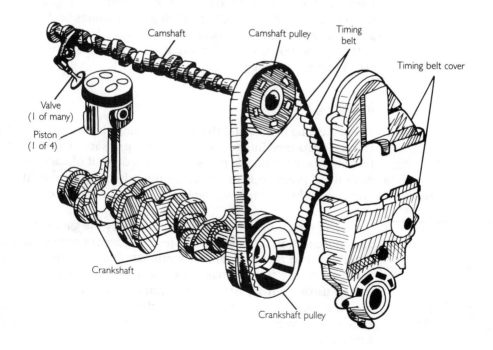

valves and pistons meeting head-on. The result of this collision is usually a bent valve and/or cracked piston. Not a pretty thought and ultra expensive to have repaired!

Happily, most of the time, Accord motors will not bend a valve when the timing belt breaks. Civic motors, unfortunately, bend a valve just about every time. I have no information on Preludes.

What does Honda Motors recommend? Although Honda Motor Co. makes no official recommendation as to when to change a timing belt, here's the unofficial word:

For models made before 1984, Honda makes no recommendation at all. Although there was no initial recommendation for 1984 and 1985 models, owners have been notified to change the timing belt every 60,000 miles. This notification was sent out as a customer service after the company found a small percentage of these models experienced timing belt failure shortly after 60,000 miles. Honda Motors, as of yet, has made no recommendation for cars made between 1986 and 1990. In 1990, Honda began advising a timing belt change on 1990 and newer models every 90,000 miles.

What's the solution? Change the timing belt every 50,000 miles, that's my solution to the problem. And, unfortunately, this interval does not guarantee the rubber timing belt will not break before the next change. Who can predict the life of a rubber belt?

I suggest you buy a timing belt from the Honda dealer and have them put it on. I imagine the dealer is stocking the highest-quality timing belt available. Installing a timing belt requires background in automotive theory and is best left to a professional. Installing the belt just one notch off will prevent the motor from running and could severely damage it.

Inspecting the tires

To ensure long tire life and the good handling characteristics of your Honda, keep tires inflated to the correct pressure. The correct air pressure for your tires is printed on the side wall of each tire. The amount of pressure is measured in pounds per square inch (PSI). Sometimes this number will be hard to see, but it's there and you'll spot it.

Fig. 6-19
Inspecting the tires for correct inflation.

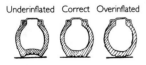

Underinflated Correct Overinflated

I recommend you purchase a good-quality tire gauge. Although all service station air hoses have pressure gauges on them, it's rare you'll find one that is accurate. Overinflation or underinflation will cause severe tire tread damage. See FIG. 6-19. If you notice a section of tire, usually a front tire, that is wearing faster or differently, take the car to an alignment shop and have the wheels aligned. Rotate the tires often—every 6,000 miles is ideal. I suggest you take it in for this service.

Checking the transmission fluid

Check the level of the transmission fluid at least once a month. Replace it after the first 3,000 miles and then every 24,000 miles thereafter. Before checking the transmission fluid level, warm up the transmission. Drive the car three or four miles, making frequent starts and stops along the way. Park your Honda on a level surface.

The automatic transmission fluid is checked with the motor running at idle speed. The fluid level in a manual transmission is checked with the motor shut off.

Automatic transmissions use Dexron-type automatic transmission fluid. Add fluid in small amounts to ensure against overfilling. Remember to start the motor and put the transmission into "Drive" before checking the fluid level. Four-speed and five-speed transmission models use motor oil in the transmission. See CHART 6-2 to determine which weight oil to use in your Honda's transmission. To select the correct weight oil for your Honda, find the arrow that best reflects the temperature range in which the new oil will be used. If you have any doubts, show CHART 6-2 to the counterperson at any auto parts store.

Checking the transmission fluid level on 1975–1979 four-speeds and all automatic transmissions

Figure 6-20 illustrates where the transmission dipstick is on four-speed and automatic models. The dipstick is on the passenger's side of the car almost directly below the battery. Dipsticks with the pull-ring top are pulled from the transmission. The pull ring is usually

Chart 6-2
Choosing the correct weight motor oil for four and five-speed transmissions.

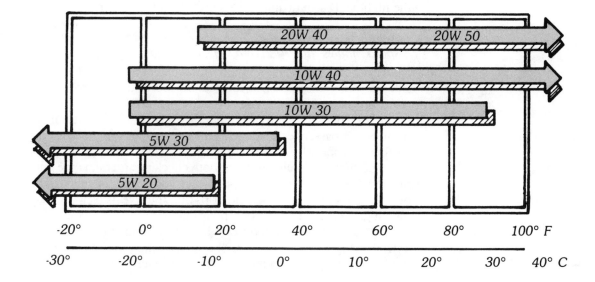

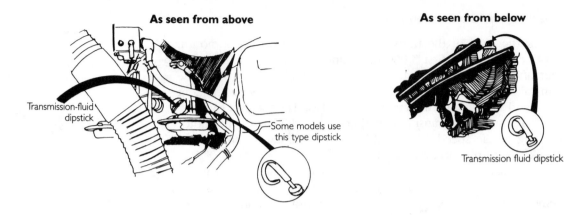

As seen from above

Transmission-fluid dipstick

Some models use this type dipstick

As seen from below

Transmission fluid dipstick

Fig. 6-20
The location of the transmission fluid dipstick on automatic transmissions and pre-1980 four-speed models.

yellow and easy to spot. Turn a dipstick with a turn-tab top counterclockwise to unscrew it from the transmission. If you are having a tough time finding the dipstick, I've included this view from below the car. You might find it easier to spot from below. Lay on the ground, just in front of the passenger's side tire and look up into the motor compartment to spot the dipstick. If your four-speed does not have a dipstick as illustrated, see the next procedure.

With the dipstick removed from the transmission, wipe it clean with a rag and reinsert it into the transmission—do not screw a turn-tab top back in. Pull the dipstick back out and check the fluid level. There are two level lines on the dipstick. It takes about 3/4 quart to bring the fluid level from the "Add" line (lower line) up to the "Full" line (upper line). A long-necked funnel is required to get the fluid into the fill hole. Discount auto parts stores stock these funnels.

Checking the transmission fluid level on all
5-speed models and 1980 and newer 4-speed models

Figure 6-21 illustrates where the 17-millimeter check/fill plug on the side of your transmission is located. To locate the check/fill plug, stand on the passenger's side of your Honda. Often, it is easier to locate the check/fill plug from under the car. Lay on the ground in front of the passenger's side tire and look up into the motor compartment to spot the check/fill plug.

The check/fill plug is used for both checking and filling the transmission fluid. Remove the check/fill plug and watch for fluid to drip out as shown in FIG. 6-21. If fluid drips out, the level is okay—replace the plug. If no fluid comes out, pour fluid into the hole from which the check/fill plug was removed. When fluid begins to drip out, wait until the dripping is very slight and replace the plug. What type of fluid goes into the transmission is discussed later in the chapter.

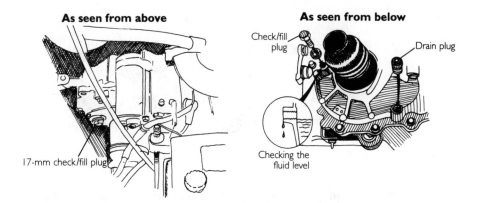

As seen from above

17-mm check/fill plug

As seen from below

Check/fill plug

Drain plug

Checking the fluid level

There are inexpensive pumps available for adding fluid to the transmission.

Fig. 6-21
The location of the transmission fluid check/fill plug on five-speed models and 1980 or newer four-speed models.

Draining and refilling the transmission fluid

The right illustration in FIG. 6-21 shows the location of the transmission fluid drain plug. Using this illustration as a guide, remove the drain plug. If the head of the drain plug has a recessed drive square as illustrated, the square drive peg of your 3/8-inch ratchet wrench should fit it. Some models use a plain bolt.

Allow the fluid to drain into a container capable of holding slightly more than 2 1/2 quarts. Replace the drain plug by starting it back into the transmission by hand. Once you're sure it's going in correctly and not cross-threading, use the wrench to tighten it securely.

On 1980 or newer four-speed transmission models and all five-speed transmission models, put the new fluid into the transmission through the 17-millimeter check/fill plug shown in FIG. 6-21. On 1979 or older four-speed transmission models and all automatic transmission models, pour the fluid in through the hole from which the dipstick unscrews on top of the transmission.

The transmission holds about 2.6 quarts, but you'll have to use slightly less because a little fluid will remain in the transmission after draining. Pour a little fluid in and check the level. If you overfill the transmission, drain some fluid through the drain plug.

Checking 4-WD rear differential fluid

To check the fluid level in the rear differential of a 4-WD Honda, remove the check/fill plug from the differential as shown in FIG.

Fig. 6-22
Checking the fluid level in the
rear differential of a 4-WD
model.

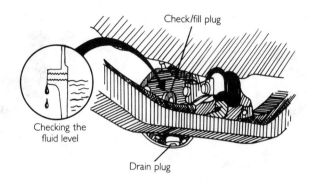

Check/fill plug

Checking the
fluid level

Drain plug

6-22. If the plug head contains a recessed drive square, the square drive of your $3/8$-inch ratchet wrench should fit it.

Remove the check/fill plug and watch for fluid to drip out as shown in FIG. 6-22. If fluid drips out, the level is okay—replace the plug. If no fluid drips out, pour fluid into the hole from which the check/fill plug was removed. When fluid begins to drip out, wait until the dripping is very slight and replace the plug.

In temperatures above 41 degrees, use Hypoid gear oil API GL5 SAE 90. In temperatures below 41 degrees, use Hypoid gear oil API GL5 SAE 80. The salespeople in any parts store will know what you want if you tell them the gear oil rating.

To change the fluid in the differential, remove both the check/fill plug and the drain plug. The rear differential holds $7/10$ quart of the specified gear oil.

There are inexpensive pumps available for adding fluid to the differential.

Miscellaneous

Other parts of your car require periodic maintenance as well. Repacking the wheel bearings (every 30,000 miles); replacing the fuel filter (every 24,000 to 30,000 miles); and checking the steering and brakes are best left to the professionals. Consult the owner's manual that came with your Honda at the time of purchase and follow the service schedule recommended for parts not covered in this chapter.

Fuel filter replacement is not covered in this chapter because of the danger of fire. This is especially true on fuel-injected models because gasoline is under a constant 30-pounds pressure in these systems.

Tools

*E*very tool mentioned in this book is described and illustrated here in this chapter. You do not need all these tools to tune-up and service your particular Honda. To learn which tools are used with your Honda, see the Tools section at the beginning of each chapter. Also, have a look at All About Tools at the front of the book. This short section fills you in on what brand tools to buy and who sells them.

Box-end and open-end wrenches

Box-end and open-end wrenches provide a slightly different service from one another (FIG. 7-1). The head of the box-end wrench completely surrounds the nut or bolt on which it is placed, gripping far more securely than the open-end wrench. This is an important advantage when a nut or bolt requires force in order for it to ''pop''

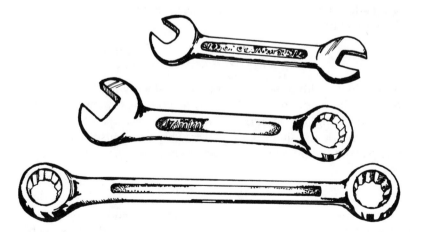

Fig. 7-1
Box-end and open-end wrenches. From top to bottom: double open-end wrench, combination open-end box-end wrench, and double box-end wrench.

Fig. 7-2
Extension bar with ³/8-inch
inside square drive.

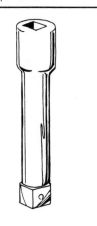

loose. An open-end wrench has its own special advantage in that it will slip into narrow spaces and is quicker and easier to use. Either type wrench will be fine for the light tune-up and servicing you'll be doing with your Honda.

The millimeter size stamped on these wrenches, such as 10 millimeter and 12 millimeter, refer to the size of the wrench. A 10-millimeter wrench fits nuts and bolts with 10-millimeter heads. Notice the different combinations of open-end and box-end wrenches in FIG. 7-1.

Extension bar with ³/8-inch drive

Figure 7-2 is an illustration of an extension bar with a ³/8-inch drive. The extension bar extends the "reach" of your ratchet wrench, enabling it to be effective in otherwise impossible-to-reach nooks and crannies of your motor. A ³/8-inch drive means that this extension bar is compatible with ratchet wrenches and socket wrenches that are also ³/8-inch drive.

Fig. 7-3
Feeler gauge.

Feeler gauge

Feeler gauges are used to measure the gap between two parts (FIG. 7-3). You will be using a feeler gauge to gap spark plugs, ignition points, and valve clearances. Each blade that folds out of the tool is a different thickness and is labeled accordingly.

For example, if I tell you to make the ignition point gap .020 inch, you simply fold out the .020-inch blade and slide it between the ignition points. If the blade slides in loosely, the gap is too big. If the blade won't slide in at all, the gap is too small.

The ignition points are in correct adjustment if the feeler gauge blade slides in with a slight drag on it, caused by the ignition points lightly touching it.

Fig. 7-4
Medium-sized screwdriver.

Medium-sized screwdriver

A screwdriver with a 6-inch shaft and a ¹/2-inch-wide blade is considered to be medium-sized (FIG. 7-4). If you already own a screwdriver that is slightly larger or smaller, you should be able to use it. I recommend purchasing a screwdriver with a well-insulated handle to help avoid the possibility of electric shock.

Offset screwdriver

An offset screwdriver makes it possible to tighten and loosen screws that are not accessible to a screwdriver with a completely straight shaft. Offset screwdrivers come with a flat head or a Phillips head (FIG. 7-5). There's nothing like an offset screwdriver for reaching tight, narrow spaces.

Fig. 7-5
Offset screwdriver.

Ohmmeter

An ohmmeter checks the resistance a wire has to the flow of electricity (FIG. 7-6). In this book, an ohmmeter is used to check the resistance of spark plug wires to the flow of electricity and is an optional tool. For more information about testing spark plug wires with an ohmmeter, see chapter 1, STEP 9.

Fig. 7-6
An ohmmeter with "alligator" clip leads (optional).

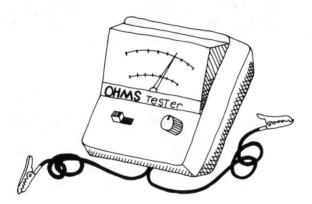

Oil filter wrench

An oil filter wrench is used to remove and replace an oil filter (FIG. 7-7). The metal band of the tool slips over the can-shaped oil filter. When you turn the handle, the metal band tightens up around the filter. As you continue to turn, the oil filter begins to unscrew from the motor.

Fig. 7-7
Oil filter wrench.

Oxygen sensor socket with ³/₈-inch drive

Fig. 7-8
Oxygen sensor socket wrench
with ³/₈-inch drive.

An oxygen sensor socket with a ³/₈-inch drive is a special socket designed to fit an oxygen sensor (FIG. 7-8). The ³/₈-inch drive allows the socket to fit onto the drive peg of your ³/₈-inch-drive ratchet wrench.

Phillips head screwdriver

Most screws in automotive use are Phillips heads (FIG. 7-9). This is because they offer a more positive gripping surface than slot-headed screws. The pointed blade of the Phillips head screwdriver fits securely into the X head of Phillips head screws. For purposes of this book, purchase a No. 2 Phillips head screwdriver. Purchase one with a well-insulated handle to help avoid the possibility of electric shock.

Fig. 7-9
Phillips head screwdriver.

Pliers

Pliers work just like a pair of kitchen tongs (FIG. 7-10). You put the jaws of the tool around an object, such as a nut or bolt, and then squeeze on the handles. Most pliers are adjustable. The tool is easily adjusted by sliding one side of the pliers up or down on the center peg.

Fig. 7-10
Pliers.

Points file

A small points file is used to file protrusions from the surface of ignition points (FIG. 7-11). Use only a genuine points file—any other type of file will cause the points to function incorrectly.

Ratchet wrench with ³/₈-inch drive

As its name implies, the ratchet wrench is a wrench that has a built-in ratchet (FIG. 7-12). This ratchet allows you to turn a part in one direction, and then turn the wrench handle back to the starting point without affecting the part.

Fig. 7-11
Points file.

Here's an example of how this ratchet works to your advantage: Imagine you have attached a 10-millimeter socket to your ratchet wrench and have begun to loosen a 10-millimeter bolt. But, after half a turn, you are stopped by a motor part in your way, preventing the wrench from turning farther. What do you do? You simply rotate the wrench handle back to a position that will again allow you to continue loosening the part.

Remember that a ratchet wrench turns in one direction and spins freely in the opposite direction. If it weren't for a ratchet wrench in the preceding example, you would have to remove your wrench after every half turn and start over again.

A 3/8-inch drive refers to the square peg of the wrench that plugs into the various ratchet wrench attachments designed to fit every screw, nut, and bolt in the universe.

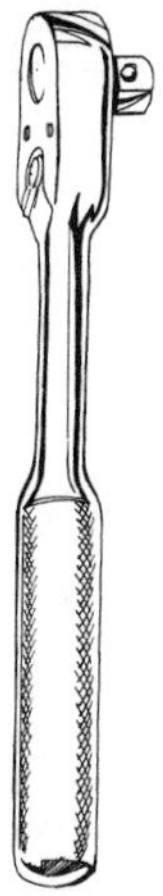

Fig. 7-12
Ratchet wrench with 3/8-inch drive peg.

Rubber hose with 3/8-inch inside diameter

A 7 or 8-inch length of rubber hose makes an excellent tool for getting spark plugs to start screwing correctly back into the motor (FIG. 7-13). If the spark plug should get started in at a slight angle, the hose will slip on the spark plug and save the threads of the motor. On motors with top-mounted spark plugs, this rubber tube is also useful for lifting spark plugs up and out of the motor.

Fig. 7-13
Rubber hose with 3/8-inch inside diameter.

Socket wrenches with 3/8-inch drive

Socket wrenches fit entirely over nuts and bolts, gripping them securely (FIG. 7-14). In addition, socket wrenches are used with your ratchet wrench, which means you get to enjoy the luxury of ratcheting back and forth as opposed to struggling along with an open- or box-end wrench.

Fig. 7-14
Socket wrenches with 3/8-inch drive.

The 3/8-inch drive of a socket wrench allows it to snap onto a ratchet wrench with a 3/8-inch drive peg. Combined with an extension bar, socket wrenches allow you to reach motor parts not accessible to open-end or box-end wrenches.

Fig. 7-15
Spark plug socket with ³/₈-inch
drive.

Spark plug socket with ³/₈-inch drive

A ³/₈-inch drive means that this tool works with wrenches and extension bars that are also ³/₈-inch drive. A spark plug socket with ³/₈-inch drive is another of the many attachments available for your ³/₈-inch-drive ratchet wrench and is used to remove and replace spark plugs (FIG. 7-15). One end of the spark plug socket plugs into the ratchet wrench (or extension bar) and the other end slips over and grips the spark plug. It's as simple as that.

Spark plugs sockets are available in ¹³/₁₆-inch and ⁵/₈-inch sizes. These numbers refer to the fact that the socket is made to grip a spark plug with a correspondingly sized nut. In the chapter on spark plugs, I tell you which size spark plug socket to get for your particular model Honda.

I recommend you purchase a spark plug socket with an insert to grip the porcelain shaft of the spark plug. This will keep the spark plug in the socket while transferring it from the motor to your hand during removal. Better to have one spark plug in the hand than three on the garage floor!

Tach-dwell meter

A tach-dwell meter is an optional tool that (see FIG. 7-16) serves two purposes. The "tach" section of the meter measures engine speed in revolutions per minute (RPM). The "dwell" section of the meter shows the distributor points adjustment in degrees. For a complete explanation of "dwell," see chapter 2, "How to adjust the points with a dwell meter."

Only 1978 and earlier Accords and Preludes and 1979 and earlier Civics have distributor points on which to check the dwell. An RPM reading is a useful aid for carburetor and timing adjustments on all model years. For a complete explanation of RPM, see "To tune or not to tune," on page xvii.

Fig. 7-16
Tach-dwell meter.

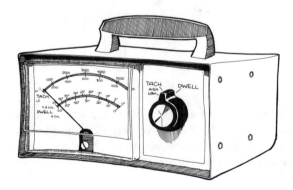

1990 – 1991 Accords and 1988 – 1991 Civics

Because your model does not have a points assembly, you will not be checking the dwell reading. If you want to connect a tachometer to your model for an RPM reading, the meter must have an inductive pick-up. Most modern tachometers now have this feature.

An inductive pick-up looks like a giant clothespin. To connect the tachometer to the motor, you clip this "giant clothespin" to any spark plug wire. Without this inductive pick-up, you would have to connect your meter directly to the ignition coil, which is not accessible on your model. More about this in chapter 3.

Timing light

A timing light is basically a strobe light (FIG. 7-17). Its strobe effect makes the timing marks on the motor appear to stand still. This is necessary to check and adjust motor timing. Remember all those dances in the sixties? Let's hope this strobe light doesn't cause any flashbacks!

There are three different types of timing lights available: an ac timing light, a dc timing light, and a neon timing light. Considering how inexpensive timing lights have become, I recommend you buy

Fig. 7-17
Timing light.

Fig. 7-18
Wire brush.

a dc timing light with an inductive pick-up. This pick-up makes it quick and easy to connect the timing light to the motor. In addition, an added feature known as an advance meter is available with a dc timing light. See chapter 3 for more information about timing lights.

1988 and 1989 carbureted Preludes

To tune-up a 1988 or 1989 Prelude equipped with a carburetor (not fuel-injected), a timing light with an advance meter is a must. This advance meter compensates for the lack of a complete timing system on these Preludes.

Wire brush

A wire brush with stiff metal bristles is great for brushing deposits from spark plug electrodes (FIG. 7-18). Any wire brush with stiff bristles will do.

Fig. 7-19
Wire gauge.

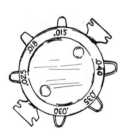

Wire gauge

A wire gauge is specifically designed to adjust and measure spark plug gap (FIG. 7-19). The different wires positioned around the tool are of various thicknesses. If my instructions tell you to gap the spark plug to .030 inch, you use the wire labeled .030″ to check this gap. The small claws on either side of the tool are used to bend the spark plug electrode and make the gap larger or smaller.

Index